Vocabulary
in use
Intermediate
with answers

Stuart Redman
with Ellen Shaw

CAMBRIDGE UNIVERSITY PRESS
Cambridge, New York, Melbourne, Madrid, Cape Town, Singapore, São Paulo

Cambridge University Press
40 West 20th Street, New York, NY 10011–4211, USA

www.cambridge.org
Information on this title: www.cambridge.org/9780521634779

First published 1999
8th printing 2005

Printed in Hong Kong, China

A catalog record for this publication is available from the British Library.

Library of Congress Cataloging-in-Publication Data
Redman, Stuart.
Vocabulary in use: intermediate / Stuart Redman, with Ellen Shaw.
p. cm.
Includes index.
ISBN-13 978-0-521-63477-9 student's book with answers
ISBN-10 0-521-63477-6 student's book with answers
1. Vocabulary – Problems, exercises, etc. 2. English language –
Textbooks for foreign speakers. I. Shaw, Ellen. II. Title.
PE1449.R4394   1999
428.2′4–dc21   96-38425
                                                     CIP

ISBN-13 978-0-521-63477-9 student's book with answers
ISBN-10 0-521-63477-6 student's book with answers

ISBN-13 978-0-521-63478-6 student's book without answers
ISBN-10 0-521-63478-4 student's book without answers

Contents

113304

iii

Connecting and linking

Topics

The world around us

People

Daily life

Work

Acknowledgments

The authors and publishers would like to thank the following for permission to reproduce copyright material in *Vocabulary in Use – Intermediate.*

p. 8, definition of "seat," p. 10, definitions of "time," "say," "tell," and "truth," and p. 38, definition of "turn": adapted and reprinted with permission from *Cambridge International Dictionary of English,* ed. Paul Proctor (Cambridge: Cambridge University Press, 1995); p. 10, definition of "treat," p. 11, definition of "raise," and p. 37, definition of "pick up": adapted from *Longman Dictionary of American English,* 2nd ed., copyright © 1997, reprinted by permission of Addison Wesley Longman, Inc.; p. 97, left-hand photograph courtesy of S. Graham, center photograph © Arthur Tilley/FPG International, right-hand photograph © Bill Bachmann/PhotoEdit; p. 110, photograph of bills © Ken Reid/FPG International, photograph of coins © Gary Randall/FPG International; p. 136, photograph of Charlie Chaplin in *Modern Times:* Photofest; p. 148, photograph of Seiji Ozawa: AP/Wide World Photos; pp. 156, 157, box shots reprinted with permission from Microsoft Corporation; p. 178, photograph of Harrah's courtesy of Harrah's Lake Tahoe; p. 180, Buckingham Palace © Travelpix/FPG International, St. Peter's © Guy Marche/FPG International, Temple Emerald Buddha © Hilarie Kavanagh/Tony Stone Images, Statue of Liberty © Rohan/Tony Stone Images, street market © Cosmo Condina/Tony Stone Images, Empire State Building © Fred George/Tony Stone Images.

Text composition by Don Williams.

Illustrations by Daisy De Puthod and Randy Jones.

Phonetic transcriptions in Index by John Bollard.

To the student

Who is this book for?

Vocabulary in Use – Intermediate is designed to help learners at this level to improve their English vocabulary. The book teaches not only new vocabulary, but also strategies for learning vocabulary that you can use after you have completed the book. It can be used by students who are studying by themselves, but it can also be used by a teacher in the classroom with groups of students.

How is the book organized?

The book has 100 two-page units. The left-hand page explains new words and expressions (most units contain approximately 25 new words or phrases), and the right-hand page gives you a chance to check your understanding through a series of exercises that practice the new vocabulary. In a few units, e.g., Units 19 and 67, the right-hand page also includes a few new words and phrases that are not explained on the left-hand page.

There is an Answer Key at the back of the book. This not only gives *correct* answers to exercises with "right" or "wrong" solutions, but also *possible answers* and *suggested answers* for exercises that have more than one correct answer.

The Index at the back of the book lists all the new words and phrases introduced in the book and refers you to the unit or units where these words appear. The Index also includes phonemic transcriptions for all words. A key to the symbols is on page 204, and page 205, "Pronunciation Problems," gives you special help with the pronunciation of approximately 200 words that present particular problems for many learners of English. Some words or phrases in the book may be pronounced in different ways by different English speakers. However, because of space limitations, only one pronunciation, used by speakers of the most common varieties of North American English, is transcribed in most cases.

The left-hand page

The left-hand page introduces the new vocabulary for each topic or area of language. First of all, the vocabulary is divided into a number of sections (A, B, C, etc.) with simple, clear titles; and then within each section, new words and phrases are usually printed in **bold type** and explained using a number of different techniques:

- A short definition. The definition follows directly after the word, or comes at the end of the phrase or sentence. It is in brackets: e.g., **unemployed** [without a job]; **make up your mind** [make a decision].
- A short explanation. This is a complete sentence that often includes the new word: e.g., **effective** – If something is **effective,** it works well and produces good results.
- A synonym or opposite: e.g., **sad** [unhappy]; **dirty** [≠ clean].
- A situation. Some words are difficult to define, and it is easier to see their meaning within a context. The following is from a text about a car accident: "Both drivers were **badly injured** and both cars were very **badly damaged.**"

- A picture or diagram. This seems the obvious way to explain a large number of concrete nouns and verbs, e.g.:

a carrot

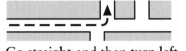

Go straight and then **turn left.**

- Sentence examples. These show the words in context in order to illustrate their meaning and their special grammatical features.

  > My girlfriend gets **jealous** when I talk to other girls.
  > The plane **appeared** in the sky, then suddenly **disappeared** behind a cloud.
  > He can't **get along with** [have a good relationship with] his parents. (v. + adv. + prep.)
  > The teams **are tied** 2–2. (*not* are tying)

Other ways of presenting the material include:

- Labels, such as *formal* and *informal:* e.g., **commence** *(formal);* **kids** *(informal).*
- A slash (/). This is often used to show that two words or phrases have similar meanings, e.g., **afraid of / frightened of.** Sometimes slashes are used to show alternative words or phrases that could be used in the same position in a sentence, although they don't mean the same thing, e.g., **Have a nice day/evening/weekend.** [to say good-bye]
- Finally, a big effort has been made to introduce new words alongside other words that often appear with them (this is called "collocation"): e.g., miss the bus; a strong accent; the car broke down; fasten your seat belt; go on vacation; to some extent; etc.

The right-hand page

The right-hand page contains the exercises to practice the new vocabulary presented on the left-hand page. In general, the first exercise practices the form of some of the new words, and then additional exercises focus on the meaning. In most units, there is at least one exercise that gives learners a chance to think about and practice new vocabulary in relation to their own lives, and/or a task that invites learners to do something with the vocabulary outside of the book (e.g., exercises 12.4, 15.4). In every unit, there is a range of exercise types to help maintain your interest.

Using the book

The first six units (or first seven units if you go to an English class) teach you some important vocabulary, but they also help you with useful ideas and techniques for vocabulary learning. Do these units first, and then work through the book, studying the units that interest you. Try to review the units you have covered on a regular basis; for example, if you study three units a week, try to review the three units at the end of the week, or every two weeks. When you review, try to make the words and expressions active, by using them in your own sentences. Be on the lookout for words you have studied, and note whenever you meet them.

What else do I need in order to work with this book?

You will need a vocabulary notebook or file where you can write the new words you are learning. (See Unit 2 for advice on how to do this.)

You will need at least one dictionary, if possible two: an English-English dictionary, preferably a learner's dictionary specifically for students whose first language is not English, and a bilingual dictionary as well. (See Units 3 and 4 for advice on using dictionaries.)

Summary of abbreviations and symbols used in the book	
n.	noun
v.	verb
adj.	adjective
adv.	adverb
prep.	preposition
pl.	word only used in the plural
s.o.	someone
sth.	something
e.g.	for example
i.e.	that is to say; in other words
etc.	and so on
(U)	uncountable word
(C)	countable word
≠	opposite
[*not* I lost the bus]	indicates that a word or an expression is wrong

Learning and reviewing with this book

Look at Exercise 1.1 on the next page before you read this page.

A · **Establish a routine**

A **routine** means doing certain things regularly in the same way. If you are using this book for **self-study** [to study alone] or if you are using it as a class text, it helps to have a routine. Decide how much time you can spend on the book each day or each week. If you are studying a unit for the first time, try to give yourself **at least** [a minimum of] half an hour or forty-five minutes; if you are **reviewing** [looking through a unit a second or third time], five or ten minutes each time is very useful. So, plan longer periods for new units, and shorter periods for **review.**

B · **Working through the book**

- Be *active* when you are learning. For example: While you are reading the left-hand page, you might use a highlighter pen to mark new or interesting vocabulary.
- Practice saying the words **silently** [without noise] in your head, and also **out loud** [making noise], to see if you can pronounce them. Put new words in your own notebook using some of the ideas from Unit 2 to do it **effectively.** [If something is **effective,** it works well and produces good results.]
- If you are using the book for self-study, you can do different things to **maintain your interest** [keep your interest high]. For example, when you do a unit, you can:
  read all of the left-hand page, then do the exercises.
  read part of the left-hand page, then do one or two exercises.
  try the exercises first, then use the left-hand page when you have a problem.

C · **Review**

It is common to learn a word one day, then find you cannot remember it a day later. If you review regularly (just for short periods), it helps you to remember words and make them part of your "active" vocabulary. Here are some ideas for reviewing with this book.

- Do exercises in pencil if you write in your book. Check your answers when you are finished, then **erase them** [remove them using an eraser]. Later, come back and do the exercises again, and use the left-hand page only if you cannot remember something.
- When you read a left-hand page for the second time and reach a new word in **bold** [darker type] that has a definition/explanation after it in **brackets** [ ] or **parentheses** ( ), cover the definition quickly and try to say what it is. Then uncover it to see if you were right.
- Review for short periods, but do it often. Five minutes a day is probably better than half an hour a week; but half an hour a week is probably better than two hours a month.
- As with learning, be *active* when you review. Look for different ways to review: Test yourself; create games for yourself; **set goals/targets** [decide on what you want to be able to do by a particular time].

Exercises

1.1   Answer these questions for yourself.

1. Is it better to plan regular self-study, or to study whenever you get some free time?
2. Do you think it's a good idea to write down new words in a notebook while you are studying a unit?
3. When you learn a new word, do you practice saying it silently, out loud, or both?
4. Is it necessary to review vocabulary?
5. Is it better to review vocabulary occasionally for long periods of time, or is it better to review frequently for short periods of time?

1.2   Finding your way around the book.

Turn to the Topic units (Units 38–90) in the Contents on pages iv–v. Take a piece of paper and cover the examples on the right-hand side of the page. Now read down the list of unit titles. For each one, try to write down your own examples – one or two for each unit. Are there any unit titles you don't understand? Are there any units where you can't think of examples? If so, turn to that unit and find out what it is about.

You could use similar titles in your own vocabulary notebook. (See Unit 2.)

1.3   *True* or *false*? If the sentence is false, rewrite it to make it true. Write your answers in pencil. Don't look at the opposite page.

1. In this book, new words are often shown in **bold** print.
2. Definitions/explanations of new words are often in **brackets** or **parentheses** after the word.
3. A **routine** means doing certain things in a different way each time.
4. If you **maintain** something, it means you keep it at the same level.
5. If something is **effective,** it doesn't work very well.
6. **At least** fifty people means a maximum of fifty people.
7. If you write something, then **erase it,** you remove it from the page.
8. If you do something **silently,** you do it without making noise.
9. **Reviewing** means studying something for the first time.
10. If you have a **goal** or **target,** you have something you want to be able to do or achieve by a particular point in the future.

Now check your answers on the opposite page and look at any wrong answers carefully. Then erase your answers and come back to this exercise tomorrow or within the next two or three days. Find out how much you can remember.

1.4   Planning your study.

Now start making your own plans for learning vocabulary with this book. Decide how much time you can spend each week, including some short periods for review. The first six units will teach you some important vocabulary, give you ideas on keeping a notebook, help you with pronunciation, and present language frequently used in class. You can use these learning strategies in the units that follow. Good luck!

Keeping a vocabulary notebook

A Organizing your notebook

Give each page or section of your notebook a title, e.g., sports, education, phrasal verbs, etc. Then, as you learn new words, **record** [write] each one on an appropriate page. You could also have a general index in the back of your book, with a space for each letter. Then, as you learn new words, you enter them alphabetically, with the title of the topic in parentheses.

B What do I need to record?

What?	*How?*	*Example*
Meaning	a. definition/ explanation	A **pond** is an area of water smaller than a lake.
	b. translation	**lembrar** = to remember (Portuguese)
	c. synonym or opposite	**awful** (= terrible); **ugly** (≠ beautiful)
	d. picture	**saucepan** 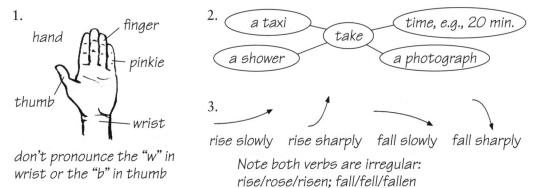
	e. example sentence	My hands were cold, so I **put on** my **gloves**.
Pronunciation	phonetic symbols *or* your own system	**ache** /eɪk/ **ache** (like "make")
Part of speech	(n.), (v.), (adj.), etc.	**gloves** (noun); **remember** (verb); **careful** (adjective), **ache** (n., v.)
Grammar	make a note + example sentence	**enjoy + -ing** form: I enjoy going to parties. **weather** (uncountable): We had beautiful **weather** in Rio.
Common partners	phrase or sentence	**make** a **mistake**; **make** a **decision**; **make** a **mess**
Special style	make a note	**purchase** *(formal)*; **kids** *(informal)*

Note: These things are important, but you won't need to record all of them for every word. You won't learn everything about a word when you first record it, so always leave space in your notebook; then you can add more information later.

C Organizing words on the page

Certain words often appear together (common partners), so it is a good idea to record them together, and not just write lists of individual words. You can do this in different ways:

1.

hand — finger
— pinkie
thumb — wrist

don't pronounce the "w" in wrist or the "b" in thumb

2. a taxi — take — time, e.g., 20 min.
a shower — a photograph

3. rise slowly · rise sharply · fall slowly · fall sharply

Note both verbs are irregular: rise/rose/risen; fall/fell/fallen

Exercises

2.1 Arrange these words into three groups, and give each one a title.

tie	ticket	fare	blouse	homeless	train	thoughtless
painful	scarf	dress	trip	station	careful	jacket
jeans	helpful	platform	put on	useless	get on	useful

Look in the Contents on pages iii–v and find the units in this book that may include these words. Then add more examples.

2.2 <u>Underline</u> the correct answer or answers.

1. I really enjoy:
   a) play tennis   b) to play tennis   c) playing tennis
2. When we were on vacation, we had:
   a) beautiful weathers   b) beautiful weather   c) a beautiful weather
3. The underlined letters in **ache** are pronounced the same as in:
   a) m<u>a</u>chine   b) <u>c</u>atch   c) <u>ch</u>emistry
4. When we were in Seoul, we .... lots of photos.
   a) did   b) took   c) made
5. The .... is also called the little finger.
   a) thumb   b) wrist   c) pinkie
6. The past tense of **fall** is:
   a) fell   b) felt   c) falled
7. You can **put on**:
   a) gloves   b) a decision   c) shoes
8. **Rise sharply** means:

   a)   b)   c)

2.3 Look again at B on the opposite page. Which would be the best way(s) to record the meaning of each word below? What other information would be useful to record with the word (e.g., pronunciation, part of speech, grammar, common partners, etc.)? Use a dictionary to help you.

| dream | concentrate | beard | nearly |
| empty | forget | rescue | knife |

2.4 Fill in the blanks with common partners for these verbs, then start a page in your own notebook for more examples. Turn to Unit 20 for help.

take   a picture   make   a mistake
       ....
       ....

do   your homework   have   breakfast
       ....
       ....

Using a dictionary (1)

A What dictionaries do I need?

If possible, you should have two dictionaries: a good bilingual dictionary and an English learner's dictionary, designed for students learning English as a second or foreign language. The bilingual dictionary is quicker and easier for you to understand, but the English learner's dictionary may give you more information about a word or phrase. It is also a good idea for you to work in English as much as possible.

B What information does a dictionary give me?

- the meaning, e.g., **homesick** [unhappy when you are away from home]
- the pronunciation, e.g., **chaos** /ˈkeɪˌɑs/, **dreadful** /ˈdred·fəl/, **island** /ˈaɪ·lənd/
- division of syllables, e.g., **stu·dent** = two syllables
- the part of speech, e.g., **dirty** *adj.* [adjective], **lose** *v.* [verb], **law** *n.* [noun]
- any special grammatical features, e.g., **advice** (U) [uncountable]
- common collocations (word partners), e.g., you **do homework** [*not* you **make homework**]
- idioms associated with a word, e.g., **take your time** with the word **time**
- example phrases or sentences, e.g., It was such a big menu, I didn't know what to **choose.**
- synonyms (where they exist), e.g., **sad = unhappy**
- opposites (where they exist), e.g., **polite** [≠ **impolite/rude**]
- labels, e.g., *formal, informal, spoken, technical, disapproving*

pronunciation part of speech grammatical feature

definition —

collocations —

idioms —

seat FURNITURE /siːt/ *n* [C] an item of furniture that has been designed for someone to sit on • *Chairs, stools, sofas and benches are different types of seat.* • *All the chairs are taken – I'm afraid you'll have to use this table as a seat.* • *A car usually has a **driver's** seat, a **front/passenger** seat and **back/rear** seats.* • *Why don't you sit down **on** that seat over there while we're waiting?* • If you tell someone to **have/take a seat** you are asking them politely to sit down: *Have a seat, Mr. Jones, and tell me what I can do for you.* • *Just calm down, take a seat, and describe what happened.*

— examples

C How should I use my dictionary?

- When you look up a word in your dictionary, put a ✓ next to it. Each time you return to a page with a ✓, look at it quickly to check that you remember the word.
- If you see an English word in a reading passage, first try to guess the meaning, and continue reading to the end of the paragraph or page to see if your guess seems correct. Then use your dictionary to check the meaning.
- If you look up a word in a bilingual dictionary and get several different words in your own language, try looking up the word in your English dictionary. This should help you decide which word in your own language is the nearest translation in this context.
- Remember that many words have more than one meaning, and the first meaning in the dictionary is not always the one you want. Read through the different meanings and check them against the context of your word.

Exercises

3.1 Use a dictionary to find/check the answers to these questions. (They all use words from the opposite page.)

1. What does **dreadful** mean?   *very bad, terrible*
2. How do you pronounce **lose?** (Is it the same as *choose* or *chose?*)
3. What part of speech is **choose?**
4. What part of speech is **homesick?**
5. **Homework** and **chaos** are both nouns, but what type of noun are they?
6. Write two adjectives that are often used before **chaos.**
7. How many syllables does **chaos** have?
8. How do you pronounce the **ch** in **chaos?** (Is it the same sound as in *character* or *change?*)
9. What two prepositions are often used after **choose?**
10. Write a sentence using **choose** with a preposition.

3.2 When you look up a word in your dictionary, you can also learn related words and phrases. Find out if your dictionary helps you to answer these questions.

1. **Choose** is a verb, but what is the noun with the same meaning?   *choice*
2. **Advice** is a noun, but what is the verb with the same meaning?
3. **Advice** is uncountable, but you can make it countable using another word. Can you complete this sentence: "He gave me a very useful .... of advice."
4. What adjective is formed from **chaos?**
5. What is the opposite of **dirty?**
6. What is the difference between **homework** and **housework?**
7. What is the opposite of **lose a game?**
8. What is the opposite of **lose weight?**
9. **Law** often appears in the phrase **law and** ....
10. If you want to invite someone to sit down in an empty **seat,** what can you say?

3.3 In the word *island* /ˈaɪ·lənd/, the letter *s* is *silent* [not pronounced]. Use the pronunciation guide in your dictionary to find the silent letters in each of these words. (Do not include the letter *e* at the end of a word.)

island   bomb   psychology   receipt
castle   doubt   wrist   knife

Note: Students often ask if the letter *t* is pronounced in **often.** Some people pronounce it, others don't. What does your dictionary say?

3.4 Do these words or phrases have labels in your dictionary?

Example: grungy – *informal*

bye-bye   incision   thereby   put someone down   childish

Using a dictionary (2)

A Finding the best meaning

Many words in English have multiple meanings, and sometimes a word can be more than one part of speech (or word class). For example, the word **treat** can be a noun or a verb, each with several different meanings. Look at these dictionary entries for **treat**:

> **treat**[1] /trit/ *v* [T] **1** to behave toward someone in a particular way: *Why do you **treat** me **like an idiot**? | She **treats** children **the same as** adults. | Mr. Parker **treats** everyone **equally/fairly**.* **2** to consider something in a particular way: *You can **treat** these costs **as** business expenses.* **3** to give someone medical attention for a sickness or injury: *Eleven people were **treated for** minor injuries.* **4** to buy or arrange something special for someone: *We're **treating** Mom **to** dinner for her birthday.* **5** to put a special substance on something or use a chemical process in order to protect or clean it: *The wood has been treated to make it waterproof.*
>
> **treat**[2] *n* **1** something special that you give someone or do for him/her: *If you're good, I'll buy you a treat.* **2** [singular] an unexpected event that gives you a lot of pleasure: *Getting your letter was a real treat.* **3 my treat** SPOKEN used in order to tell someone that you will pay for something: *Put away your money – dinner's my treat.*

When you meet a new word, you first need to decide which part of speech it is. Then read all the definitions for that part of speech and select one that makes sense for the sentence: "These crops have been <u>treated</u> with insecticide." (verb, definition #5)   "You're always taking me out. This time it's *my* <u>treat</u>." (noun, definition #3)

B Finding phrases in a dictionary

Dictionaries explain the meanings of single words and compound words, but they also explain a large number of phrases, e.g., **take your time, for the time being, to tell (you) the truth, on the tip of my tongue, sooner or later, How are you?**, etc.

Where do you find them?

1. If a phrase contains a **noun** (or nouns), that is the first place to look. For example, **take your time** and **for the time being** are both explained under *time*. **On the tip of my tongue** is under *tip* and *tongue*.

   > **time** PERIOD /taɪm/ *n* . . . • *Leave the ironing **for the time being** (=for a limited period) – I'll do it later.* • *If you **take** your **time,** you do something slowly: Take your time, there's no hurry.* • *He's certainly taken his time in answering my letter.*

2. If there is a **verb,** that is the next place to look. For example, **you can say that again** is under *say;* **to tell (you) the truth** is usually under both *tell* and *truth*.

   > **say** *(obj)* SPEAK /seɪ/ *v past* **said** /sed/ • *(saying)* "You can say that again" means I completely agree with you.
   > **tell** /tɛl/ *v* **told, told, telling** . . . **13 to tell (you) the truth** said in order to emphasize or admit that what you are saying is true: *I don't know how you cope, to tell you the truth.*
   > **truth** /truθ/ *n* . . . **4 to tell (you) the truth** SPOKEN used when you admit something or tell someone your true opinion: *To tell you the truth, I don't care where she went.*

3. If there is no noun or verb (or only the verb *be*), look up the first word in the phrase (except for prepositions and articles). For example, **sooner or later** is usually explained under *sooner;* **How are you?** is under *how*.

(See also Unit 5.)

Exercises

4.1 Some learner's dictionaries have *guide words* at the beginning of the definition, which give core meanings so you can find a simple definition quickly. Most of the dictionary entries below for *raise* use guide words.

Read the entries and the sentences below them. For each sentence, identify the best definition of *raise* by writing a guide word or a brief definition.

---

raise[1] /reɪz/ *v* [T]
1 ▶MOVE◀ to move or lift something to a higher position or to an upright position: *The flag is raised at school every morning.* | **Raise your hand** *if you know the answer.*
2 ▶INCREASE◀ to increase an amount, number, or level: *a plan to raise taxes* | *Don't **raise your voice** at me, young man.* (=speak loudly and angrily)
3 ▶IMPROVE◀ to improve the quality or standard of something: *This bill is all about raising standards in our schools.*

4 ▶CHILDREN/ANIMALS/CROPS◀ to take care of children, animals, or crops until they are fully grown: *They've raised seven children.* | *He wants to try raising corn.*
5 ▶GET MONEY/SUPPORT◀ to collect money, support etc. so that you can use it to help people: *We've raised $10,000 for cancer research.*
6 raise a question/objection etc. to begin to talk or write about something that you want someone to consider: *Maryann raised the issue of marriage again.*

---

1. We <u>raised</u> a lot of money at the Walk for Cancer last weekend.
   get money/support
2. She was <u>raised</u> on a farm, but later she moved to the city.
3. Our <u>salaries</u> haven't been <u>raised</u> in four years.
4. They <u>raise</u> corn and wheat on this farm.
5. If you want better quality, you need to <u>raise</u> your standards.
6. I know you're angry, but please don't <u>raise</u> your voice.
7. At the meeting, employees <u>raised</u> questions that management couldn't answer.
8. If you have any questions <u>about</u> the lesson, please <u>raise</u> your hand.

4.2 Look up *raise* in your own dictionaries (both bilingual and English) and compare the entries with the ones in 4.1 above. Do your dictionaries show the same features (e.g., part of speech, grammar, pronunciation) and in the same way? If not, how are they different?

4.3 Use your English dictionary to find these phrases and expressions. Which word(s) did you find them listed under?

Example: on the tip of my tongue   *tip; some dictionaries list it under both "tip" and "tongue."*

1. in other words
2. better late than never
3. on second thought
4. break a promise
5. no hard feelings
6. every now and then
7. the sooner the better
8. a matter of opinion/time
9. beside the point

4.4 Dictionary quiz: Answer these questions using an English dictionary.

1. You bought half a **dozen** eggs. How many did you buy?   *six*
2. When you went out, it was very **chilly.** Were you hot or cold?
3. When you are **feeling blue,** are you happy or sad?
4. Your friend was **climbing the walls** last night. How did your friend feel?
5. If you are **bilingual,** how many languages can you speak?

English language words

Parts of speech

nouns	e.g., chair, information, happiness
verbs	e.g., choose, tell, complain
adjectives	e.g., happy, tall, dangerous
adverbs	e.g., slowly, carefully, often
prepositions	e.g., in, at, on
pronouns	e.g., me, you, him, we, it, she
articles	e.g., definite article *(the)*; indefinite article *(a, an)*

Special terms

uncountable noun (U): a noun that has no plural form and cannot be used with the indefinite article, e.g., *information*. See Unit 28.

plural noun (pl.): a noun that has a plural form but no singular form and cannot be used with the indefinite article, e.g., *scissors*. See Unit 28.

infinitive: the base form of a verb used with *to*, e.g., *to work, to stop, to be.*

phrasal verb: a verb + adverb and/or preposition, e.g., *turn on, look over, give up, put up with.* See Units 17 and 18.

idiom: a group of words with a meaning that is different from the individual words, e.g., *have second thoughts, have something in mind, keep an eye on something.*

transitive verb: a verb that needs a **direct object,** e.g., "Police caught the thief" (*the thief* is the direct object of the verb *caught*). See Unit 18.

intransitive verb: a verb that does not need a direct object, e.g., "The books arrived on time" (there is no direct object after *arrive*). See Unit 18.

Word building

In the word *uncomfortable, un-* is a **prefix,** *comfort* is a **root,** and *-able* is a **suffix.** Other common prefixes include: *re-, in-,* and *dis-;* common suffixes include: *-ity, -ment,* and *-ive.* Many words also have **synonyms,** which are words with the same meaning. For example, *big* is a synonym of *large.* The **opposite** is *small.*

Pronunciation

Dictionaries show the pronunciation of a word using **phonetic symbols,** e.g., book /bʊk/, before /bɪˈfoʊr/, computer /kəmˈpjut·ər/, and so on.

Each word contains one or more **syllables:** *book* has one syllable; *before* has two syllables (be-fore); *computer* has three syllables (com-put-er). The **stress** is on the second syllable in be<u>fore</u> and in com<u>pu</u>ter.

Note: Dictionaries mark stress in different ways: in bold (**return**); or with a ' before the stressed syllable (reˈturn); or with a ' after the stressed syllable (re turnˈ). Make sure you understand how your dictionary shows stress.

Punctuation

period	.	comma	,	parentheses	( )
brackets	[ ]	hyphen	-	question mark	?

Exercises

5.1 There is one word missing in each line of this text. Where does the missing word go? And what type of word is it (noun, verb, etc.)? Can you guess the word? Look at the example first.

Last year I went to͜for my vacation. I spent the first
week Seville staying with a couple of friends, and
then I took a train to Barcelona, where spent another
ten days. It is beautiful city and I had a marvelous
time. I stayed in a very hotel right in the center of
town, but I didn't mind spending a lot money
because it is a wonderful and also very convenient.
My brother recommended it; he goes Spain a lot
and he stays anywhere else.

1. *Spain (noun)*
2. ....
3. ....
4. ....
5. ....
6. ....
7. ....
8. ....
9. ....

5.2 In the dialogue below, can you find at least one example of: an uncountable noun; a plural noun; a phrasal verb; an idiom?

A: What time is it?
B: Eight o'clock, so we'd better get a move on if we're going to meet Keiko at the airport.
A: That's all right. Her flight doesn't arrive until 8:30.
B: Yeah, but it'll take us an hour to get there – you know what the traffic is like.
A: OK. I'll just go and change clothes.
B: What's wrong with those shorts?
A: I don't like driving in shorts. I'm going to put some jeans on.

5.3 Look at the underlined verbs in these sentences. Which are transitive, and which are intransitive?

1. She broke her leg.   *transitive*
2. I got up at 7:30.
3. We arrived late.
4. Take off your jacket.
5. She doesn't like Chinese food.
6. He told me to sit down.

5.4 How many syllables are there in each of the words in the box? Mark the main stress in each word.

English	noun	informal	education
understand	adjective	decide	pronunciation
before	opposite	preposition	comfortable

5.5 Look at these words, then answer the questions.

happy   correct   lucky   sure   possible

1. What part of speech are these words?
2. Change each one into an adverb.
3. Can you think of a synonym for at least three of the words?
4. Which prefix can you use to form the opposite of each word? (three different prefixes)
5. Which word has the main stress on the second syllable?

UNIT
6 Problems with pronunciation

A **Phonetics**

With many languages you can look at a word and know (more or less) how to pronounce it. With English it can be difficult to know the pronunciation of a word by looking at it. For example:

c<u>ough</u> (sounds like *off*); en<u>ough</u> (like *stuff*); thr<u>ough</u> (like *too*); th<u>ough</u> (like *so*)

One way you can be sure about the pronunciation is to learn some phonetic symbols. Dictionaries use them, and there is a table of phonetic symbols, with examples, on page 204. Phonetic symbols are used next to most words in the index, and there is a special list of words on page 205 that cause pronunciation problems for English learners.

B **Word stress**

When a word has two or more syllables, one of them has the main stress. If you put the stress on the wrong syllable, it may be difficult to understand you. In these examples, the main stress follows the symbol ' :

'accent   pre'fer   edu'cation   'necessary   Ja'pan   Japa'nese

C **Schwa /ə/**

Schwa /ə/ is probably the most important sound in English, because it is often the pronunciation of the letters **a, o,** and **e** if they are not part of a stressed syllable.

ma'chine /mə'ʃin/   'mother /'mʌð·ər/
po'tato /pə'teɪt·oʊ/   ba'nana /bə'næn·ə/

D **Key letters and sounds**

A common problem is that a single letter or combination of letters has more than one pronunciation, e.g., -ough in section A. Here are some more examples:

the letter **o** is often /ɑ/ as in **hot;** or /oʊ/ as in **no;** /ʌ/ as in **some;** or /ə/ as in **melon**
the letter **a** is often /æ/ as in **hat;** or /eɪ/ as in **same;** or /ə/ as in **across**
the letter **u** is often /ʌ/ as in **run;** or /ʊ/ as in **put;** or /u/ as in **ruler**
the letter **i** is often /ɪ/ as in **sit;** or /ɑɪ/ as in **side;** or /i/ as in **police**

E **Silent letters and short syllables**

There are many words in English where a letter is not pronounced:

fas<u>t</u>en   plum<u>b</u>er   woul<u>d</u>   <u>k</u>nee   <u>w</u>rong   com<u>b</u>

There are also words where we almost "eat" one of the syllables, so that a vowel sound disappears or almost disappears. For example:

interested /'ɪn·trəst·ɪd/   fattening /'fæt·nɪŋ/   vegetable /'vedʒ·tə·bəl/
chocolate /'tʃɔ·klət/   laboratory /'læb·rə,toʊr·i/   every /'ev·ri/

14

Exercises

6.1 Using your dictionary or the index of this book, fill in the pronunciation of the vowels in these words (put the symbols between the / /). Then practice saying the pairs of words, making sure you know the difference.

1. row /oʊ/   cow /   /   3. soup / /   soap / /

2. back / /   bacon / /   4. pot / /   pole / /

6.2 Look at the underlined letters in these words. Circle the odd one out.

1. br<u>ea</u>d   (dr<u>ea</u>m)   spr<u>ea</u>d   d<u>ea</u>d
2. sp<u>oo</u>n   f<u>oo</u>d   fl<u>oo</u>d   ch<u>oo</u>se
3. f<u>a</u>st   phr<u>a</u>se   bl<u>a</u>me   sunb<u>a</u>the
4. c<u>ou</u>sin   w<u>ou</u>nd (n.)   r<u>ou</u>gh   tr<u>ou</u>ble
5. v<u>i</u>rus   p<u>i</u>lot   d<u>i</u>et   s<u>i</u>nce
6. h<u>y</u>phen   s<u>y</u>mptom   t<u>y</u>pe   ps<u>y</u>chology

6.3 Which syllable has the main stress in these words? Put them in the correct column. How many examples of the schwa /ə/ sound can you find?

cathedral   policy   palace   desert (n.)   competition   organize
opposite   police   understand   attractive   assistance   education

First syllable	*Second syllable*	*Third syllable*
opposite		

Note: Some English speakers may pronounce the reduced sound in some of these words as either /ə/ or /ɪ/, e.g., *palace* could be /'pæl·əs/ or /'pæl·ɪs/.

6.4 Look at the underlined letters in these pairs of words. Is the pronunciation the same or different?

<u>k</u>now / <u>k</u>nife *same*   mus<u>c</u>le / s<u>c</u>issors   <u>h</u>onest / <u>h</u>ope
lis<u>t</u>en / wes<u>t</u>ern   ans<u>w</u>er / s<u>w</u>ear   <u>w</u>rong / <u>w</u>rist
is<u>l</u>and / Is<u>l</u>am   clim<u>b</u> / bom<u>b</u>   col<u>d</u> / coul<u>d</u>

UNIT 7 Classroom language

A Equipment

These are some things you may use in your classroom or school.

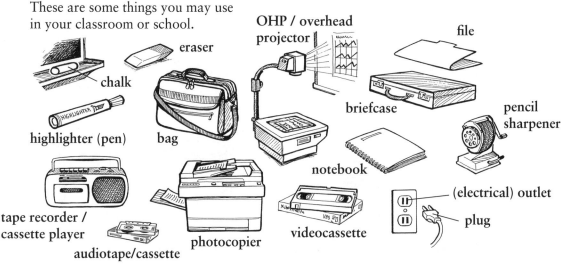

Note: We can use some of these nouns as verbs with little or no change: **to (video)tape** [to record a program on video], **to (photo)copy** [to use the photocopier], **to highlight,** and **to file** [to put things in a file].

B Classroom activities

Things students or teachers do in the classroom:

Look up a word if you don't understand it. [find the meaning of a word in a dictionary]
Borrow someone's dictionary or eraser. [use it and then return it]
Plug in the tape recorder. [put the plug in the outlet]
Turn up the tape recorder if you can't hear it. [increase the volume]
Erase things **from** a notebook / the board. [remove writing from a notebook / the board]
Correct students' English. [give the correct English if students make mistakes]

Things a teacher may ask students to do in the classroom:

Could you **erase** the board, Carlos? [remove all the writing from the board]
Write these words **down.** [Write these words on a piece of paper / in a notebook.]
Kim, could you **share** a book with Lorena? [use it together and at the same time]
Repeat this sentence after me. [say it again]
If you have a question, **raise your hand.** [hold up your arm]

C Questions about vocabulary

What does X mean? (*not* What means X?)
How do you pronounce it?
How do you spell *bicycle?*
How do you use *anyway* in a sentence?
What's the difference between X and Y?

Exercises

7.1   Label these pictures. Then check your answers on the opposite page.

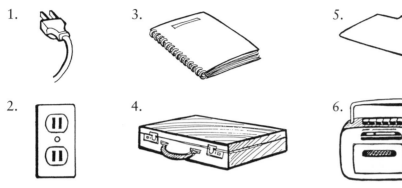

1.

2.

3.

4.

5.

6.

7.2   Answer these questions.

1. Why do you turn up a tape recorder?   *to make it louder*
2. What do you put in a tape recorder?
3. What do you use a photocopier for?
4. What do you keep in a file?
5. What do you put in a briefcase?
6. What do you put in an outlet?
7. What do you use a dictionary for?
8. What do you use an eraser for?

7.3   Match the verbs on the left with the nouns on the right.

1. look up	a classmate
2. turn up	a word
3. borrow	mistakes
4. share with	an exercise
5. videotape	a dictionary
6. do	the OHP
7. make	the tape recorder
8. plug in	a program

7.4   Think about your last class. Did you do any of these things?

use an eraser	look up a word
borrow something	make or correct a mistake
raise your hand	write something down in a notebook

7.5   Here are some answers. What are the possible questions?

A: ....?   B: It means to use something that belongs to someone else and then return it.

A: ....?   B: /ˈbɑr·oʊ/ Like *tomorrow*.

A: ....?   B: B-O-R-R-O-W.

A: ....?   B: If you borrow something, you take it. If you lend something, you give it.

Prefixes

A With the meaning "not"

Prefixes (**un-**, **im-**, **in-**, **il-**, **ir-**, and **dis-**) are often used to give adjectives (and some verbs and nouns) a negative meaning. Here are common examples:

happy	**un**happy	like (v.)	**dis**like (v.)
possible	**im**possible	legal	**il**legal [against the law]
correct	**in**correct	regular	**ir**regular, e.g., irregular verbs

un- is used with many different words, e.g., **unfriendly**, **unable**, **unemployed** [without a job], **unreasonable**, **unknown**.

im- is used before some words beginning with **m** or **p**, e.g., **impolite** [rude], **impatient** [someone who is **impatient** wants things to happen now; they cannot wait].

il- is used before some words beginning with **l**, e.g., **illegible** [cannot be read because the writing or the copy is very bad].

ir- is used only before words beginning with **r**, e.g., **irresponsible**.

dis- is used before some adjectives, e.g., **dishonest**, and a few verbs, e.g., **dislike**, **disagree**.

in- is used before a limited number of words, e.g., **invisible** [cannot be seen].

Note: A prefix does not usually change word stress, e.g., happy/unhappy; possible/impossible.

B Verb prefixes: *un-* and *dis-*

These prefixes have two meanings: They can have a negative meaning (as above), but they can also mean "the opposite of an action" or "to reverse an action."

I **locked** the door when I left, but then I lost the key, so I couldn't **unlock** it.

I had to **pack** my suitcase [put clothes, etc., in it] very quickly, so when I **unpacked** [took everything out] at the hotel, most of my clothes looked terrible.

The plane **appeared** in the sky, then suddenly **disappeared** behind a cloud.

In the morning you **get dressed** [put on your clothes]. Before you go to bed, you **get undressed** [take off your clothes].

C Other verb prefixes with specific meanings

re- [again]	My homework was all wrong, so I had to **redo** it. The store closed down, but it will **reopen** next month. I failed my exam, but I can **retake** it next year.
over- [too much]	You can get a stomachache from **overeating**. I went to bed late and **overslept** this morning. [slept too long] The cashier **overcharged** me. [charged me too much money]
mis- [badly or incorrectly]	I'm sorry, but I **misunderstood** what you said. Two of the students **misread** the first question. A lot of people **misspell** the word *misspell*.

MAYBE I OVERATE.

Exercises

8.1 Write the prefix that forms the opposite of these words. (The words on the
bottom line are all verbs; the rest are adjectives.)

....*un*..happy	........patient	........polite	........legal
........correct	........regular	........visible	........possible
........legible	........friendly	........employed	........honest
........pack	........lock	........agree	........appear

8.2 Agree with these statements, using words from the opposite page that have the
same meaning as the underlined words.

Example: A: He doesn't have a <u>job</u>, does he?

B: No, ...*he's unemployed*........ .

1. It's <u>against the law</u>, isn't it?
   Oh, yes, ...
2. This bill can't be right. They've <u>charged me way too much</u>.
   You're right. They've .... you.
3. <u>Bacteria can't be seen</u> without a microscope.
   That's right. They're practically ....
4. This handwriting is <u>impossible to read</u>.
   Yes, I know, ...
5. She <u>can never wait for five minutes</u>, can she?
   No, ...
6. I thought it was <u>rude</u>, didn't you?
   Yes, it was very ....

8.3 Complete the verbs in these sentences.

1. I'm sorry, I mis.*understood*.. her message completely.
2. We un....................... as soon as we got to the hotel, then went out for a walk.
3. She was here a minute ago, but then she dis....................... . I don't know
   where she went.
4. We usually have similar opinions, but I totally dis....................... with him on
   this subject.
5. My homework was so bad that I had to re....................... it.
6. Her alarm clock didn't go off and she over....................... .
7. She finally managed to un....................... the door, and we were able to go
   inside.
8. I dis....................... the movie, but everyone else enjoyed it.
9. I don't think I'll pass the exam, but I can re....................... it in September.
10. He wrapped my present so well that it took me five minutes to
    un....................... it.
11. I was so tired that I fell asleep without getting un....................... .
12. My spell checker corrects my mistakes whenever I mis....................... a word.

8.4 Keep a few pages in your notebook for verbs or adjectives that combine with
these prefixes. Each time you add a new word, read through your list of words
with that prefix, then close your book and see how many you can remember.

Noun suffixes

A   Verb + suffix

Many nouns are formed by adding a suffix to a verb.

Verb	Suffix	Noun
improve [get better]	-ment	improvement
manage [e.g., a store or business]	-ment	management
elect [choose somebody by voting]	-ion	election
discuss [talk about something seriously]	-ion	discussion
inform [give someone facts; *formal*]	-ation	information
administer [manage a company, government, etc.]	-ation	administration
spell [e.g., S-P-E-L-L]	-ing	spelling

Note: Sometimes there is a spelling change, for example, the omission of the final e before the suffixes **-ion** and **-ation:** organize – organization; translate – translation.

B   Adjective + suffix

Nouns are also formed by adding a suffix, such as **-ness** or **-ity,** to an adjective. Notice that the y changes to **i** before the suffix **-ness:** happy – happiness.

Adjective	Suffix	Noun
weak [≠ strong]	-ness	weakness
dark [e.g., at night, when you can't see]	-ness	darkness
happy	-ness	happiness
stupid [≠ intelligent, smart]	-ity	stupidity
punctual [always arrives on time]	-ity	punctuality
similar [almost the same; ≠ different]	-ity	similarity

C   Pronunciation

Adding a suffix to a verb or an adjective may change the pronunciation. Nouns ending with **-ion** or **-ity** have the main stress on the syllable before, so the stress may change:

Verb	Noun	Adjective	Noun
educate	education	similar	similarity
inform	information	stupid	stupidity
discuss	discussion	punctual	punctuality

D   *-er, -or,* and *-ist*

These common noun suffixes, added to nouns or verbs, describe people and their occupations. Notice the common spelling changes: translate – translator, economy – economist, psychology – psychologist.

-er	-er	-or	-ist
dancer	driver	actor	artist
singer	manager	director	economist
teacher	writer	translator	psychologist
farmer	employer	operator	journalist

Exercises

9.1 Complete the tables and mark the stress in each word. Some words are not on the opposite page – do you know or can you guess them?

Verb	Noun	Adjective	Noun
educate	*education*	stupid	....
improve	....	dark	....
discuss	....	weak	....
govern	....	similar	....
spell	....	punctual	....
hesitate	....	happy	....
arrange	....	popular	....

9.2 Combine the suffixes on the right with the words on the left. Then complete the paragraph below. (You may need to make small spelling changes.)

improve	televise	elect
educate	weak	manage
administer	stupid	

-ment	-ion
-ation	-ness
-ity	

In her first broadcast on (1) *television* .... since she won the
(2) .... last month, the president promised to make health and
(3) .... two of her top priorities. And in a strong attack on the
previous (4) ...., she said that the current (5) ....
of the nation's economy was caused entirely by (6) .... and bad
(7) .... She said she would act immediately and she hoped the
people would be able to see clear signs of an (8) .... in the
economy by the end of the year.

9.3 Write the name of the person who does these things.

1. farm *farmer*
2. employ ....
3. act ....
4. sing ....
5. drive ....
6. psychology ....
7. economics ....
8. translate ....
9. manage ....

9.4 Look at the two examples and then complete the rest of the definitions.

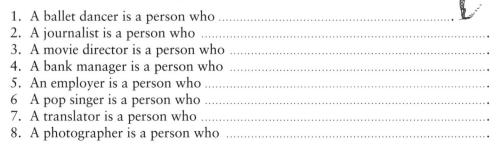

Examples: An actor is a person who *acts in movies, plays, and on TV.*
A taxi driver is a person who *drives a taxi.*

1. A ballet dancer is a person who ....
2. A journalist is a person who ....
3. A movie director is a person who ....
4. A bank manager is a person who ....
5. An employer is a person who ....
6 A pop singer is a person who ....
7. A translator is a person who ....
8. A photographer is a person who ....

10 Adjective suffixes

Suffixes change word class, e.g., from verb to noun or noun to adjective, but they can also change meaning (see sections B and C below).

A Noun or verb + suffix

Noun or verb	Suffix	Adjectives
danger, fame	-ous	dangerous, famous [well known]
music, politics, industry, economics	-al	musical, political, industrial, economical [saves you money]
cloud, fog, sun, dirt	-y	cloudy, foggy, sunny, dirty [≠ clean]
attract, create	-ive	attractive [pretty, nice to look at]; creative [able to produce new ideas; with imagination]

Note: Sometimes there is a spelling change. Here are common examples:
double the consonant, e.g., sun – sunny, fog – foggy
leave out the final **e**, e.g., create – creative, fame – famous
leave out the final **s** before **-al**, e.g., politics – political; economics – economical
change **y** to **i** before **-al**, e.g., industry – industrial

B *-able* and *-ible*

These suffixes (pronounced /ə·bəl/) can form many adjectives from nouns or verbs: **enjoyable, comfortable, knowledgeable** [knows a lot], **flexible** [can be bent].

Often, **-able** and **-ible** have the meaning "can be done." For example, something that is **washable** "can be washed." Other examples include: **drinkable, comprehensible** [can be comprehended or understood], **reliable** [can be relied on or trusted].

Words ending with **-able** quite often express the opposite meaning by adding the prefix **un-**: **undrinkable, unreliable, unbreakable** [cannot be broken], **uncomfortable.**

Words ending with **-ible** add the prefix **in-**: **incomprehensible, inflexible** [somebody who is inflexible cannot change quickly or easily]; **inedible** [cannot be eaten].

C *-ful* and *-less*

The suffix **-ful** often means "full of": If you are **careful**, you are full of care; if you are **helpful**, you are full of help. Other examples are: **painful** [hurts a lot], **useful,** and **thoughtful** [someone who is thoughtful is kind and always thinks about others].

thoughtful   **painful**

The suffix **-less** means "without": If you are **careless**, you do something "without care." Other examples are: **painless, useless** [has no use or function], **thoughtless, hopeless,** and **homeless** [with nowhere to live].

Note: You can see that **-ful** and **-less** are often used with the same words to form opposites. But this is not *always* true: A person with a home is *not* "homeful."

Exercises

10.1 Cover the opposite page. Then write an adjective (or adjectives) from these nouns or verbs.

Example: thought *thoughtful, thoughtless*

industry	dirt	pain	comfort
attract	care	knowledge	fame
create	danger	comprehend	rely
fog	politics	sun	wash
home	enjoy	music	break

10.2 Fill in the blanks with adjectives from the opposite page.

1. You have to be very .... when you drive in wet weather.
2. Everyone in my country has heard of her; she's very ....
3. The people in the tourist information office were very .... and answered all our questions.
4. This is a very .... road; there were three serious accidents on it last year.
5. It was very .... when I hit my leg against the corner of the table.
6. We haven't had any problems with our TV in ten years; it's been very ....
7. The factory is in the middle of the .... part of the city, surrounded by other factories.
8. I made some coffee, but it was horrible. In fact, my sister said it was ....
9. Unfortunately my working hours are very ....; I have to start at exactly the same time every day and finish at the same time every day.
10. It's terrible that there are so many .... people living in a city with thousands of empty houses.

10.3 Which of these words can form opposites with the suffix *-less*?

painful	wonderful	useful	hopeful
beautiful	tactful	awful	thoughtful

Can you think of words that mean the opposite of the other words (the ones without *-less*)?

10.4 Choose three adjectives from this unit to describe each of these people or things. (You can use the same adjective more than once.)

1. the weather *cloudy, sunny, foggy* ....
2. someone who is a very bad driver ....
3. Wolfgang Amadeus Mozart ....
4. a large city ....
5. Albert Einstein ....
6. a new car ....
7. a speech ....
8. yourself ....

Nouns, verbs, and adjectives with the same form

A   What are nouns and verbs with the same form?

Many words in English can function as a noun and a verb, or a noun and an adjective, or a verb and an adjective, with no change in form. The meaning is not always the same, but this unit looks at examples of words with the same form and the same meaning.

What's the **answer?** (noun)
Please **answer** the question. (verb)

I don't like the **cold.** (noun)
I don't like **cold** weather. (adjective)

I have to **clean** my room. (verb)
It's a **clean** room. (adjective)

I didn't **reply** to the letter. (verb)
I wrote a **reply** to the letter. (noun)

Note: Other examples in the book are marked like this: ache (n., v.), damage (n., v.), dry (v., adj.). Keep a record of them in your notebook.

B   Noun and verb

You may know these words as one form but not the other. (The definitions are for the verb.)

brake [stop a car using the **brake** on the floor]
diet [eat less and lose weight]
guess [give an answer when you're not sure of the facts]

call [telephone]
push [≠ **pull**]
murder [kill someone]

Note: Other words in this group include **stay, drink, rest, look, cost,** and **wait.**

C   Which verb?

When you use these words as nouns, you need to choose the correct verb to use with them.

Verb	*Noun*
We **rested** for a while.	We **took/had** a short rest.
She **braked** quickly.	She **hit** the brakes quickly.
He needs to **diet.**	He needs to **go on** a diet.
I'll **call** you next week.	I'll **give** you a call next week.
I **dreamed** about you last night.	I **had** a dream about you last night.

Exercises

11.1 Rewrite these sentences using the underlined nouns as verbs. The meaning must stay the same.

Example: There was a lot of rain yesterday.
        It rained a lot yesterday.

1. We had a long wait.
   ....

2. Can you give me an answer to my question?
   ....

3. This orange has a strange taste.
   ....

4. The cost of the vacation was about $800.
   ....

5. I wrote a reply to his letter yesterday.
   ....

6. When the door gets stuck, you have to give it a push.
   ....

11.2 Now rewrite these sentences using the underlined verbs as nouns. The meaning should stay the same.

Example: I'll call her tonight.
        I'll give her a call tonight.

1. If I put on weight, I diet, but then I always gain it back again.
   ....

2. It was very hot, so we rested after lunch.
   ....

3. I braked, but I still couldn't stop in time.
   ....

4. I dreamed about you last night.
   ....

11.3 Sometimes the same word form can be a verb and a noun but with a very different meaning. Read these pairs of sentences. Does the verb have the same meaning as the noun, a similar meaning, or a completely different meaning?

1. We had a long wait for the bus.
   If we wait any longer, we may miss the train.
2. Could we have another bottle of water, please?
   I asked her to water the garden.
3. I gave him the book.
   Have you booked our flight yet?
4. They always take a break after an hour's work.
   Did he break his leg skiing?
5. I go for a run most mornings.
   I was late, so I had to run to get to school on time.

Compound nouns

A **Formation**

A compound noun is made up of two nouns, or an adjective and a noun.

earring   alarm clock   traffic light   parking meter   can opener

stop sign   dining room [the room where you eat meals]
credit card   movie star (e.g., Leonardo DiCaprio, Harrison Ford)
table tennis   brother-in-law [your sister's husband; your spouse's brother]
T-shirt   income tax [the tax you pay on your salary or earnings]
haircut   writing paper [paper for writing letters]
sunglasses   washing machine [a machine for washing clothes]
running shoes   checkbook [a "book" that holds checks]
raincoat   baby-sitter [he/she watches children when the parents are out]
math teacher   box office [where you buy tickets in a theater]
*first aid   *mother tongue [your first language]
*personal computer   *science fiction [stories about technology, space travel, etc.]

Note: The compounds marked * all have stress on both parts.

B **One word or two?**

Compound nouns are sometimes written as two words (e.g., credit card), other times as one word (e.g., sunglasses). Occasionally they are joined by a hyphen (e.g., baby-sitter). Unfortunately there is no rule for this, so you may need to check in a dictionary. *Note:* Frequently used compounds often become one word over time.

C **Pronunciation**

The main stress is usually on the first part (e.g., <u>park</u>ing meter), but sometimes it is on both parts (e.g., <u>mo</u>ther <u>tongue</u>). Some dictionaries show the stress on compounds.

D **Forming new compounds**

Often, one part of a compound forms the basis for many different compound nouns.

post/ticket/box **office**   **traffic** light/jam/cop
brother/sister/father/mother-**in-law**   dining/living/waiting **room**
movie/pop/rock **star**   **coffee** break/cup/pot/shop

Exercises

12.1 Find compound nouns on the opposite page connected with each of these topics.

Money	Roads	People	Things we wear
credit card			

12.2 Complete these sentences with compound nouns, then see if you can find them on the opposite page.

1. I'm late because there was a terrible .... in the center of town.
2. Marilyn Monroe was a famous .... in the 1950s and early 1960s.
3. My .... didn't go off this morning; I didn't wake up until noon!
4. I had to sit in the .... for an hour before I could see the dentist.
5. We really wanted to see the movie, but we couldn't find a .... for the children, so we had to stay home.
6. When I'm driving, I always wear .... if it's very bright and sunny.
7. In most countries, you have to pay .... on your salary; the amount usually depends on how much you earn.
8. I often have the same problem: I park the car next to a ...., and then I realize that I don't have the right change.

12.3 Take the first or the second word (or part) from each compound and create a new compound. Use a dictionary if necessary.

1. brother-in-law   *mother-in-law*
2. table tennis   *table leg*
3. movie star   ....
4. credit card   ....
5. toothpaste   ....

6. dining room   ....
7. traffic light   ....
8. sunglasses   ....
9. post office   ....
10. hairbrush   ....

Now mark the main stress in each of the compound nouns you created.

12.4 Try creating your own compound nouns. Choose two or three common words and then try to form compound nouns from them. Then check a dictionary to see if your words exist. Start with these.

.... book   *or*   book ....
.... card

Compound adjectives

Formation and pronunciation

A compound adjective is made up of two different words, and occasionally three. The second part of the compound is often a present participle (e.g., *looking*) or a past participle (e.g., *known*). Some compound adjectives use a hyphen before a noun (e.g., a **good-looking** man; a **well-known** actress), but not after a noun (e.g., He is **good looking**. That actress is **well known**.). The stress is usually equal on both parts of the compound.

Describing people

Many compound adjectives describe a person's appearance, character, and situation.

This is Bill. He isn't **well known** [famous], he isn't **well off** [rich], and I've never heard anyone say he was **good looking** [handsome/attractive]. But he's a very nice man – kind, friendly, and **easygoing** [relaxed]. In this picture he's wearing a **short-sleeved** shirt and a **brand-new** [completely new] hat.

Well and *badly*

Well and **badly** combine with many past participles to form compound adjectives. You can use them in front of the past participle.

a well-directed movie	a badly paid job [a low salary]
a well-made pair of shoes	a badly behaved child [acting in a bad way]
a well-written story	a badly dressed student [wearing horrible clothes]
a well-known writer	[There is no opposite for *well-known* using *badly*.]

A "five-minute" walk

We can combine a number and a singular noun to form a compound adjective. *Note:* We say **a five-minute walk** (*not* a five-minutes walk).

It's a **fifteen-minute** drive to the beach. [a drive of fifteen minutes]
He works in a **four-star** hotel. [a hotel with a rating of four stars]
I gave her a **five-dollar** bill. [a bill with a value of five dollars]
The winner was a **ten-year-old** girl. [a girl who is ten years old]
There was a **two-hour** delay on our flight. [The plane was two hours late.]

Common compounds

She used to have a **part-time** job in the mornings, but she changed to a **full-time** job.
The city is **northwest** of here. (also **northeast, southeast,** and **southwest**)
Most people are **right-handed,** but about 10% are **left-handed.**
On trains and planes you can buy a **first-class** ticket, if you are willing to pay a lot more.
Mary bought a **second-hand** car. [The car was used, not **brand new.**]

Exercises

13.1 Match words from the left-hand box with words on the right to form twelve compound adjectives.

Example: *good-looking*

good	well
easy	north
ten	short
brand	badly
part	left
first	second

new	known
written	class
looking	sleeved
hand	handed
going	east
time	dollar

13.2 Cover the left-hand page. Then fill in the blanks to form compound adjectives.

well *known*............   badly .... handed

....

.... time   .... east   .... class

....

13.3 Complete the compound adjectives in these sentences.

1. We stayed in a five-........................ hotel.
2. There is a shop in Toronto that sells things for left-........................ people.
3. We just bought a brand-........................ car.
4. The airport is about ten miles south........................ of the city.
5. One little girl was very badly ....; she kept shouting during lunch and then threw food all over the floor.
6. He just got a ....-time job; he works three hours a day on Mondays, Wednesdays, and Fridays.
7. It was a very badly .... article: I noticed several mistakes and the meaning wasn't clear.
8. They're very well ...., so they can afford to go to expensive restaurants.
9. It's a twenty-........................ walk to the house, but it's much faster by car.
10. When I saw her last night, she was dancing with a very good-........................ young man in a white suit.
11. What would you do if you found a hundred-........................ bill in the street?
12. I had a nice time with my cousin – he's good company and very easy........................ .

13.4 Write ten sentences about yourself, using a different compound adjective in each one. You can describe yourself, your personality, your family, your clothes, the place where you live, the trips you take, etc. Try to do this exercise with a friend and read each other's descriptions. Are they accurate?

Collocations (word partners)

 A **What is collocation?**

In each language, certain words go together. For example, in English we say:

I **missed the bus.** [*or* I didn't **catch the bus;** *not* I lost the bus.]
He **made a mistake.** [*not* He did a mistake.]
a **serious illness**
She **committed a crime.** [*not* She did a crime.]
Rescuers did everything **humanly possible** to save the people trapped in the
    building. [everything a person is able to do]

B **Verb + noun**

The meaning of these examples may be clear, but did you know these verbs and
nouns go together? Is it the same or different in your language?

start the car [turn on the engine]   start a family [have your first child]
tell a story   tell the truth [≠ tell a lie]
tell a joke   run a store/company [manage/control it]
get on a bus [≠ get off]   get in(to) a car [≠ get out (of) a car]
miss a person [be unhappy because that person is not there]
miss a class [when you don't come to a class]

C **Adjective + noun**

a soft drink [nonalcoholic drink]   a soft voice [≠ a loud voice]
strong coffee [≠ weak coffee]   a strong/heavy accent [≠ a slight accent]
hard work [hard physically or mentally]   a great success [very successful]
heavy traffic [a lot of cars on the road]   heavy rain [raining a lot]

I can't understand his English because he has such a **strong accent.**
It was **hard work** organizing the conference, but I think it was a **great success.**
There's always **heavy traffic** during rush hour.

D **Adverb + adjective**

In these sentences, all the adverbs mean "very," but we often use them with
certain adjectives. (You could still use **very** in these examples if you wish.)

I was **terribly/awfully sorry** to hear about your accident.
It's **highly unlikely** he'll come now. [I'm almost sure he will not come.]
She was **bitterly disappointed** when she didn't get the job.

E **Collocation in dictionaries**

Good dictionaries (especially learner's dictionaries) list some common
collocations, but they do it in different ways – sometimes they are in bold print
after the definition; sometimes in italics after the definition; and sometimes in the
definition and examples. (See Unit 3, section B.)

Exercises

14.1 You can keep a record of common collocations by using "bubble networks."
These are very clear, and you can add to them in your notebook. Complete these.

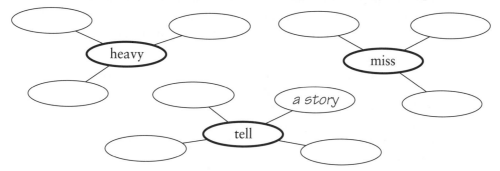

14.2 Write the opposite of these phrases and expressions.

1. a heavy accent – *a slight accent*
2. strong coffee
3. a soft voice
4. get on the bus
5. tell the truth
6. catch the bus

14.3 Fill in the blanks with an appropriate word from the opposite page.

1. I'm .... sorry to be late, but I .... the bus.
2. He .... everyone the same joke, and nobody laughed.
3. It was freezing during the night, and I couldn't .... the car this morning.
4. Michael is the owner, but his sister Jane .... the company. She has about fifty employees working for her.
5. I think they want to get married and .... a family.
6. That's the third mistake he's .... today.
7. A person who .... a crime should be punished.
8. If this .... rain continues, I think it's .... unlikely she'll come.
9. The doctors did everything .... possible to save the child's life.
10. I really .... my family when I went away to college.

14.4 The adjectives on the left can all mean "very big," but we often use them specifically with the nouns on the right. Try to find the correct collocations (a learner's dictionary can help), then complete the sentences.

wide	large
broad	vast

shoulders	range
majority	size

1. I used to be medium, but now I need a ...*large*... .... because I've put on weight.
2. Fortunately most clothing stores have a .... of clothes to choose from.
3. I also have very ...., but my waist is fairly small.
4. A few men can't find clothes to fit them, but the .... are small, medium, or large.

Verb or adjective + preposition

Verb (+ preposition)

The verbs below are usually followed by a particular preposition. You will probably know most of the verbs, but do you always get the preposition right? Pay special attention to any that are different in your language.

I **listen to** the radio a lot.
My brother never **agrees with** me. [He never has the same view/opinion as me.]
I may go to the beach; it **depends on** the weather. [The weather will decide for me.]
She **suffers from** a type of diabetes. [has the unpleasant/bad experience of]
He **got married to** a woman he met in Brazil.
I'm going to **apologize for** the mistakes we made. [say I'm sorry]
She has **applied for** a new job. [made a written request]
They were **waiting for** me when I arrived.
Don't **worry about** your exam; it'll be OK. [be nervous]
She **complained to** the waiter **about** the food. [said she was not satisfied] (You complain **to** someone **about** something.)
He **spends** a lot of money **on** clothes and CDs.
That dictionary **belongs to** Maria. [It is Maria's dictionary.]

Changes in meaning

Sometimes a different preposition changes the meaning of the verb:

He **shouted to** me. [communicated from a distance]

He **shouted at** me. [He was angry with me and spoke loudly.]

She **threw** the ball **to** me. [for me to catch it]
She **threw** the ball **at** me. [in order to hit me; maybe she was angry]

Adjective (+ preposition)

I was never very **good at** math.
He is **afraid of** flying. [frightened of]
I'm **crazy about** cats. [I like cats very much.]
She is **similar to** [almost the same as] her sister, but very **different from** her brother.
He's very **interested in** antique furniture.
I was **surprised at** (*or* **by**) his reaction. I thought he'd be happy to hear the news.
I think she is **aware of** the problems in her class. [knows about]
I'm **tired of** studying foreign languages. [I've had enough and I want to stop.]
The streets are **full of** trash. [There is trash everywhere in the streets.]
There is something **wrong with** this TV. [The TV is not working/functioning properly.]

Exercises

15.1 Complete these questions with the correct prepositions; then write a short answer (from your imagination) for each one.

Examples: A: What is she worried ..*about*..?   B: *Her exams, I think.*
A: Which sports is she good ....*at*....?   B: *Soccer and tennis.*

1. A: Who is she waiting ....?   B: ....
2. A: What job is she applying ....?   B: ....
3. A: What program is she listening ....?   B: ....
4. A: What did she complain ....?   B: ....
5. A: What did she apologize ....?   B: ....
6. A: Does this car belong .... her?   B: ....
7. A: I know she was angry, but who was she shouting ....?   B: ....
8. A: Is she interested .... any kind of music?   B: ....
9. A: What will the decision depend ....?   B: ....
10. A: What is she afraid ....?   B: ....

15.2 Match the words to form sentences.

1. He suffers
2. She wasn't aware
3. I was very surprised
4. He complained
5. That suit is similar
6. She applied
7. He threw a book
8. He said it depends
9. The suitcase was full
10. She apologized

a. at me, but it missed.
b. from a rare illness.
c. for a job in Puerto Rico.
d. on me.
e. for the mistake.
f. at his choice.
g. of clothes.
h. to the one she's wearing.
i. about the bad service.
j. of her mistakes.

15.3 Complete these sentences with your own ideas.

1. My steak was overcooked, so I complained *about it to the waiter* .
2. I work hard, but I'm not very good ....
3. I want to work in the travel business, so I've applied ....
4. When I was a child, I sometimes wore clothes that belonged ....
5. In the summer, a lot of people suffer ....
6. I've always been interested ....
7. A lot of people are afraid ....
8. People in my country are very different ....

15.4 A good dictionary tells you if a verb or an adjective is usually followed by a special preposition. Sometimes the preposition is shown after the verb or adjective; sometimes it is in the example sentences. Use a dictionary to find the preposition that often follows these words.

fond (adj.)   concentrate (v.)   responsible (adj.)   rely (v.)

Preposition + noun

A Common patterns

Many expressions are formed by a preposition + noun.

a play **by** Shakespeare, a movie **by** Steven Spielberg, a song **by** Madonna
You can go **for** a walk, **for** a drive, **for** a run, **for** a swim.
You can go **in** the morning, **in** the afternoon, **in** the evening (but **at night** / **at noon**).
You can travel **by** car, **by** plane, **by** bus, **by** train, **by** taxi (but **on foot**).
I heard it **on** the radio; I saw it **on** TV; I spoke to her **on** the phone (but I read it **in** the newspaper, **in** a magazine).
the man **in** the dark suit [wearing the dark suit]; the woman **in** the red dress / **in** red

B Fixed expressions

Sometimes it is difficult to know why particular prepositions are used, so you have to learn them as fixed expressions.

I took your pen **by mistake.** [an error; I didn't mean to take it.]
I did all the work **by myself.** [alone; without help from others]
The workers are **on strike.** [They refuse to work because of a dispute with management.]
I met them **by chance.** [It wasn't planned; it was luck.]
We're **on vacation.** [taking a vacation; away from work, school, etc.]
There were **at least** fifty people at the party. [a minimum of fifty]
I can't talk now; I'm **in a hurry.** [need to do things quickly; have no time]

He broke the glass **by accident.** [He did not want to do it; it was a mistake.]

He broke the glass **on purpose.** [He wanted to do it and intended to do it.]

C *In time* or *on time?*

Sometimes two prepositions can be used with the same noun, but the meaning is different.

We got home **in time for** / **in time to** see *Baywatch* on TV. [early enough]
Class begins at 8:30 and I always arrive **on time.** [at 8:30] (*not* on time to/for)

In the end, we went home. [finally, after a long period]
At the end of the book, they get married.

The two people are **in business.** [They are businesspeople.]
The two people are in Mexico **on business.** [They are there for work, not on vacation.]

I'll see you **in a moment.** [very soon]
I can't speak to you **at the moment.** [right now]

Exercises

16.1 Cover the opposite page. Then complete these sentences with the correct preposition.

1. I saw it .... TV.
2. They came .... car.
3. They are all .... strike.
4. She is here .... business.
5. I went there .... myself.
6. It was written .... Cervantes.
7. We went .... a walk.
8. I read it .... a magazine.
9. He's .... vacation this week.
10. She took it .... mistake.

11. I went .... the afternoon.
12. He came .... foot.
13. I'm .... a hurry and can't stop.
14. She broke it .... accident.
15. He did it .... purpose.
16. I'll see you .... a moment.
17. I'm very busy .... the moment.
18. It's very quiet here .... night.
19. We met .... chance.
20. She's .... least 25 years old.

16.2 Replace the underlined words with a prepositional phrase.

Example: The meeting was planned for 11 a.m. We got here at 11 a.m. *on time.*

1. Did you get to the theater before the movie started?
2. She's making a phone call.
3. I saw the advertisement when I was watching TV last night.
4. He opened her letter because he thought it was addressed to him (but it wasn't).
5. The project was difficult for everyone, but finally it all worked out.
6. She gets killed in the last scene of the movie.
7. I'm afraid I'm very busy right now.
8. I saw her yesterday but I didn't plan to see her.

16.3 Respond to these questions with a negative answer and a prepositional phrase from this unit.

Example: Was it the woman wearing the blue blouse?
No, the woman in the white blouse.

1. Did she hit him on purpose?
....
2. Did they go by car?
....
3. Are they here on vacation?
....
4. Did you read about the accident in the newspaper?
....
5. Did anyone go with him?
....
6. Do you want to sit down and rest?
....

16.4 Translate the prepositional phrases in this unit into your own language. Which ones are exact translations and which ones aren't?

Phrasal verbs (1): form and meaning

Formation

Phrasal verbs are verbs that combine with a particle (an adverb or a preposition) and occasionally with more than one particle.

The price of coffee may **go up** again next week. [increase]
He **fell down** as he was running for the bus. [fell to the ground]
She promised to **find out** more about the new project. [learn/discover]
If you don't understand the meaning, you can **look** it **up**. [find the meaning in a
    book – especially a dictionary]
He can't **get along with** his parents. [have a good relationship with] (v. + adv. + prep.)

Meaning

Sometimes the meaning of a phrasal verb is very similar to the base verb, and the adverb just emphasizes the meaning of the base verb, e.g., **stand up, wake up, save up, hurry up, sit down, lie down,** and **send off** (e.g., a letter). On other occasions, the adverb adds the idea of completing the action of the verb, e.g., **drink up** [finish your drink], **eat up** [finish eating], **use up** [use completely], **finish off** [use or eat the last part].

But more often, the meaning of a phrasal verb is very different from the base verb, e.g., **go up** [increase] doesn't mean the same as **go**; **look up** is different from **look**; and **find out** is different from **find**. A particle can therefore change the meaning of a verb. For example:

It took her a long time to **get over** her illness. [get better / recover from]
I finally decided to **give up** smoking. [stop]
I can't make any sandwiches because we've **run out of** bread. [There is no more
    bread.]
My neighbor had to come and **put out** the fire. [extinguish/stop]

Multiple meanings

Many phrasal verbs have more than one meaning. Note that in most cases, the phrasal verb is much more natural (or less formal) than the explanation in brackets.

It was hot, so I **took off** my jacket. [removed]
I am always nervous when the plane **takes off**. [leaves the ground]

I don't know how I'll **get through** this difficult time. [survive]
I tried calling you all afternoon, but I couldn't **get through**. [reach by telephone]

I **picked up** the trash and put it in the garbage can. [lifted it]
I had to go to the store to **pick up** my photographs. [go and get]

They want to **bring up** their children in a peaceful environment. [raise]
Whenever you **bring up** the subject of food, I get hungry. [introduce a topic]

My alarm clock didn't **go off** this morning. [ring]
The bomb could **go off** at any minute. [explode]

go off

Exercises

17.1 Fill in the blanks to complete the phrasal verbs.

1. We went around the neighborhood and ....*picked*.... **up** all the trash.
2. I don't think they ever .... **out** how the prisoner escaped.
3. Did you manage to .... **through**, or is the line still busy?
4. They had a bad relationship at first, but they are .... **along** very well now.
5. The price .... **up** three times last year.
6. If you are not sure how to pronounce a word, ... it **up** in the dictionary.
7. Didn't your alarm clock .... **off** this morning?
8. This photocopier always .... **out of** paper because the paper tray is so small.

17.2 Complete these sentences in a logical way.

1. It will take him a long time to get over *his illness / his wife's death* ....
2. Oh, no! We've run out of ....
3. She had to look it up ....
4. I don't really get along with ....
5. He came in and took off ....
6. I had to put out ....
7. The plane took off ....
8. My rent is going up ....

17.3 Look at the dictionary entry for *pick up,* and match the meanings with the sentences below.

---

pick up[1] *phr v*
1 ▶LIFT UP◀ [T **pick** sb/sth ↔ **up**] to hold someone or something and lift him, her, or it from a surface: *Pick me up, Daddy!* | *kids picking up shells at the beach* | *I picked up the phone* (=answered the phone) *just as it stopped ringing.*
2 ▶GO GET SB/STH◀ [T **pick** sb/sth ↔ **up**] to go somewhere, usually in a vehicle, in order to get someone or something: *I'll pick up my stuff around six, okay?* | *What time should we pick you up at the airport?*
3 ▶BUY◀ [T **pick** sth ↔ **up**] INFORMAL to buy something: *Will you pick up something for dinner on your way home?* | *The company is picking up the bill for my computer.* (=it is paying for it)

4 ▶CLEAN A PLACE◀ [I,T **pick** sth ↔ **up**] to put things away neatly, or to clean a place by doing this: *Straighten your room and pick up all those papers.* | *He never picks up after himself.* (=he does not put away the things he has used)
5 ▶GET BETTER◀ [I] to improve: *Sales should pick up before Christmas.*
6 ▶INCREASE◀ [I,T **pick up** sth] to increase or get faster: *The car was gradually picking up speed.* (=going faster) | *The wind had picked up considerably.*
7 ▶LEARN◀ [T **pick** sth ↔ **up**] to learn something without deliberately trying to: *Craig picked up the guitar from his dad.*
8 ▶ILLNESS◀ [T **pick** sth ↔ **up**] to get an illness from someone: *She's picked up a cold from a child at school.*

---

1. I said I would pick them up at the train station.   *definition 2*
2. Could you pick up some milk on the way home?
3. Where did he pick up that strange accent?
4. Business was bad at the beginning of the year, but it's picking up now.
5. I hurt my back when I tried to pick up that suitcase.

17.4 Cover the opposite page. Then write two sentences for each of these phrasal verbs to show their different meanings.

pick up   take off   go off   bring up

UNIT 18

Phrasal verbs (2): grammar and style

Look at Unit 17 before you do this unit.

A   Grammar: intransitive verbs

Some phrasal verbs are intransitive and do not need a direct object. These verbs are not usually separated, e.g., you can say "The children are **growing up** fast." (*not* "The children are growing fast up.")

Don't wait out there. Please **come in**. [enter]
I **stayed up** late last night. [went to bed late]

B   Grammar: transitive verbs

Many phrasal verbs are transitive and *do* need a direct object. With some of these, you can put the object between the verb and the adverb:

Put on your shoes.	**Turn on** the TV.
Put your shoes **on**.	**Turn** the TV **on**.

If the object is a pronoun, it *must* go between the verb and the adverb.

Put them **on**. [*not* Put on them.]   **Turn** it **on**. [*not* Turn on it.]

Note: Most dictionaries will show you if you can put a word between the verb and adverb:

> **turn** *(obj)* |SWITCH| *v* [always + adv/prep] to use a control to switch (a piece of equipment) on or off or to increase or reduce what it is producing • *Turn* ***off/out*** *the light.* • *Who turned the TV* ***on****?* • *I asked him to turn* ***down*** *the heat.* • *Turn the sound* ***up*** *– I can't hear what they're saying.*

C   Style: formal or informal?

Some phrasal verbs can be used equally in written and spoken English.

I always **wake up** early, even on weekends.
The car **broke down** on the freeway. [stopped working]
The plane couldn't **take off** because of bad weather.
Burglars **broke into** the house and took all the money and jewelry. [entered by force]

D   Informal phrasal verbs

Many phrasal verbs are informal and are more common in spoken English. In written English, there is often a more formal word with the same meaning.

We had to **make up** a story. [**invent**, i.e., create from our imagination]
I can usually **get by** on about $500 a week. [**manage**]
You can **leave out** question 7. [**omit**, i.e., you don't need to do question 7]
I can't **figure out** this math problem. [**solve**]

Exercises

These exercises also practice and test some of the phrasal verbs from Unit 17.

18.1   Complete these sentences in a logical way.

1. I'm not very good at making up ..*excuses/stories*...
2. I'm tired today because I stayed up ....
3. Would you please turn on ....?
4. Two burglars tried to break into ....
5. Why did you leave out ....?
6. Unfortunately the car broke down ....
7. Can you get by ....?
8. I grew up ....

18.2   Is it possible to separate the two parts of the phrasal verb in the sentences below?
If the answer is *yes,* rewrite the phrasal verb.

Examples: I forgot to **get off** the bus.   *no*
              Why did he **take off** his coat?   *yes (take his coat off)*

1. She tried to **put out** the fire.
2. Could you please **turn on** the radio?
3. Could you go to the store for me? We just **ran out of** coffee.
4. I think she **made up** that story.
5. I can't **get by** on the money my parents give me.
6. Children **grow up** very quickly these days.
7. I **turned off** the light when I went to bed.
8. Can we **leave out** this question?
9. What time did you **wake up** this morning?
10. *(to a child)* **Pick up** your toys right now!

18.3   Make these texts more informal by changing the underlined verbs to phrasal
verbs with the same meaning.

1. The cost of living is increasing *going up* all the time. It's hard to manage on my salary.

2. She told me to enter, but then I had to remove my shoes and extinguish my cigarette.

3. The teacher told the class to invent a story to go with the picture in their books. She
   said they could omit the next exercise.

4. He introduced the topic of inflation, pointing out that prices are not increasing as
   quickly as before.

18.4   There are many phrasal verbs in other units. Can you find:

1. three phrasal verbs in Unit 22 on p. 46?   4. three phrasal verbs in Unit 57 on p. 116?
2. three phrasal verbs in Unit 48 on p. 98?   5. three phrasal verbs in Unit 63 on p. 128?
3. three phrasal verbs in Unit 49 on p. 100?   6. three phrasal verbs in Unit 75 on p. 152?

(See Unit 5 for more on transitive and intransitive verbs.)

Idioms and fixed expressions

A   What is an idiom?

An idiom is a group of words (or a compound) with a meaning that is different from the individual words, and often difficult to understand from the individual words. Many of the phrasal verbs in Units 17 and 18 are idiomatic. Here are some more common idioms.

The teacher told us to **get a move on.** [hurry; be quick]
My wife and I **take turns** cooking. [I cook one day, she cooks the next, etc.]
I don't know the answer **offhand.** [without looking it up or asking someone]
I'm not very good at **small talk.** [social talk; not about serious things]
I'm sorry I can't **make it** on Friday. [come]
I asked her to **keep an eye on** my suitcase while I went to the bathroom. [watch]

B   Fixed expressions

There are also expressions in English where the meaning is easy to understand, but the same idea in your language may need a completely different expression. If you translate each word from your language, you may say something in English that is completely wrong. For this reason, you need to learn certain fixed expressions as idioms. For example:

A: What was wrong with the hotel?
B: Well, **for starters,** it was next to a freeway and very noisy. And **to make matters worse,** there was a factory across the street, which stayed open 24 hours.

It's a good **short-term** [temporary, for now] solution, but **in the long run** [over a longer period of time] we will need to think about it.

C   Using idioms

Idioms are important to know, but they can be difficult to use correctly. With many idioms, if you make just a small mistake, it can sound strange, funny, or completely wrong. For example: get the move on, offhands, small talks, put an eye on, etc.

Idioms often have special features: They may be informal or funny or ironic; they may be used by certain people (e.g., young children, or teenagers, or elderly people); they may appear only in limited contexts; they may have special grammar. For these reasons, you can sometimes "learn" the meaning of an idiom but then use it incorrectly. For example, "I was sorry to hear that your father **kicked the bucket.**" This idiom means *died,* but it is used humorously, never in a serious situation. It would be completely inappropriate when offering sympathy.

D   Some easy idioms to use

Some idiomatic expressions are used alone, or with just one or two other words.

A: Can I borrow your dictionary?
B: Sure, **go ahead.** [it's OK; do it]

A: I don't know which one to choose.
B: Well, **make up your mind.** [decide]

A: **What's up?** [What's new/wrong?]
B: Nothing.

A: Are you coming?
B: Yeah. **Right away.** [soon]

Exercises

19.1   It can be difficult to guess the meaning of an idiom. Look at these examples (they are not presented on the opposite page).

1. I **feel like** having a soft drink.
2. They're gone **for good**.
3. I **changed my mind**.
4. I'm **tied up** all afternoon.
5. I can **make do** with what I'm getting.

Here is a fuller context for each idiom. Can you guess the meaning now?

1. A: Are you hungry?
   B: No, but I'm thirsty. I feel like having a soft drink.
2. A: Do you think they'll ever come back?
   B: No, they're gone for good.
3. A: You want to go out? You just said you wanted to stay home.
   B: I changed my mind.
4. A: Do you have a lot of clients to see?
   B: Yes, I'm tied up all afternoon.
5. A: Are you going to ask for a raise in salary?
   B: No, because I know I won't get it. I can make do with what I'm getting.

19.2   Replace the underlined words with idioms from the opposite page. (But try to do the exercise before looking at the opposite page.) Can you think of similar expressions in your language?

1. A: Could I borrow this for a minute?
   B: Yes, take it.   *go ahead*
2. A: Sorry I can't come on Thursday.
   B: Don't worry. It's OK.
3. A: What's the matter?
   B: Nothing. Why?
4. A: Do we have to leave now?
   B: Yes, hurry, or we'll be late.
5. A: You'll have to decide soon.
   B: Yes, I know, but it's very difficult.
6. A: Would you watch my things for a minute?
   B: Yeah, sure.

19.3   Complete the expressions in these sentences.

1. It wasn't a very successful vacation. **For** ....*starters*...., the beach was a long way from our hotel; then **to make** .... **worse**, the car broke down on the third day and we had to walk to the beach for the rest of our stay.
2. We **take** .... walking the dog.
3. She asked me about the train schedule, but I couldn't tell her **off**.............................
4. I don't enjoy parties where you just stand around and make .... **talk** with lots of people you don't know.
5. We can probably **make** .... with a one-bedroom apartment for now, but **in the long** .... we will have to move into a bigger place.

19.4   Find at least three idioms below. What do they mean?

I went to stay with my cousin last week. We are the same age but have very little in common: He loves sports and I hate them; I'm crazy about music and he's not interested in it. As you can imagine, we didn't have a very good time together, and by about Thursday we were really getting on each other's nerves, so I decided to go home.

Make, do, have, take

A Things we make

a mistake	She **made** a few **mistakes** on the exam. [errors]
a meal	I had to **make** my own **dinner** last night. [prepare and cook something to eat]
money (U)	He **made** a lot of **money** when he worked in California. [earned money]
friends	It's not easy to **make friends** in a new place.
a decision	We can take the red one or the green one, but we have to **make a decision** (choose the red or green) now.
noise (U)	I can't work when the children **make** a lot of **noise.**
progress (U)	Her English is good now; she's **made** a lot of **progress.** [improvement]

B Things we do

homework (U)	I forgot to **do** my math **homework** last night.
the housework (U)	My father **does** all **the housework** in our house. [the cleaning]
the shopping (U)	I always **do the shopping** on weekends. [buy food]
research (U)	She's **doing research** in genetics. [detailed study]
(someone) a favor	Could you **do me a favor** and pick up a newspaper on your way home? Thanks. [do something to help someone]
something/anything/ nothing	I didn't **do anything** last night. / Those kids are so lazy – they **do nothing** all day long.

C Things we have

food and drink	I **had** [ate] **steak** but Paula just **had** [drank] **a cup of coffee.**
a meal [breakfast, lunch, dinner]	We **had lunch** at noon.
a look	Could I **have a look** at your newspaper?
a party	I'm **having a party** for my birthday.
a baby [be pregnant or give birth]	Sandy is **having a baby** next month.
a nice/good/great/terrible time	We **had a great time** in Mexico last year.
a fight / an argument	I **had an argument** with my parents again.

D Things we take

subjects [study subjects]	Did you **take English** in high school?
a course	I **took** a one-week **course** in word processing.
an exam	I'm going to **take** four **exams** next month.
a photo/picture	We **took** lots of **photos/pictures** on our vacation.
a bus/train/plane/taxi	We were late, so we **took a taxi** to the airport.
a nap [a short sleep]	I like to **take a nap** in the afternoon.
a bath/shower	I always **take a bath/shower** in the morning.

Notice the use of **be + adjective** (*not* **have** + noun) in these expressions:

She **was lucky.**   I'm **hungry.** [I want to eat.]   I'm **thirsty.** [I want a drink.]

Exercises

20.1 Circle the correct verbs in these sentences.

1. I couldn't (do)/ make the homework last night.
2. She's going to take / have a party for her birthday.
3. Did he do / make many mistakes?
4. I often make / do the housework.
5. Did you make / take many photos on your trip?
6. When do you take / make your next exam?
7. They did / made a lot of noise during the party.
8. I want to take / make a course in English.
9. We'll have to do / make a decision soon.
10. He is doing / making research in chemistry.

20.2 Replace the underlined word(s) with a word or an expression from the opposite page.

Example: I want to eat something. *I'm hungry.*

1. I rode on a bus to get to work.
2. I'm going to prepare lunch tomorrow.
3. I'll clean the house on the weekend.
4. I ate a pizza in the restaurant.
5. I want a drink.
6. I usually buy my food on Saturdays.

7. They both want to become rich.
8. When are they going to decide?
9. I think she enjoyed herself last night.
10. He is definitely improving. How many driving lessons has he had now?

20.3 Describe these pictures using expressions from the opposite page.

1. **John / on Saturday**
   Example: John went shopping on Saturday.

2. **Maria / after dinner**

3. **Bill / after lunch most afternoons**

4. **the Lees / on their vacation**

5. **Nancy / next month**

20.4 Test yourself. Without looking at the opposite page, write at least twelve things (three for each verb) you can . . .

make *a mistake*   do ....   have ....   take ....

Give, keep, break, catch, see

Some of these verbs combine with specific nouns, e.g., give someone a call, break the law, keep the change, etc. You can learn these as expressions.

A   ## *Give*

I'll **give** you **a call** this evening. [telephone you]
Could you **give** me **a hand?** [help me]
Please **give my regards to** Paul. [say "hello" to him from me]
Don't make your decision immediately; **give it some thought.** [take time to consider it]

B   ## *Keep*

The coat will **keep** you **dry;** the gloves will **keep** your hands **warm.** [The coat/gloves will help you to stay dry/warm.] (**keep** + noun/pronoun + adjective)
I **keep** losing my glasses. [I lose my glasses again and again.] (**keep** + **-ing**)
Please **keep in touch.** [stay in contact, e.g., call or write to me sometimes]
The school **keeps records / keeps a record** of student absences. [written information]
That's OK, just **keep the change.** [You can give a tip for services with the "change," or coins you get back for a payment, e.g., $4.25 from a $5 bill gives 75 cents change.]
Always try to **keep** your **promises.** [do what you have promised to do]

C   ## *Break*

He **broke the** world **record** again. [created a new record, e.g., He ran the 100 meters in 9.85 seconds, which is 0.1 second faster than anyone else.]
Many people **break the law** at some point in their life. [do something against the law]
In my first lesson with a new class, I usually do something to **break the ice.** [to make people feel more relaxed when they first meet strangers]
After elections, politicians often **break** their **promises.** [don't do what they promised]

D   ## *Catch*

We can **catch the bus** at the corner. [get on the bus]
How did you **catch that cold?** [get that cold]
Catch the ball and throw it to Sue.

E   ## *See*

A: It's easier to carry two smaller suitcases.
B: Yes, **I see what you mean.** [I understand what you are saying.]

A: Do you think we should rent a car?
B: I don't know. **I'll see** what the others say. [I'll ask and find out.]

I'll **see to it** that no one disturbs you. [make sure/certain]
(**I'll**) **see you later. / See you.** [*informal;* good-bye]

Exercises

21.1 Match the verbs on the left with the nouns on the right to form common word partners. (There are two nouns you need to use twice each.)

break (3)	keep (3)
catch (3)	give (2)

the ball	the law	a cold
me a hand	a bus	in touch
a record	a promise	my regards to . . .

Example: break a record

21.2 Fill in the blanks with the correct verbs.

1. I'll .... to it that your mail is collected while you're away.
2. These boots should .... your feet warm and dry.
3. Please .... my regards to your mother when you go back home.
4. Before we make a decision, let's .... what Antonio says.
5. A: .... you later. B: Bye.
6. I don't know what the problem is, but I .... getting headaches.
7. I didn't really enjoy the vacation because I .... a cold on the second day and spent most of the week sneezing and blowing my nose.
8. When you organize a conference, I think you need something to .... the ice; otherwise people can be nervous and shy.
9. I .... what you mean, but I'm not sure I agree with your point of view.
10. These suitcases are pretty heavy. Can you .... me a hand?
11. Let's get together for lunch next week. I'll .... you a call.
12. Whenever I meet people on vacation, I always promise to .... in touch, but I never do.
13. I can't give you an answer yet. I need to .... it some thought.
14. You said you would get home early tonight, but you .... your promise.

21.3 What expressions are represented by these pictures?

1. 2. 3.

21.4 Look through the expressions on the opposite page again. Can you translate them into your own language? If so, do you use the same verb in your own language? Concentrate on the ones that are different.

Get: uses and expressions

A   Meanings

Get is an informal word, so it is more common in spoken English than in written English. It has many meanings. Here are some of the basic ones:

receive	I got a letter this morning.
	You'll get a certificate at the end of the course.
obtain/find [*sometimes* buy]	She's trying to get a new job.
	Where did you get those shoes?
become [a change in state]	It gets dark very early at this time of year.
	My hands are getting cold.
arrive	When did you get here?
	I'll call when I get home.
bring / take / pick up	Could you get those books from the shelf?
	She went to get the children from school.

B   *Get* + past participle

We sometimes use **get** + past participle:

get married [marry]	They got married in Canada.
get divorced [divorce]	They got divorced last year. [The marriage ended officially.]
get dressed [dress]	I got dressed quickly and went out.
get undressed [undress]	He got undressed and got into bed.
get lost [lose one's way]	I got lost on my way to the station.

C   Common collocations

Get is so common with certain words that it is a good idea to learn them as expressions.

It's getting hot/cold.
     dark/light.
     late.
     better/worse.
     crowded.

I'm getting hot/cold.
     tired.
     better/worse.
     hungry.
     ready. [preparing]

Note: The expression **getting better** sometimes describes an improvement in your health, e.g., She was very ill, but she's **getting better** now. [≠ **getting worse**]

D   Phrasal verbs and special expressions with *get*

I **get along** very well **with** my sister. [I have a very good relationship with my sister.]

It's hard to **get to know** people in a foreign country. [meet people and make friends]

I want to **get rid of** all my old CDs. [sell them, throw them away, or give them away]

My alarm goes off at 7 a.m., but I don't usually **get up** until 7:15. [get out of bed]

I don't **get it.** [understand] Why would you want to live in a tent?

Exercises

UNIT
22

22.1 Write a synonym for *get* in each of these sentences.

1. Where can I get something to eat around here?   *buy/obtain*
2. Could you please get me some milk while you're in the kitchen?
3. What time did they get here last night?
4. He got very angry when I told him what you did with his CDs.
5. I couldn't get a room; all the hotels were full.
6. We normally get five weeks' vacation.
7. This book is getting very interesting.
8. I have to get some stamps before I go home.
9. She sent the letter last week, but I didn't get it until yesterday.
10. Try to get here on time.

22.2 Write appropriate sentences using *I'm getting* + adjective or *it's getting* + adjective.

IT'S GETTING COLD IN HERE.

1. A: *It's getting cold in here.*
   B: Yes, it is. I'll turn on the heat.
2. A: ....
   B: Me too. Let's have something to eat.
3. A: ....
   B: I am too. I'll open the window.
4. A: ....
   B: Yes, it is. I think I'll go to bed.
5. A: ....
   B: Well, I'll turn the lights on.
6. A: ....
   B: Yes, it is. A lot of people come here on the weekend.

22.3 Rewrite each of these sentences using an expression with *get*. The meaning must stay the same.

1. They're preparing to go out.
   They're ....
2. I had to put on my clothes very quickly.
   I had to ....
3. How do you meet people and make friends in this country?
   How do you ....?
4. I have a good relationship with my boss.
   I ....
5. We're going to throw away most of these chairs.
   We're going to ....
6. You just don't understand, do you?
   You just don't ....?

22.4 Write some examples of *get* that you see or hear, then try to group your sentences according to the different meanings. This will help you get [obtain] an idea of the ways this important word is used in English.

23 *Go:* uses and expressions

A   *Come* vs. *go*

Go usually expresses a movement away from the position the speaker is in now; **come** expresses a movement toward the speaker.

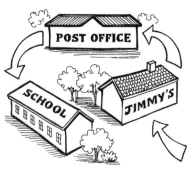

Imagine you are at school. The time is 9:30 a.m.

I had to **go** to Jimmy's to pick up some books; then I **went** to the post office before I **came** to school.

Sometimes the speaker is in one place but imagines being in another place. For example, when Claudio meets Marta in Buenos Aires, he invites her to São Paulo, Brazil. He says:

"Would you like to **come** and visit me in São Paulo?" (He imagines he is there, and so her movement is toward him.)

Note: It is a similar difference between **bring** and **take**:

"Could you **take** this deposit to the bank for me? And remember to **bring** back the receipt."

B   **Different meanings of *go***

- When you leave a place in order to do an activity, you often express it either with **go** + **-ing** or **go** (**out**) + **for a** + noun. Here are some common examples:

We could go	shopping. riding (horses).	They went	sightseeing. swimming (*also* for a swim).
She wants to go	(out) for a walk. out for coffee.	Let's go	(out) for a drive. out for dinner.

- **Go** is followed by certain adjectives to describe a change in state (usually to a worse state) with the meaning "become" (**get** is also used with some adjectives).

  My father is **going bald**. [losing his hair] My hair is **going** (*also* **turning**) gray.
  The company **went bankrupt** last year. [lost all its money and had to stop operating]
  My grandmother is **going deaf**. [losing her ability to hear]
  He'll **go crazy/nuts** if you wear his jacket. [*informal*; get very angry]

- When you want to say/ask if a road or form of transportation takes you somewhere:

  Does this bus **go** to the National Gallery? [take me]
  I don't think this road **goes** to the station. [leads]

- We use the expression **How's it going?** [*informal*; How are you?] as a greeting. You can use the same question if you want to know if something is easy, difficult, enjoyable, etc. For example, if you are doing an exercise in class, your teacher may ask: **How's it going?** (*also:* **How are you getting along?**)

Exercises

23.1 Complete the dialogue with correct forms of these verbs: *come, go, bring, take.*
(There are two verbs that can be used in one of the answers.)

A: What time are you (1) .*going*........ to Jim's party tonight?
B: I'm not sure, because Chris is (2) .... here first, and then we'll
(3) .... together.
A: Oh. Is there going to be music?
B: Yeah. Jim asked me to (4) .... some CDs. I'll probably leave the party
early, though, so could you (5) .... my CDs back here tomorrow?
A: Yeah, sure. What time?
B: Well, I want to (6) .... shopping in the morning. Could you
(7) .... before ten?
A: No problem.

23.2 Replace the underlined words and expressions. The meaning must stay the same.

1. Hi Toshi. How's it going?
2. Excuse me. Does this road go to the bus station?
3. I think this bus goes to the shopping mall.
4. A: How's it going?
   B: OK. We're nearly finished with the first exercise.

23.3 Complete these sentences with an *-ing* noun (e.g., *riding*), or *for* + noun (e.g., *for a walk*).

1. I went .*shopping*.............. this morning and bought some books and clothes.
2. We didn't have any food in the house this morning, so we went out
   ....
3. Why don't we go .... at the new pool this weekend?
4. I wanted to go .... because I had never seen Venice before,
   but the others wanted to rent a car and go .... in the country.
5. There are some stables near where we live with about a dozen horses, and we
   go .... most weekends.

23.4 Complete these sentences. Use a dictionary to help you.

1. You can wear a hearing aid if you go ....
2. If business doesn't improve, they could go ....
3. You can dye [change the color of] your hair if you start going ....
4. And you can wear a wig if you go ....
5. If the kids ride their bicycles over her flowers, she'll go ....

23.5 Look back at the different meanings of *go* (as verb and noun) on the opposite
page. Translate these meanings into your own language. How many meanings use
the word for *go* in your language? Concentrate on the ones that are different.

23.6 Now look up *go* in a good English dictionary. You will find many meanings
(including phrasal verbs and idioms), but just concentrate on two or three that
you think may be useful to you. Try to learn them.

Apologies, excuses, reassurances, and thanks

A Apologies

We can apologize [say we are sorry] in different ways in different situations:

Apology	*Situation*
(I'm) sorry. *(formal)* I beg your pardon.	a general apology, e.g., you close the door in someone's face, interrupt someone, etc.
I'm very/terribly/so/awfully sorry.	a stronger apology, e.g., you step on someone's foot or spill liquid on them
I'm really sorry I'm late. / I'm very sorry to be late.	when you are late for an appointment
Sorry to keep you waiting. I won't be long. [I will talk to you soon.]	when someone is waiting to see you and you are busy, e.g., talking to someone else

Note: In formal situations (especially in writing), we often use **apologize** and **apology:**

I **apologize for** being late. I would like to **apologize for** the delay.
Please accept our apologies for the mistakes in your order. We tried to . . .

B Excuses

If the situation is important, we usually add an explanation or **excuse** after the apology. An **excuse** is the reason for the apology, which may or may not be true. (If it is not true, it should still be a reason that people will believe.) Here are some common excuses:

I'm sorry I'm late, but I **was delayed / held up** in traffic. [late because of a problem that is out of your control]
I'm sorry I'm late, but my flight was **canceled.** [The flight was scheduled but did not fly.]

If you are responsible for a problem, you can offer or promise to do something about it:

I'm sorry **about** the mess in here. **I'll clean it up.** [make it neat and clean]

C Reassuring people

When people apologize to us, it is very common to say something to **reassure** them [tell them that "everything is OK," and that we are not angry]. Here are some common expressions. Note that we often use two of them to emphasize the fact that "it's OK."

A: I'm sorry I'm late.
B: **That's OK. Don't worry. / Never mind. It doesn't matter. / That's OK. No problem.**

D Thanks

A: I'll mail those letters for you.
B: Oh, **thank you. That's very kind of you.**

A: I'm so glad you could come.
B: It was a lovely dinner. **Thank you for everything / for inviting me / for your hospitality.**

A: Here's your pen. B: **Thanks very much. / Thanks a lot.**

Exercises

24.1 Complete these dialogues with expressions from the opposite page.

1. A: I'm *very/terribly/really/awfully/so* sorry.
   B: That's OK. Don't worry.
2. A: I'm sorry .... late, but I got .... up.
   B: That's OK. No ....
3. A: Sorry to .... you waiting.
   B: That's OK. Never ....
4. A: I'll carry your bags for you.
   B: Oh, thank you. That's very .... of you.
5. A: I have to .... for missing the meeting.
   B: That's OK. It doesn't ....
6. A: I'm busy right now, but I won't be ....
   B: .... mind. I'll come back later.
7. A: I .... your pardon.
   B: It's OK. Don't ....

24.2 What could you say in these situations? If it is an apology, give an explanation/excuse if you think it is necessary.

1. You get on a bus at the same time as another person and he/she almost falls over.
   I'm terribly sorry. / I beg your pardon.
2. You arrange to meet some friends downtown but you are twenty minutes late.
   ....
3. You are pushing your car into a side road and a stranger offers to help you.
   ....
4. A friend borrows a pen from you and then loses it. When your friend apologizes, you want to reassure him/her.
   ....
5. Some American friends invite you to dinner. How could you thank them as you leave their house at the end of the evening?
   ....
6. Your company promised to send information about new products to a customer last month. You still haven't sent the information and must now write to explain.
   ....

24.3 Write what you think the person in each picture should say.

1.   2.

24.4 Do you apologize, reassure, explain, and thank people in similar ways in your own language? Read the opposite page again and think about any differences between English and your language.

UNIT 25

Requests, invitations, and suggestions

A **Requests and replies**

We use different expressions to introduce a request – it depends on who we are talking to, and the "size" of the request ("big" or "small"). These are some of the most common (the "small" requests first), with positive and negative replies.

A: **Could you** pass me the salt?   A: **Could I** borrow your dictionary?
B: Yes, **sure.**   B: Yes, **of course.**   *or*   Yes, **help yourself.**
     [Yes, take it.]   *or*   **Go ahead.**

A: **(Is there) any chance you could** lend me five dollars?   *or*
     Would you mind lending me five dollars? (*Note:* **mind + -ing**)
B: Yes, **sure.**   *or*   **I wish I could, but** I don't have any money on me at all.
           I'm sorry, but . . .

A: **I was wondering if I could** leave work half an hour early today?   *or*
     Would you mind if I left work . . . ? / **(Do you) mind if I leave** work . . . ?
B: **No problem.**   *or*   **Well, I'd rather you didn't** because . . .

B **Invitations and replies**

A: **Would you like to** go out this evening?
B: Yeah, **great / I'd love to.**   *or*
     I'm sorry, I can't.

A: We're going out to dinner **and we were wondering if you'd like to** come with us.
B: **I'd love to, but** I can't tonight. I have to finish this report.

C **Suggestions and replies**

Asking for / making suggestions:
What would you like to do tonight? **Where should we go** this evening?
How about (*or* **What about**) a movie?
How about (*or* **What about**) staying home? (*Note:* **How/What about + -ing**)
We could go to the student center and watch the game on a big-screen TV.
Why don't we try that new cafe downtown?

Responding:
Yeah, **great / fine / OK / that's a good idea.**
Sounds good/great/terrific.
I don't know. [I don't really want to.] **(It) sounds kind of boring.**
Yeah, **if you like.** [If you want to go, then I am happy to go.]
I think **I'd rather** stay home and watch videos. [**I would prefer to**]

Exercises

25.1 Correct the mistakes in this dialogue.

A: ~~Do~~ *Would* you like to go out this evening?
B: I wish I can, but I don't have any money.
A: That's OK, I'll pay. How about go to a movie?
B: Yeah, great.
A: Why we don't go see that new romantic comedy playing downtown?
B: I don't know. Sounds like kind of boring. I think I'd rather to see an action movie.
A: Well, what like the latest disaster movie?
B: Great! I'd love.

25.2 Complete these dialogues with an appropriate word or phrase.

1. A: .... you open that window? It's very hot in here.
   B: Yeah, ...
2. A: The Satos are here and we were .... if you'd like to come over
   and join us for dinner this evening?
   B: Yes, I'd ....
3. A: What .... we do this evening?
   B: Gee, I don't know. Any ideas?
   A: Why .... we go dancing? We haven't done that in ages.
   B: Yeah, that's a ....
4. A: Where .... we go on Saturday?
   B: .... going to the beach if the weather is nice?
   A: Yeah. Or we .... play golf.
   B: Mmm. I think I'd .... go to the beach.
   A: OK, if you ....
5. A: What .... you like to do this weekend?
   B: How .... a barbecue?
   A: Yeah. .... good.

25.3 Respond to these requests, invitations, or suggestions as fast as you can. If
possible, do this activity with someone else: One asks the questions, the other
answers. Alternate positive and negative answers.

1. Could I borrow a pen for a minute?   *Sure, go ahead.   or*
   I'm sorry, but I need it right now.
2. Would you mind mailing a letter for me?
3. I was wondering if you have a suitcase you could lend me.
4. Would you like to go out this evening?
5. I've got tickets for a concert tonight and I was wondering if you'd like to go
   with me.
6. How about going to a baseball game this weekend?
7. Why don't we meet this afternoon and practice our English for an hour?
8. We could invite some other people from our English class to meet us too.

25.4 Try using English expressions in place of your first language to respond to
requests, invitations, and suggestions. If your friends don't understand, you can
teach them a little bit of English.

Opinions, agreeing, and disagreeing

A   Asking someone's opinion

What do you **think of** his new book?
How do you **feel about** working here?
What are your **feelings** *(pl.)* **about** the change in schedule?
What's your (**honest**) **opinion of** that painting?

B   Giving your opinion

I think Carla had the best idea.
I don't think he knows much about the subject.
Personally, I think his first book is trash.
In my opinion, we should sell the old car and buy a new one.
As far as I'm concerned, the whole evening was a waste of time. (*Note:* This can
    mean "This is my opinion and I don't care what anyone else thinks.")

Note: To say something *isn't* a good idea, you usually make "think" negative: **I
don't think** it's a good idea. [*not* I think it's not a good idea.]

C   Agreeing with someone

We often agree with someone by adding to their opinion or argument.

A: I think we should concentrate on this one project.
B: Yes, it's better to do one thing well than two things badly.

But if we want to make it very clear that we agree, we can use these expressions:

Yes, **I agree (with you).** (*Note:* **Agree** is a verb in English; *not* I am agree.)
Yes, **I think you're right.**

D   Disagreeing with someone

It is very common in English to begin with a short expression of agreement, and
then give a different opinion. Here are some expressions used to introduce the
disagreement:

I see/know what you mean,   but I'm not sure that . . .
Yes, maybe/possibly/perhaps, but don't you think . . . ?
Yes, that's true,   but what about . . . ?
Yes, you could be right,   but don't forget . . .

Personally, I think . . .   Yes, that's true, but . . .

If you disagree strongly, you can say: I'm sorry, but **I totally disagree (with you).**

Note: When we want to disagree, but not completely, we can use these phrases:

Yes, I agree (with you) **somewhat,** but . . .
I agree **to some extent / to a certain extent,** but . . .

Exercises

26.1 Complete these sentences in at least three different ways to ask people their opinion.

1. .... the proposed changes?
2. .... the new building?
3. .... the subway system?
4. .... the new labor law?

26.2 Fill in the blanks (one word only).

1. A: What did you think .... it?
   B: Well, ..., I didn't like it very much.
2. In my ...., we should start right away.
3. I agree with her to a certain ....
4. As far as I'm ...., the plan will never work.
5. I'm sorry, but I .... disagree with you.
6. I see what you ...., but I'm not sure I agree with you.

26.3 Rewrite these sentences without using the underlined words and phrases. The meaning must stay the same.

1. In my opinion, you can't learn a language in three months.
   Personally, I don't think you can learn a language in three months.
2. I think the club needs to buy a new computer.
   ....
3. Yes, I think you're right.
   ....
4. What are your feelings about our new workplace?
   ....
5. I agree with her to some extent.
   ....

26.4 Agree or disagree with the statements below. If you agree with the point of view, add to the argument. If you introduce a different point of view, remember to start with a short expression of agreement first.

1. A: A lot of women are perfectly happy to stay home and be housewives.
   B: *I agree to some extent, but there are a lot of women who can't afford to stay home.   or*
      Yes, some women find it more rewarding to raise a family.
2. A: The government shouldn't give money to people who don't want to work.
   B: ....
3. A: Watching a lot of TV is bad for young people.
   B: ....
4. A: Animal experimentation is immoral and should be banned.
   B: ....
5. A: Students shouldn't have to pay any tuition for their courses.
   B: ....

UNIT 27 Greetings, farewells, and special expressions

A Greetings

Neutral to formal:	*Less formal:*
A: Hi./Hello. How are you?	A: Hi/Hey. How are things? /
B: Fine, thank you. / Fine, thanks.	How's it going? / How're you doing?
. . . How are you? / How	B: Pretty good. / OK. / All right. /
about you?	I'm good. . . . How about you?

We sometimes use these greetings at different times of day:

Good morning. / Good afternoon. / Good evening. [We don't use **Good night** as a greeting.]

When meeting someone for the first time, we can say:

Nice to meet you. [The answer could be **Nice to meet you too. / Same here.**]
How do you do? / Pleased to meet you. *(formal)*

Nice to meet you.

Same here.

B Farewells

Good-bye. *(neutral to formal)*
Take care. / Take it easy. / So long. / Bye. / See you. *(less formal)*
See you later. / See you soon. [if you plan to see someone again, soon]
Good/Nice to see you. [a greeting or a farewell to someone you already know]
Nice meeting you. [to say good-bye to someone you've just met for the first time]
Good night. [to say good-bye late at night or if one or both of you is going to bed]
Have a nice day/evening/weekend. [to say good-bye to a friend or colleague or to a customer in a store; the response could be: **You too.**]

C Special expressions

Excuse/Pardon me.	(a) To get someone's attention. (b) To get past someone who is in your way. (c) To say you are sorry, e.g., if you stand on someone's foot. [*or:* **I beg your pardon.**] (d) Say **Excuse me** (*not* **Pardon me**) before you leave the room.
Excuse/Pardon me? / I beg your pardon?	To ask someone to repeat what was said.
To your health. / Cheers.	A toast when people have a drink together. It could also be **To your new job. / To friendship. / To romance.** etc.
Good luck!	To wish someone success, e.g., on exams / a job interview / a contest.
Congratulations.	To someone who has achieved something or had good fortune, e.g., found a job, graduated, got a raise. Also **Good job!** or **Nice going!** *(informal)*
Bless you.	To someone when they sneeze. They can reply: **Thank you. / Thanks.**
Happy birthday. / Happy New Year.	To wish someone well on their birthday / on or soon after New Year's Day (often printed or written on greeting cards).

Exercises

27.1 **What would you say or write to a friend in these situations?**

1. Your friend turns 21 tomorrow.   *Happy birthday! / Congratulations!*
2. It is January 1st or soon after.
3. Your friend has just passed an important exam.
4. Your friend is going to take a driving test next week.
5. You know you are going to see your friend again in a few hours.

27.2 **Complete the conversations in a logical way.**

27.3 **What would you say in these situations? (Don't use "Excuse me" more than twice.)**

1. You are in a meeting. Someone comes in to say you have an urgent telephone call. What do you say as you leave?   *Excuse me. This won't take long.*
2. Someone says something to you, but you don't hear all of it.
3. You are on a crowded bus. It is your stop and you want to get off. What do you say to the other passengers as you move past them?
4. You are staying with friends. You leave the room in the evening to go to bed.
5. A friend tells you she has just won a contest.
6. Another friend is going for a job interview this afternoon.
7. You met a new business client for the first time an hour ago, and now you are both leaving.
8. While shopping, you meet an old friend (by chance), who you haven't seen in ages.

27.4 **When do we use these expressions? Do you have similar ones in your language?**

Say "cheese."   Watch out.   I have no idea.   Good for you!

Uncountable nouns and plural nouns

A Uncountable nouns

Uncountable nouns (e.g., information, advice, weather):

- cannot be used with **a/an**, e.g., **information** [*not* an information]
- cannot be made plural, e.g., **some advice** [*not* some advices]
- take a singular verb, e.g., **The weather is** very nice today. [*not* The weather are . . .]

Countable nouns are nouns that we can count, e.g., **one book, two books, three books,** etc. They can be used with a/an and made plural, e.g., **a book, some books.**

These uncountable nouns in English are often countable in other languages:

She couldn't give me any **information** about the hotel.
He gave me lots of **advice** about the best dictionary to buy.
We are going to sell all the **furniture.** [tables, chairs, sofas, etc.]
My **knowledge** of Korean is very limited.
You need a lot of **equipment** for camping. [tent, sleeping bag, cooking utensils, etc.]
She is making good **progress** in her English. [Her English is improving / getting
    better.]
We had fabulous **weather** in Mexico.
The teacher gave us a lot of **homework** last night.
I never take much **luggage/baggage** when I go on vacation. [bags and suitcases]

B In dictionaries

Learner's dictionaries usually show countable nouns with a (C) and uncountable nouns with a (U). Some nouns can be countable with one meaning and uncountable with another.

book (C)   The books are on the table.
housework (U)   I did a lot of housework this morning.
hair (U)   My hair is getting very long. I need to get it cut.
hair (C)   There is a hair on my dinner plate.

C Plural nouns

Plural nouns (e.g., pants, pajamas):

- have only a plural form and cannot be used with **a/an**, e.g., **pants** [*not* a pant]
- usually take a plural verb, e.g., **These pants are** too long. [*not* These pants is . . .]
- can usually be made singular using **a pair of**, e.g., **a pair of pants/pajamas**

Here are some other nouns that are usually plural:

I bought a new pair of **jeans** when I went shopping.
When it's sunny, I wear **sunglasses** for driving.
The **headphones** on my personal stereo are great.
These **shorts** don't fit me.
The **scissors** are on the table.

Exercises

28.1 Correct the mistakes.

1. I need some informations. *I need some information.*
2. We had a great weather.
3. I'm looking for a new jeans.
4. Your hairs are getting very long.
5. I can't find my sunglass.
6. We had a lot of homeworks yesterday.
7. Do you think she's making a progress with her English?
8. These pajamas is too big for me.

28.2 Are these nouns countable (C), uncountable (U), or both? Use a dictionary to help you. If they can be both C and U, write sentences to show the difference.

Examples: dish   *C*   time   *U: I don't have time to take a break.*
rice   *U*   time   *C: I've seen "Star Wars" at least ten times.*

butter   cup   paperwork   insurance   television   vocabulary
spaghetti   coffee   grape   work   money   people

28.3 Complete these dialogues using a plural noun or an uncountable noun from the opposite page. Make sure the form of each word is correct.

Example: A: It's too hot for jeans.
B: You need *a pair of shorts / some shorts.*

1. A: I have to cut this paper into three pieces.
   B: You need ....
2. A: I can't see because the sun is in my eyes.
   B: You need ....
3. A: I don't know what to do when I graduate.
   B: You need ....
4. A: My room looks so empty.
   B: You need ....
5. A: I can't play my music loud because my mother always complains.
   B: You need ....
6. A: My teacher said my English wasn't getting any better.
   B: Maybe you need to do more ....

28.4 Read this radio news broadcast. Can you find three uncountable nouns and two plural nouns (i.e., nouns that are always plural for this meaning)? These words are *not* on the opposite page.

> Traffic has been heavy throughout the day because of construction on Pacific Coast Drive, on the outskirts of town, causing long delays for motorists heading into the city. The authorities are advising drivers to avoid the area if at all possible. We will keep you informed of the situation with the latest news every half hour, so don't go away.

Verb + *-ing* form, infinitive, or base form

A **Verb + *-ing* form**

Some verbs are followed by an **-ing** form if the next word is a verb:

enjoy **finish** **imagine**
(don't) mind **can't stand** [hate] **feel like** [want/desire]
give up [stop doing something]
avoid [If you avoid something, you stay away from it.]
admit [If you **admit** something, you agree it is true, and often it is something bad.]
deny [You say something isn't true; ≠ **admit.**]

I stayed home last night, but I **feel like going** out tonight.
At the police station, he **admitted** stealing the money but **denied** taking the computer.
I've lived in Texas all my life; I can't **imagine** living anywhere else.
Some people **can't stand** working at night, but I **don't mind.** [It's not a problem.]
I **don't mind** driving during rush hour, but I **avoid** taking crowded freeways.

B **Verb + infinitive**

Some verbs are followed by an infinitive if the next word is a verb:

offer **want** **seem** **decide** **hope** **need**
mean [intend, plan] **expect** [think or believe something will happen]
manage [be able to do something, even when it is difficult]
refuse [say "no" when someone asks you for something]
promise [say you will definitely do something, or that something will definitely
  happen]

We were very busy, but we **managed to finish** before 6 p.m.
It was getting late and there were no buses, so I **offered to take** them home in my car.
She hit one of the boys, but she didn't **mean to do** it. I **meant to call** you, but I forgot.
I asked her to carry the suitcases, but she **refused to help.**
I don't **expect to see** them before next week.

C **Verb + base form**

Two common verbs followed by an object + base form are: **make** someone do
something, and **let** someone do something.

My parents always **make** me **do** my homework. [They **force** me **to do** my
  homework.]
My parents **let** me **go** out on weekends. [They **allow/permit** me **to go** out.]

D **Verb + *-ing* form or infinitive**

Some verbs can be followed by an **-ing** form or infinitive, but the meaning is very
similar, e.g., **love, like, hate, try,** and **prefer:** "I like going to the movies. / I like to
go to the movies." But with some verbs there is a difference in meaning:

I **remembered to buy** a present for my brother. [I didn't forget to buy a present.]
I **remember buying** him a present. [It's in my memory; it happened and I remember.]

Exercises

UNIT 29

29.1 Circle the correct answer(s). In some sentences, both choices are correct.

1. We decided (to work) / working during our vacation.
2. She promised to help / helping us.
3. I don't feel like to go / going for a walk right now.
4. We need to make / making plans for the holidays.
5. Don't you hate to drive / driving when it's wet?
6. I can't imagine to eat / eating eggs every day of the week.
7. Most of the time she prefers to work / working at home.
8. I don't remember to go / going to the zoo when we visited San Diego.
9. He hopes to finish / finishing his thesis by the end of the month.
10. He gave up to smoke / smoking for health reasons.

29.2 Complete part (c) of each number in a logical way.

1. Most people want:
   a) to be rich   b) to get married   c) _to be happy_
2. A lot of people can't stand:
   a) getting wet   b) getting up early   c) ....
3. Many people enjoy:
   a) going to parties   b) lying on a beach   c) ....
4. Most people expect
   a) to be happy   b) to find a job they will like   c) ....
5. Some people don't mind:
   a) washing dishes   b) ironing   c) ....
6. Some parents make their teenage children:
   a) wear certain clothes   b) do housework   c) ....
7. Other parents let their teenage children:
   a) wear what they like   b) stay out all night   c) ....

Do you think the statements above are true, and are they (or were they) true for you? If possible, compare and discuss your answers with someone else.

29.3 Read the story and answer the questions below.

When Julie was 17, her father said she could go on vacation with two school friends. He also said he would lend her the money for a hotel, but she would have to pay for the airfare and her entertainment herself. Julie was delighted and said she would bring him back a wonderful present and pay him back in six months. But first she and her friends had to decide where to go. They looked at lots of brochures and finally agreed on a two-week vacation in the Caribbean. They had a great time, but unfortunately Julie spent all her money and forgot to buy a present for her father.

1. What did Julie's father let her do when she was 17? He let ....
2. And what did he offer to do? He offered ....
3. But what did he refuse to do? He refused ....
4. In return, what did Julie promise? She promised ....
5. What did the three friends decide? They decided ....

61

Verb patterns

A Verb + object

subject	verb	object	
She	proposed [*formal*; suggested]	the plan	at the meeting.
The travel agent	confirmed [said it was sure]	my reservation.	
They	discussed [talked about]	the movie	for hours.

B Verb + object + question word

subject	verb	object	question word	
I	told	them	where	to find it.
She	asked	us	why	we wanted it.

Note: A common mistake is: "He explained me what to do." After **explain** + question word, there is no direct object. We say: "He explained what to do / what I had to do."

C Verb + object + infinitive

subject	verb	object	infinitive	
She	asked	everyone	to leave.	
They	told	us	to wait	outside.
The doctor	advised	him	to stay	in bed.
I	wanted	the others	to help	us.
He	persuaded	me	to go	to the party.
She	warned	them	to be	careful.

persuade [make someone do or believe something by giving good reasons; **convince**]
warn [tell someone of a possible danger or problem]

D Verb + (object) + (that) clause

She warned me that it was dangerous.

subject	verb	object	(that) clause
He	said	–	(that) it was good.
She	suggested	–	(that) we go together.
He	insisted	–	(that) we work late.
They	told	him	(that) it was expensive.
She	warned	me	(that) it was dangerous.

insist [demand something strongly and not accept refusal]
We can also use **-ing** after **suggest**, e.g., She **suggested** going there together.

E Verb + (object) + preposition

He **insisted on** paying the bill. (*Note:* Use the **-ing** form of the verb after a preposition.)
They **blamed** me **for** the accident. [They said I was responsible / it was my **fault**.]
She **complained** (to the manager) **about** the bad service. [She said she was not satisfied.]
The manager **apologized** (to the customer) **for** the bad service. [The manager said, "Sorry."]

Exercises

30.1 Correct the mistakes in these sentences. (Most are the result of translating from the first language.)

1. She said me the movie was terrible.   *She said the movie was terrible.*
2. He told it was not possible.
3. Can you explain me what to do?
4. He suggested us to go to an Italian restaurant.
5. I want that he leaves.
6. I need to confirm me the flight.
7. I apologized my mistake.
8. She advised me buy a dictionary.

30.2 Fill in the missing verb in each sentence. (There may be more than one answer.)

1. They watched the movie together; then they ..*discussed*.......... it in small groups.
2. Her room was very noisy, so she called the hotel manager to ....
3. It was a terrible thing to say to him, but she refused to ....
4. He knew it was dangerous, but he didn't .... me.
5. I didn't want to go at first, but she .... me.
6. She advised them not to leave, but they .... on going.
7. I booked the flight by telephone, but I asked the travel agent to .... it in writing anyway.
8. It wasn't his fault, but they still .... him.

30.3 Complete these sentences in a logical way.

1. Some of us were getting hungry, so I suggested ..*that we go out to eat.*.........
2. They were making a lot of noise next door, and I told ....
3. She went to that new Chinese restaurant and said ....
4. We read the book for homework and discussed ....
5. The streets are dangerous at night, so I insisted ....
6. It was only a few minutes to the beach, but I still couldn't persuade ....
7. He wasn't feeling very well, and the teacher advised ....
8. The whole team played badly, but most of the newspapers blamed ....
9. The water there can make you sick, and I warned ....
10. If you don't understand the instructions, someone will explain ....

30.4 When you learn a new verb, look at the grammar information about it in a good dictionary. Always look carefully at the example sentences, and then write one or two of your own. Do this for these three verbs below. Which patterns from the opposite page are used after these verbs?

Example: ask   1) *+ object + question word: I asked her who was coming to the party.*
              2) *+ object + infinitive: He asked me to mail the letter.*
              3) *+ preposition: Don't be afraid to ask for help.*

order   recommend   prevent

Adjectives

Adjectives ending in *-ing* and *-ed*

There is a large group of adjectives that can have an **-ing** or **-ed** ending. The **-ing** ending is often used on adjectives that describe a person, thing, or situation; the **-ed** ending is often used on adjectives that describe the effect of this person, thing, or situation.

It was such a **boring** party; I was **bored,** and so was everyone else.
I didn't think the movie was very **frightening,** but the children were **frightened** by it.
I think the students are **depressed** because the weather is so **depressing.**

Other examples of common adjectives ending in **-ing** and **-ed** include:

astonishing/astonished exhausting/exhausted
confusing/confused fascinating/fascinated
disappointing/disappointed interesting/interested
embarrassing/embarrassed surprising/surprised
exciting/excited terrifying/terrified

Jane isn't very good at English, so I was very **surprised** when she passed the exam. And I was absolutely **astonished** when I heard that she'd gotten 99%.
In Tokyo there are lots of streets with no names, and it's very **confusing** if you are a tourist. Another problem is that it's a huge place. We walked everywhere on our last trip, and we were **exhausted** by the end of each day. But it's a very **exciting** city, with so much to do.
It's been a terrible week for Carlos. He was very **disappointed** last Saturday because he played badly in an important tennis match. Then on Monday, his girlfriend left him for someone else, so he's very **depressed** right now.
One of our teachers can never remember our names. It seemed funny at first, but now it's becoming kind of **embarrassing.**

"Scale" and "limit" adjectives

(absolutely) terrible	(very) bad	OK	(very) good	(absolutely) fabulous
awful				marvelous
horrible				terrific

Some adjectives, such as **good** and **bad,** can be described on a scale from weak to strong. We can use **very** before "scale" adjectives, e.g., very good, very bad. Other adjectives, such as **awful** and **terrific,** are not measured on a scale: They are usually limited to "all or nothing." We can use **absolutely** before "limit" adjectives, e.g., absolutely awful, absolutely terrific. (You cannot say "very awful"; you cannot say "absolutely good.") Here are some more examples:

Scale	Limit	Scale	Limit
big	enormous/huge	hot	boiling
hungry	starving	cold	freezing
surprised	astonished	frightened [afraid of something]	terrified

Exercises

31.1 Complete these dialogues using a different adjective from speaker A, in the correct form (*-ing* or *-ed*).

1. A: I was very interested in her talk. B: Yes, it was absolutely ...*fascinating*...
2. A: Was it very tiring? B: Yes, we were absolutely ....
3. A: Maria said it was a frightening film. B: Yes, it was absolutely ....
4. A: It was a surprising decision, wasn't it? B: Yes, I was absolutely ....
5. A: Was it very cold? B: Oh yes, it was ....

31.2 Can you think of an adjective from the opposite page to describe how the people felt in each of these situations?

1. They walked about ten miles in the morning, then spent the afternoon helping some friends cut down trees. *exhausted*
2. From the description in the travel brochure, they expected a big, beautiful villa on the beach. In fact it was small, not very clean, and miles from the ocean.
3. They decided to wear jeans to the party, but when they arrived, everyone else was wearing formal evening dress.
4. One person told them the street was on the left, another told them to turn right, and a third person said they had to go back to the station.
5. She spent $1 on a lottery ticket. The next week, she discovered that she'd won $1 million!

31.3 Write at least one limit adjective for these scale adjectives. Cover the opposite page before you begin.

1. big ...*enormous/huge*.................
2. cold ....
3. surprised ....

4. hot ....
5. bad ....
6. frightened ....

31.4 Rewrite this postcard using limit adjectives instead of the underlined words to give a more positive and/or more extreme effect.

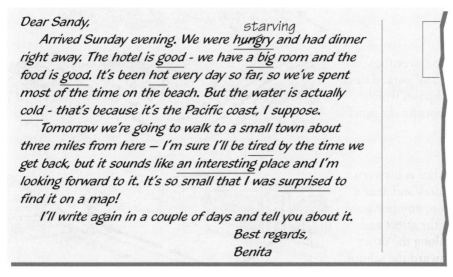

Dear Sandy,
    Arrived Sunday evening. We were hungry and had dinner [*starving*] right away. The hotel is good - we have a big room and the food is good. It's been hot every day so far, so we've spent most of the time on the beach. But the water is actually cold - that's because it's the Pacific coast, I suppose.
    Tomorrow we're going to walk to a small town about three miles from here — I'm sure I'll be tired by the time we get back, but it sounds like an interesting place and I'm looking forward to it. It's so small that I was surprised to find it on a map!
    I'll write again in a couple of days and tell you about it.
                    Best regards,
                    Benita

Prepositions: place

A   ***At, on, in***

at a point/place	I met her at the bus stop. She lives at 43 Lake Drive. He is at work / at home / at school. They are at a party tonight.
on a surface	The book is on the desk. We sat on the floor.
in an area or space	Congo is a country in Africa. She lives in Taipei. He is in the kitchen. The key is in my pocket. Put it in the box.

B   **Opposites**

up ↑   down ↓   into   out of

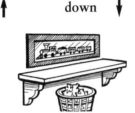 

The picture is **over/above** the shelf.   The bus is **in front of** the car.
The wastebasket is **under/below** the shelf.   The car is **behind** the bus.

Note: **Over/above** and **under/below** usually mean the same thing, but **over** and **under** sometimes suggest movement, e.g., "He jumped **over** the fence" or "I pushed the note **under** the door."

When we flew **over** the city, we couldn't see much because we were **above** the clouds. **Below** us was the river, which ran **under** the bridge.

C   **Other common prepositions of place**

We drove **along** the river, **around** the lake, **past** the old fort, and **through** the town.

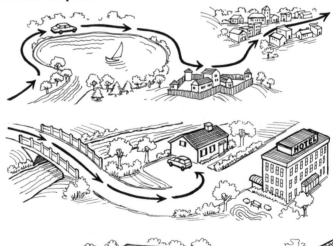

We came **over** the bridge and parked **next to** the house, which was **opposite** the hotel.

Our office is **between** two stores and **near** a bus stop; you just go **across** the street and walk **along** the other side **toward** the school.

Exercises

32.1 Fill in the blanks with *at, on,* or *in.*

1. The ice cream is ..*in*..... the freezer, where it won't melt.
2. We saw them .... the bus stop.
3. I met her .... a party.
4. She works .... Mexico City.
5. The dictionary is .... my desk, next to the telephone.
6. I left my briefcase .... work.
7. There was still a lot of snow .... the ground when I arrived.
8. He lives .... a very nice area.

32.2 Answer the questions using the opposite preposition.

1. Was he standing in front of the statue? No, ...*behind the statue.*...............
2. Is his house up the hill? No, ...
3. Did you climb over the fence? No, ...
4. Did you see her get into the car? No, ...
5. Did you fly below the clouds? No, ...
6. Does she live in the apartment above you? No, ...

32.3 Look at the map and complete the description of the route you took.

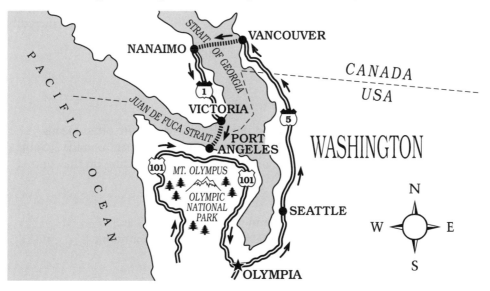

We took Route 101 (1) ...*around*.... Olympic National Park, which is (2) ....
Washington state. We drove (3) .... Port Angeles, without stopping, and
then south to Olympia, the state capital. From there we headed north to Seattle,
then drove (4) .... the border, (5) .... Canada. We drove all the
way up to Vancouver, where we stayed overnight. The next morning, we took the
ferry (6) .... the strait to Nanaimo. From there, we drove (7) ....
the island's eastern shore to beautiful Victoria, where we went sightseeing and
stopped for tea (8) .... a charming tearoom. Later we took another ferry
(9) .... the strait to Port Angeles.

Adverbs: frequency and degree

A **Frequency (how often)**

100%   *0%*

always	frequently	regularly	sometimes	occasionally	seldom *(formal)*	never
	usually	fairly often			hardly ever	
		generally			rarely	

Adverbs of frequency go before the <u>main</u> verb with the exception of the verb *to be*:

I **rarely** see them.   They **hardly ever** go to the movies.
She is **often** late these days.   I've **never** tried Korean food.

Sometimes and **occasionally** can go at the beginning or end of a sentence:

My parents give me money **sometimes**.   I play tennis **occasionally**.
Sometimes my parents give me money.   **Occasionally** I work on weekends.

B **Degree (how much)**

less   *more*

slightly	kind of	rather	quite		extremely
a (little) bit	somewhat	fairly	pretty	very	terribly
					incredibly

Kind of, pretty, and **incredibly** are mostly used in spoken English:

That car is **incredibly** expensive.
The food was **pretty** good. [almost "very" good]
I'm **kind of** curious. [fairly; in some ways]

Rather is sometimes more formal than the other words. **Quite** often means
"very," but not "extremely," e.g., "It's quite warm [very warm] outside." Some
speakers use *quite* to mean "fairly" or "moderately," depending on the context.

C *Almost/nearly*

It's **almost/nearly** five o'clock. [It is a minute or so before five.]
I **almost/nearly** lost the game. [I won, but only by a small amount.]

D *Hardly*

Hardly + a positive often has the same meaning as **almost** + a negative:

I **hardly** had **anything** to eat for lunch. [I had almost nothing.]
She could **hardly** walk after her operation. [She almost couldn't walk.]
We **hardly ever** go to the beach. [We almost never go to the beach.]

Note: In the first two sentences above, you can also use **barely** with the same
meaning.

Exercises

33.1 Make sentences from these scrambled words.

1. brother   often   us   Sundays   visits   on   my
My brother often visits us on Sundays.
2. me   ever   calls   she   hardly
3. visit   saw   I   hardly   his   him   during
4 get   occasionally   I   early   up
5. have   smoked   never   I

33.2 Replace the underlined adverb with an adverb that has a similar meaning.

1. She seldom goes to conferences.   *hardly ever / rarely*
2. I can barely remember the first house we lived in.
3. There were almost fifty people at the party.
4. I thought the play was kind of disappointing, didn't you?
5. I'm sorry, but I'm extremely busy next week.

33.3 Change the underlined adverbs to make the first three sentences a little less negative, and the last two sentences a little more positive.

1. John said the apartment was very small.   *John said the apartment was
kind of / fairly / a bit small.*
2. They said it was fairly boring.
3. The clothes were very expensive.
4. I thought they were very good.
5. He's been getting pretty good marks on his exams.

33.4 Put a frequency adverb into each sentence to make a true sentence about yourself.
Compare your answers with someone else if possible.

1. I buy clothes I don't like.   *I never buy clothes I don't like.*
2. I polish my shoes.
3. I remember my dreams.
4. I give money to people on the street if they ask me.
5. I speak to strangers on buses and trains.
6. I'm rude to people who are rude to me.

Now think about each of your answers to the above sentences (and if possible,
your partner's answers). Do you think they are:

a) very typical?   c) slightly unusual?
b) fairly typical?   d) extremely unusual?

33.5 Think of something you . . .

1. always do.   *I always wash my hands before meals.*
2. usually do in the morning.
3. sometimes do in the evening.
4. would never do.
5. would like to do more often, but hardly ever have a chance to do.

Time and sequence

A · *When* and *as soon as*

I'll call you **when** I get home. / **As soon as** I get home, I'll call you.
When you've finished, you can leave. / You can leave **as soon as** you've finished.

Note: The two linking words/phrases above can be followed by the present tense or the present perfect [but *not* **will**: You cannot say "As soon as I will finish . . ." or "When I will finish . . ."] **As soon as** suggests that the second action will happen *immediately* after the first.

B · Two things happening at the same time

Pat wrote some letters **while** I cooked dinner. [two actions in the same period of time]
The accident happened **while** I was on my way to work. [Here "on my way to work" is a longer action than "the accident." We can also use **when** or **as** here.]
I saw him (**just**) **as** I was coming out of the office. [For two short actions we use **as** (*not* **while**), and we often use **just as** to emphasize that these two short actions happened at exactly the same moment: "He opened the door **just as** I touched the doorknob."]

C · One thing after another

We met them at the cafe, and **then/afterward/afterwards** we went to the concert.
After my visit to New York, I decided to relax for a few days.
We had something to eat **before** we went out.

Note: We can also follow **before** and **after** with an **-ing** form:

After visiting New York, I decided to relax for a few days.
We had something to eat **before** going out.

D · A sequence of actions

We had a great vacation. **First (of all)**, we went to San Francisco. **Then / After that / Afterward(s)**, we drove to Los Angeles. **Finally,** we went to San Diego.

Note: If something happened after a lot of time and/or problems, you can use **eventually** or **in the end**, e.g., I made several wrong turns, but **eventually** I got there.

E · A sequence of reasons

There are different combinations of words and phrases we can use here:

SON: Why can't we go away this weekend?
DAD: **First / First of all,** because I'm busy this weekend. **Second(ly),** you've got a lot of schoolwork to do. And **third(ly),** we're planning to go away *next* weekend.

Note:
- We can also start with the phrases **To begin with / To start with.**
- In spoken English, we can start with **For one thing,** followed by **And for another (thing).**
- For the second or final reason, we sometimes use (**And**) **Besides** or **Anyway,** e.g., "We can't go to that club because it's too far. **And besides,** I'm not a member."

Exercises

34.1 Circle the correct answer. Sometimes both answers are correct.

1. I'll give them your message as soon as I (get)/ will get there.
2. Mary cleaned the kitchen just as / while I cleaned the bathroom.
3. I'd like to visit that gallery before to leave / leaving the city.
4. I had a lot of problems at the store, but eventually / finally they gave me a refund.
5. I did my homework. After / After that, I went out.

34.2 Complete these sentences in a logical way.

1. We played tennis, and afterward *we went for a swim.* ....
2. I'll meet you as soon as ....
3. Remember to lock the back door before ....
4. I think I dropped the letter as ....
5. I looked up half of the words in my dictionary while ....
6. We had to wait for hours, but eventually ....
7. My car is too big for you to drive. And besides, ...
8. I saw the burglar breaking the window just as ....

34.3 Add a final sentence (starting with a linking word or phrase from the opposite page) to each of these mini-conversations.

1. A: Why do you want to stay home this evening when we could go to Karl's party?
   B: Well, for one thing, my ex-boyfriend will be there and I really don't want to see him. ....
2. A: What did you do on your trip?
   B: First of all, we spent a few days in Tokyo. After that, we took the train to Osaka and stayed there overnight. ....
3. A: Why can't we send one of our staff members to the conference?
   B: Well, to begin with, I don't think the company should send anyone to the conference. And ....

34.4 Imagine you spent a weekend at a hotel and had these problems in the restaurant:

- There was very little variety in the food.
- The service was very slow.
- When you mentioned these things to staff members, they were very rude.

The manager (Ms. Watson) was away during your stay, so you have decided to write her a letter of complaint. Complete this letter.

```
Ms. M. Watson
Manager, Park Royal Hotel

Dear Ms. Watson:

I have just returned from a weekend at the Park Royal
Hotel, and I am writing to express my dissatisfaction
with the food and service in your restaurant.
```

Addition and contrast

A *In addition, furthermore, etc. ("and")*

When you add a second piece of information in a sentence to support the first piece of information, you can use **and**, e.g., "The food is excellent **and** the prices are reasonable." When you put this information in two sentences, you can use these linking words and phrases:

The food is excellent. **Furthermore / What's more,** the prices are reasonable.
The fixed price menu is $10, which is very reasonable. **In addition,** you get a free beverage.
The restaurant has a reputation for excellent food. The prices are **also** reasonable.
The food is excellent in that restaurant. The prices are reasonable **as well / too.**

Note: **Furthermore** and **in addition** are more common in written English.

B *Although, in spite of, etc. ("but")*

When you want to contrast two pieces of information in a single sentence and say that the second fact is surprising after the first, you can use these linking words:

She still won the game, **although / though / even though** she had a bad knee.
They still went out **in spite of the fact that** it was raining hard / **in spite of** the rain.
He still failed the exam **despite the fact that** he'd studied hard / **despite** study**ing** hard.

Note: In the above examples you can also begin the sentence with the linking word(s), e.g., "**Although** she had a bad knee, she still won the game."

It is common to use **still** in these sentences to emphasize the surprise (as in the examples).

After **although, though,** or **even though,** you must use a clause [subject + verb], e.g., **Although** she had a bad knee, . . . / **Although** her knee was bad, . . .

C *Whereas*

Whereas shows that something is true of one thing but not true of another.

Pat is very careful, **whereas** Chris makes lots of mistakes.
The south is hot and dry, **whereas** the north gets a lot of rain.

D *However*

You can use **however** or **on the other hand** to contrast two ideas in two sentences. **However** is more appropriate when the second sentence is surprising after the first.

I don't agree with all of her methods. **However,** she is a good teacher.
We didn't like the hotel at all. **However,** we still enjoyed ourselves.
Sam liked the movie a lot. Joe, **however / on the other hand,** thought it was stupid.
Most big cats, such as tigers and leopards, are very solitary creatures. Lions, **however / on the other hand,** spend much of their time in groups.

Exercises

35.1 Circle the correct answers. Sometimes both answers are correct.

1. <u>Although / In spite of</u> we left late, we still got there on time.
2. It was a fantastic evening <u>although / in spite of</u> the terrible food.
3. We decided to go <u>in spite of / despite</u> the cost of the tickets.
4. They enjoyed the course, <u>even though / whereas</u> it was very difficult.
5. I love the ocean, <u>furthermore / whereas</u> most of my friends prefer the mountains.
6. We found a lovely bungalow near the lake that we can rent. <u>In addition, / However,</u> it has its own swimming pool, and we have free use of a car.
7. We both told John the car was too expensive. <u>However, / On the other hand,</u> he still decided to buy it.
8. Most people we met tried to help us. They were very friendly <u>too / as well.</u>

35.2 Connect parts from each column to form five short sentences or groups of sentences.

A	B	C
He went to school today	even though	the pay isn't very good.
He always did his best at school,	in spite of	he's the most experienced.
He has the right qualifications.	However,	the help I gave him.
He didn't pass the exam	whereas	he didn't feel very well.
He decided to take the job.	What's more,	most of his classmates were very lazy.

35.3 Fill in the blanks with a linking word or phrase.

1. *Despite / In spite of* taking a map, they still got lost.
2. It took me two hours to do it, ... the others finished in less than an hour.
3. The hotel has a very good reputation. ...., it is very reasonable.
4. She managed to get there .... she had a broken ankle.
5. It's not the best dictionary you can buy; ...., it's better than nothing.
6. She's younger than the others in the group, and she's better than most of them ....

35.4 Complete these sentences in a logical way.

1. I was able to follow what she was saying even though *she spoke very quickly.*
2. I was able to follow what she was saying, whereas ....
3. We enjoyed the vacation in spite of ....
4. If you buy a season ticket, you can go as often as you like. Furthermore, ...
5. The exam was very difficult. However, ...
6. Although it was a very long movie, ...

35.5 Write all the linking words and phrases from the opposite page that you can remember. Then organize them into groups according to meaning. Write your own examples for each one and keep them on one page in your notebook. In the future, you can add more examples as you meet them.

Similarities, differences, and conditions

 A   ### Similarities

Joe is **similar to / like** his brother in many ways. Joe and his brother are very **similar.**
Joe and his brother are (**very much**) **alike.**
Sue and Pat **both** passed their exams. [Sue passed and Pat passed.] But **neither**
(**one**) wants to go to college. [Sue doesn't want to go, and Pat doesn't want to
go either.]
The two boys **have a lot in common.** [They have many things, e.g., hobbies,
interests, beliefs, that are the same or very similar.]

B   ### Differences

Paula is **not at all like / (quite) unlike** her sister Pam.
   [very different from]

Paula   Pam

They **have nothing in common.** [no interests, beliefs, etc., that are the same]
His early movies are (**quite**) **different from** his later ones.

C   ### Using *compare*

We want to **compare** the prices of all the cameras before deciding which one to buy.
They made a **comparison** of average salaries in different parts of the country.
Our new home is very big **compared with/to** our old one.
If you **compare** this one **with** the others, I'm sure you'll see a difference.

D   ### Exceptions

When we make a general statement about things or people, and then say that one
thing or person is not included or is different from the others, we use these words
and phrases:

It snowed everywhere **except** on the west coast.
The two girls are very similar, **except** that Marie has slightly longer hair.
The museum is open every day **except** (**for**) / **apart from** Sunday(s).
Everyone heard the fire alarm **except** (**for**) / **apart from** the two boys in Room 7.

Note: **Except** can be followed by different words (nouns, prepositions, etc.), but
except for and **apart from** are followed by nouns or noun phrases. **Apart from** is
more formal.

E   ### Conditions

Notice the tenses underlined in the examples.

We will be late **unless** we hurry. [We will be late if we don't hurry.]
Unless the weather improves [if the weather doesn't improve], we won't be able
   to go.
I have to go now; **otherwise** I'll miss the last bus. [if I don't go now]
You can borrow it **as long as*** you bring it back by Thursday. [**on condition that**]
Take your umbrella **in case** it rains. [because it may rain later]

Note:* The meaning is very similar to **if here, but the use of **as long as** shows that
the condition is very important to the speaker.

Exercises

36.1 Read the information, then complete the sentences using the words/phrases from A and B on the opposite page.

MICHAEL . . .
is 21 and lives with his parents. He works in a store. He is shy, hard working, and very good at sports. He would like to become the manager of a sports shop.

PHILIPPE . . .
is 22 and lives alone. He is in college. He is smart but lazy and spends most of his time at parties. He has no plans for the future.

PAUL . . .
is 18 and lives with his parents. He is a trainee in a bank, but he would like to be the manager someday. He is very good at golf.

1. Michael and Paul are very _..similar_.
2. Philippe is quite .... the other two.
3. Paul and Michael have ....
4. Paul and Philippe have almost nothing ....
5. Paul and Michael both ....
6. Neither of them ....

36.2 Rewrite these sentences. Keep the meaning the same.

Example: She's a lot like the others.
She's _very similar to the others_ . (similar)

1. Hong is not at all like her sister.
   Hong is very .... (different)
2. When you see the houses, you realize that the apartments are a very good value.
   The apartments are a very good value .... (compare)
3. In her class, Carla was the only one who didn't pass the exam.
   Everyone .... (except)
4. The two boys have completely different interests.
   The two boys have .... (common)

36.3 Fill in the blanks with a linking word or phrase from E opposite.

1. You'd better write these words down; _otherwise_ you might forget them.
2. I made extra food for the party .... more people come than we expect.
3. I can meet you for dinner tonight .... I have to work late at the office.
4. I agreed to buy my son a dog .... he takes it for a walk every day.
5. We'd better leave early; .... we'll be stuck in traffic.

36.4 Complete these sentences in a logical way.

1. You can't go into that club unless you _are a member_ .
2. I want to finish this report today; otherwise I'll ....
3. You can borrow the money as long as you ....
4. I cleaned the guest room and made the bed in case ....
5. I'm not going to work overtime unless ....

UNIT
37

Reason, purpose, and result

A   Reason

I went home early **because/since/as** I was feeling tired.

Note: It is common to put **since/as** at the beginning of the sentence, e.g., **Since/As** I was feeling tired, I left early.

We always go there **because** the scenery is so beautiful. [**because** + clause: subject + verb]
We always go there **because of** the beautiful scenery. [**because of** + noun or noun phrase]

Due to means the same as **because of,** and is often used to explain the reason for a problem:

The plane was late **due to** bad weather. [**Due to** is often used after the verb *to be.*]

B   "Cause" and "result" verbs

Police think the bus driver **caused / was responsible for** the accident. [made it happen]
The extra investment should **lead to / result in** more jobs. [make it happen]

"Cause" and "result" verbs sometimes appear together in this way:

Police think a cigarette **caused** the fire, which **resulted in** the destruction of the building.

C   Purpose

A "purpose" is an intention, an aim, or a reason for doing something, e.g., **The purpose of** buying this book **is** to improve my English.

But we often introduce a purpose using **so (that)** or **in order to:**

I bought this book **so (that)** I can improve my English.
We moved to this neighborhood **so (that)** we could send our children to this school.
They went home early **in order to** beat the traffic.

Note: In spoken English, people often just say **so** (without **that**). It is also very common (as in the examples) to use a modal verb, e.g., **can** or **could,** in a clause after **so that.**

D   Result

I left the ticket at home, **so** I had to buy another one.
The manager was out sick. **As a result,** there was no one to make decisions.
I forgot to send the letters. **Consequently,** some people didn't know about the meeting.
She worked extremely hard and **therefore** deserved the promotion.

Note: **So** is the most common of these linking words in spoken English, and usually links ideas in a single sentence. **As a result** and **consequently** are more formal and usually connect ideas in two separate sentences (as in the examples). **Therefore** (also more formal) can be used in a single sentence (as in the example), but it may also connect two sentences.

Exercises

37.1   Combine the two sentences into one sentence using *so, so that, because, as,* or
since. More than one answer is possible in some sentences.

1. I didn't call you. It was very late.   *I didn't call you because it was very late.*
   or   It was very late, so I didn't call you.
2. I turned up the radio in the living room. I could hear it in the kitchen.
3. The restaurant was full. We went to the coffee shop next door.
4. The company has poor management. There has been a drop in profits.
5. It is a very large city. You have to use public transportation a lot.
6. I learned to drive. My mother didn't have to take me to school every day.

37.2   Rewrite the sentences with *because of.* Make changes if necessary.

1. He couldn't play soccer because he had an injured shoulder.
   He couldn't play soccer because of his injured shoulder.
2. She got the job because her qualifications are excellent.
3. The weather was awful, so we couldn't eat outside.
4. She had to stay home because she had a broken ankle.
5. The flowers died because it was so dry.
6. The traffic was heavy. I was half an hour late.
7. It started raining, so the referee had to stop the game.

37.3   Complete this memo from a manager to the staff. Use words from the opposite page.

To:	All staff	***Date:***	August 9th
From:	The Manager	***Subject:***	Temporary road work

Starting next Monday (and continuing all week), there will be construction on
the major roads leading to the factory. (1) *Because / Since / As* this will
(2) .... delays, please try to leave home a few minutes early
in the morning (3) .... everyone arrives on time. The
construction could also (4) .... severe traffic congestion.
(5) ...., you may want to consider using public transportation
instead of driving.

Thank you for your cooperation.

37.4   These sentences are about learning English. Complete them in a logical way.

1. I want to improve my English because *I will need it in my job very soon.*
2. I bought myself a personal stereo so that I ....
3. I study English on weekends since ....
4. I always write words down in my notebook in order to ....
5. I don't get many opportunities to practice my English. Consequently, ...
   ....
6. My brother has a lot of American and Canadian friends. As a result, ...
   ....

The physical world

A The solar system

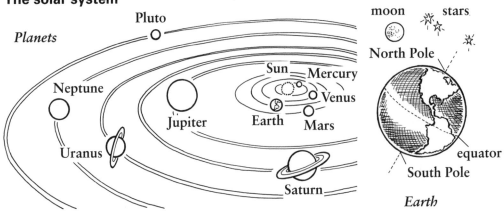

Planets

Pluto
Neptune
Jupiter
Uranus
Saturn
Sun
Mercury
Venus
Earth
Mars

moon stars
North Pole
equator
South Pole

Earth

B Physical features

continents: Asia, Europe
countries: Thailand, Hungary, Brazil
islands: Sicily, Manhattan, Hong Kong
group of islands: the Bahamas, the West Indies
oceans: the Atlantic Ocean, the Pacific Ocean
seas: the Adriatic Sea, the Red Sea
lakes: Lake Michigan, Lake Titicaca
rivers: the Rio Grande, the Mississippi
falls: Niagara Falls, Angel Falls
mountains: Mount Everest, Mount Fuji
mountain ranges: the Andes, the Rockies
jungles: the Amazon (also called the Amazon Rain Forest)
deserts: the Sahara, the Gobi

Note: Sometimes you need the definite article *the,* e.g., the Atlantic Ocean, the
Andes; sometimes no article is used, e.g., Mount Everest and Lake Titicaca.
Compare this with your own language.

C Natural disasters

A **disaster** is when something terrible happens, which often results in death,
destruction, and suffering. A **natural disaster** is caused by nature, not by humans.

volcano /
volcanic eruption

earthquake

flood

hurricane

Exercises

38.1 Match the items in the box with the descriptions below.

Earth	moon	planets	stars
equator	North Pole	South Pole	sun

1. Mars, Jupiter, and Pluto are all ..*planets*......
2. It revolves around the Earth.
3. The Earth revolves around it.
4. The Big Dipper is a group of ....
5. It divides the Earth into northern and southern halves.
6. It's the most northern point on the surface of the Earth.
7. It's the most southern point on the surface of the Earth.
8. It rotates around the sun every 365 days.

38.2 Complete the sentences.

Example: The Nile is ..*a river*...................................

1. The Atlantic is ....
2. The Alps are ....
3. Japan is ....
4. The Sahara is ....
5. The Amazon is ....
6. The Mediterranean is ....
7. The Bahamas are ....
8. Africa is ....
9. Australia is a ....
10. Everest is the highest .... in the world.

38.3 Fill in the blanks with *the* if necessary or Ø if no article is necessary.

My trip took me across (1) ..*the*.. Atlantic Ocean from (2) ..*Ø*.... Europe to
(3) .... South America. I traveled through (4) .... Amazon rain forest and
down through the interior of (5) .... Brazil, and then into (6) .... Paraguay.
From there I headed north again, through Bolivia, around (7) .... Lake Titicaca,
and up to Cuzco. Then I crossed (8) .... Andes and finally arrived in Lima. For
the last part of the journey I flew to (9) .... Jamaica in (10) .... West Indies.

38.4 What kind of disaster is described in each of these sentences?

1. It lifted a car about ten feet off the ground, and then we saw it disappear.
2. It was about six feet deep, and we watched as most of our furniture just
   floated away.
3. The walls began to move visibly, and large cracks opened up in the ground.
4. We could see the lava slowly advancing toward the town just ten miles away.

38.5 Can you name any other natural disasters besides the ones on the opposite page?

Weather

Weather conditions

Here are some common weather words. You can often form adjectives by adding **-y**.

Noun	Adjective	Noun	Adjective
sun	sunny	wind	windy
cloud	cloudy	ice	icy
fog	foggy	rain	rainy
heat	hot	humidity	humid

A light rain, which comes down in fine drops, is a **drizzle**. When it rains for a short time, we call it a **shower**, e.g., "We had a few showers yesterday." When it is raining a lot (or **raining hard**), we often say it's **pouring**. A **drought** is a long period without rain.

Temperature

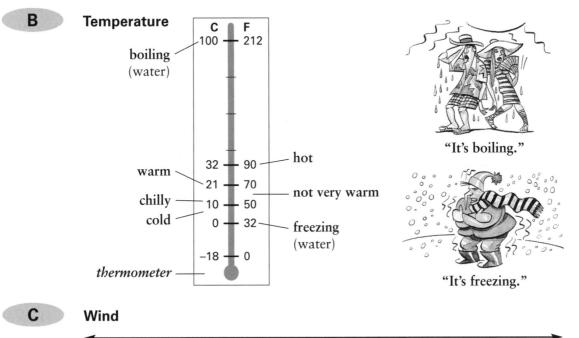

C F
- boiling (water): 100 — 212
- warm: 32
- 21 — 70
- chilly: 10 — 50
- cold: 0
- hot: — 90
- not very warm: — 70
- freezing (water): — 32
- −18 — 0
- thermometer

"It's boiling."

"It's freezing."

Wind

a **breeze**   a **wind**   a **strong wind**   a **gale**   a **hurricane**

A **breeze** is a gentle and pleasant wind; a **hurricane** is a severe storm with violent winds over 75 miles per hour.

It was a hot day, but there was a nice **breeze**.
The **wind** blew my hat off.
A **hurricane** caused severe damage in Puerto Rico.

Thunderstorms

A **spell** [period] of very hot weather often ends with a **thunderstorm.** First it becomes very **hot** and **humid** [wet air], then you get **thunder and lightning** [loud noise and flashes of light during a storm], and finally, very **heavy rain** [it pours]. Afterward, it is usually cooler and feels fresher.

Exercises

39.1 Identify the weather conditions in these pictures.

1. ....   3. ....

2. ....   4. ....

39.2 *True* or *false?* If a sentence is *false,* write a true sentence about the weather.

1. It frequently pours in the desert.   *false: It hardly ever pours in the desert.*
2. It can get very chilly in the desert at night.
3. Thunder makes a noise.
4. Lightning can kill people.
5. A shower is a light breeze.
6. A spell of hot weather may end in a thunderstorm.
7. When it is humid, the air is very dry.
8. Below 32° F / 0° C, water turns to ice.
9. Drought is a long period of rain.
10. When it's foggy, you need sunglasses.

39.3 Complete these scales.

.... → wind → strong wind → .... → hurricane
.... → hot → warm → not very warm → cold → ....

39.4 Complete the paragraph with words from the box.

blows	heavy	hot	humid	snows	spell	winds

The single greatest influence on Japanese weather is the wind. During the summer it
(1) *blows* .... from the Pacific, causing (2) .... and humid
weather. In winter, however, the northwesterly (3) .... from Siberia
are very cold, and it (4) .... heavily in the mountains of the northwest.
The southeastern parts receive cold dry air. Between June and mid-July, there is a
(5) .... of wet weather when the rice fields get the water vital for
growth. After that, there is less (6) .... rain, but the air is still
(7) .... Autumn, however, is drier, and usually very pleasant.

Write a paragraph about the weather in your own country, or a specific part of
your country, using as many words as possible from the opposite page.

Using the land

A — Ground and soil

When we walk, our feet are on the **ground.** [the general word for the surface of the earth] The top part of the ground, where grass and flowers grow, is called **soil.**

There were no seats in the park, so we had to sit on the **ground.**
The **ground** is very hard because it hasn't rained for weeks.
Plants don't grow very well here because the **soil** is too dry.

B — Above the ground

Some land is used for parks and gardens, where we **grow** trees and **plants** [living things with **roots** and **leaves,** smaller than trees, which grow in the soil]. First, you **plant** the tree or plant [put the tree or plant in the ground], then you **water** it [give it water].

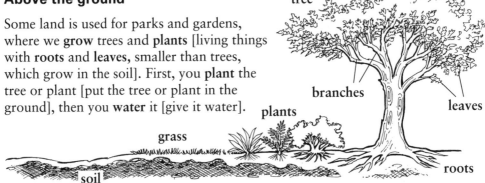

Land in the country is often used for **agriculture/farming.** Some farms concentrate on **dairy production,** e.g., milk, butter, and cheese. Other farms **raise** animals, which are **slaughtered** [killed] for their meat, e.g., cattle, pigs, and lambs. Some farms use the land to **grow fruit,** e.g., apples and grapes; **vegetables,** e.g., potatoes and carrots; and **grains** [seeds from plants], e.g., wheat, rice, and barley. When they are ready, farmers **pick the fruit** and **harvest** [collect and bring in] the other **crops** [a general word to describe plants that are grown to be eaten]. This period of time is also called the **harvest.**

C — Below the ground

One of the main activities below the ground is **mining.** This is the process of **extracting** [*formal*; removing or taking out] different materials, e.g., **coal** or **gold,** from below the **ground.** We call the place a **mine,** e.g., a coal mine or gold mine.

These are some of the **metals** we take out of the ground:

gold: a **precious** [valuable] yellow metal used to make coins and jewelry
silver: a **precious** [valuable] whitish metal used to make coins, jewelry, utensils
iron: usually takes the form of a hard, dark gray metal, and is used in building and to make tools. It is also used to make **steel.**
tin: a softer metal often used to cover other metals and used to make containers
copper: a soft reddish metal. It permits heat and electricity to pass through it easily.

Exercises

40.1 Which nouns on the right often go with the verbs on the left? (There may be more than one noun for some of the verbs.)

1. plant	coal
2. water	animals
3. pick	wheat
4. extract	apples
5. grow	crops
6. raise	trees

40.2 Are these statements *true* or *false*? If *false*, correct them.

1. Roots grow above the ground.   *false: Roots grow under the ground.*
2. Plants are slaughtered for food.
3. If you extract something, you remove it.
4. The harvest is the period when we plant the crops.
5. Soil is the top part of the ground.
6. Iron is used to make silver.

40.3 Complete the descriptions of these objects with a "metal."

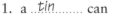

1. a ...*tin*.... can

3. a knife with a
.... blade

5. a .... ring

2. a .... spoon

4. a frying pan with
a .... bottom

6. strong .... bars

40.4 Complete these sentences with the correct "general" word.

1. Apples, oranges, and bananas are all types of ...*fruit*.........
2. Potatoes, beans, and carrots are types of ....
3. Silver, tin, and copper are types of ....
4. Milk, butter, and cheese are all .... products.
5. .... are the seeds from wheat, rice, barley, etc.
6. We use the word .... as a general word for plants that are grown to be eaten.

40.5 Answer these questions about your own country.

1. Which are most important to your economy: agriculture, mining, or fishing?
2. Are any precious metals found in your country?
3. What are some of the main crops grown in your country? Which are imported?

Animals, insects, and other creatures

A Pets and farm animals

Many people keep **pets** [domestic animals that live with people]. In the U.S. and Canada, the most common pets are **dogs** and **cats**. Some people keep birds, such as **parakeets**; fish, such as **goldfish**; and furry animals, such as **hamsters**.

Farm animals include: **sheep, pigs, cows, horses, chickens,** and **goats.**

Note: The word **sheep** is both the singular and plural form, i.e., a sheep or two sheep. A young sheep is called a **lamb.**

dog pig goldfish goat cat sheep horse

B Wild animals

In a zoo or **in the wild** [in a natural area, outside human control], you will find these wild animals.

gorilla elephant tiger giraffe bear zebra camel lion leopard monkey

C Common insects and other small creatures

bee ant mosquito butterfly fly spider

D In the water, in the air, and on the ground

Here are some **creatures** [living things, e.g., animals, birds, fish] that swim, fly, or move along the ground.

whale shark eagle snail snake

Exercises

41.1 Look at the underlined letters in each pair of words. Is the pronunciation the same or different?

Examples: whale   animal   *different* /eɪ/, /æ/
         cat   camel   *same* /æ/

1. lion   tiger   5. spider   wild
2. bear   eagle   6. monkey   butterfly
3. goat   mosquito   7. camel   snake
4. gorilla   giraffe   8. leopard   shark

41.2 Arrange the words into three groups: farm animals, wild animals, and insects.

monkey	tiger	fly	gorilla	elephant	bear
butterfly	goat	sheep	cow	leopard	mosquito
horse	bee	lion	ant	pig	chicken

41.3 Start each sentence with a creature from the opposite page.

1. ......*Eagles*.......... can fly at great heights.
2. .... can swim very long distances.
3. .... can understand lots of human commands.
4. .... can run very fast.
5. .... can travel through the desert for long distances without water.
6. .... can be as long as 100 feet (about 30 meters).
7. .... can eat fruit from tall trees.
8. .... change their skin several times a year.
9. .... can pick things up with their trunk.
10. .... provide us with wool.

41.4 Complete each sentence with a logical word.

1. They have lots of pets: two dogs, four cats, and a ..*parakeet*................. .
2. Their farm animals include cows, sheep, and ....
3. The children love to see the "big cats" at the zoo, such as lions, tigers, and ....
4. I hate most insects, but especially mosquitoes and ....
5. We saw some really large animals at the Wild Animal Park: elephants, giraffes, and ....

41.5 Can you match these creatures with their maximum speeds?

lion	spider	elephant
rabbit	pig	snail
shark	golden eagle	

40 mph	0.03 mph	50 mph
35 mph	25 mph	6.5 mph
168 mph	1.17 mph	

Countries, nationalities, and languages

A   Who speaks what and where?

Country	Nationality	Language
Argentina	Argentinean	Spanish
Australia	Australian	English
Brazil	Brazilian	Portuguese
Canada	Canadian	English and French
Chile	Chilean	Spanish
China	Chinese	Mandarin Chinese / Cantonese
Egypt	Egyptian	Arabic
El Salvador	Salvadoran/Salvadorian	Spanish
France	French	French
Great Britain	British	English
Greece	Greek	Greek
Hungary	Hungarian	Hungarian
Indonesia	Indonesian	Indonesian
Israel	Israeli	Hebrew
Italy	Italian	Italian
Japan	Japanese	Japanese
Korea	Korean	Korean
Mexico	Mexican	Spanish
Panama	Panamanian	Spanish
the Philippines	Philippine/Filipino	Tagalog/English
Russia	Russian	Russian
Spain	Spanish	Spanish
Taiwan	Taiwanese	Mandarin Chinese / Taiwanese
Thailand	Thai	Thai
Turkey	Turkish	Turkish
the United States	American	English
Venezuela	Venezuelan	Spanish
Vietnam	Vietnamese	Vietnamese

B   The people

When you are talking about people in general from a particular country, there are some nationalities that you can make plural with an **s**, but others can be formed only with **the** (and no plural **s**):

(The) Brazilians, Koreans, Italians, Mexicans, Canadians, Greeks } are (usually very . . .)

The Chinese, The French, The Spanish, The Japanese, The Vietnamese, The British } are (usually very . . .)

- With both groups you can use "people": Korean people, Mexican people, etc.
- When you talk about one person from these countries, you need to add woman/man/person to the group on the right: a Brazilian *but* a Chinese person; a Korean *but* a Japanese person, etc.

Exercises

42.1   **Answer these questions without looking at the opposite page.**

1. Name at least four countries where the national language is English.
2. What language is spoken in Brazil?
3. What are people from El Salvador called?
4. What language is spoken in Egypt?
5. What nationality are people from Thailand?
6. What language is spoken in Argentina?
7. What are people from Korea called?
8. Where do people speak Mandarin Chinese?
9. Name at least three countries where Spanish is spoken.
10. What are the people of the Philippines called?

42.2   **Mark the main stress in these words and practice saying them.**

Example: Italian

Japan	Japanese	Brazilian	Egyptian	Arabic
Chinese	Australia	Indonesia	Indonesian	Vietnamese

Which syllable is stressed in the words above ending -ian and -ese?

42.3   **Complete these sentences with the names of the people from the countries in the box.**

1. I've worked with many ..*Venezuelans*.....
2. *The Spanish*..... have late mealtimes; for example, dinner is usually after 10 p.m.
3. Many .... speak or understand both French and English.
4. .... are well known for their classic cuisine.
5. On my visit to Mexico City, I found .... very warm and charming.
6. .... have a healthy diet compared to many people in Western countries: They consume a lot of fish, rice, and vegetables.
7. Some people say that .... are reserved, but it's not always true.
8. I met a lot of .... on my trip to Rio de Janeiro.

Brazil
Canada
France
Great Britain
Japan
Venezuela
Mexico
Spain

42.4   **Complete these sentences.**

1. Bangkok is the capital of *Thailand*.
2. Buenos Aires is the capital of ....
3. Ankara is the capital of ....
4. Seoul is the capital of ....
5. Manila is the capital of ....
6. Taipei is the capital of ....
7. Athens is the capital of ....
8. Moscow is the capital of ....
9. Madrid is the capital of ....
10. Tokyo is the capital of ....

42.5   **Have you ever met someone from any of the countries on the opposite page? Go through the list and check the ones you have.**

The body and what it does

A Parts of the body

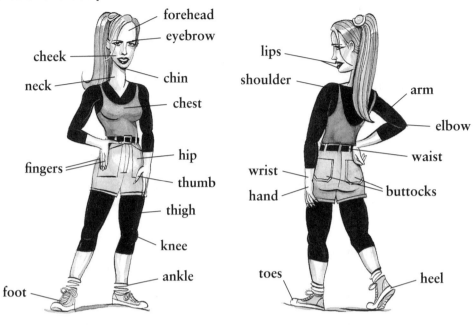

forehead
eyebrow
cheek
chin
neck
chest
fingers
hip
thumb
thigh
knee
ankle
foot

lips
shoulder
arm
elbow
waist
wrist
hand
buttocks
toes
heel

B Physical actions

You can **breathe** through your nose or your mouth.
People **smile** when they're happy or think something
is funny, or to be polite. They **laugh** at something
very funny; they may **cry** when they're sad; they
yawn when they're tired or bored.
Many people **nod** their head (up and down) to mean
"yes," and **shake** their head (side to side) when
they mean "no."
When you pick up something heavy, you should
bend your knees and keep your back straight.

C Common expressions

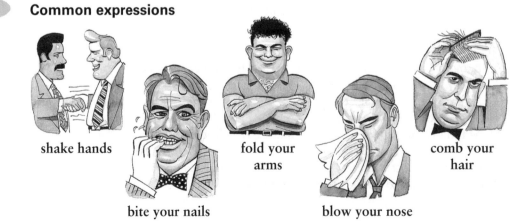

shake hands

fold your
arms

comb your
hair

bite your nails

blow your nose

Exercises

43.1 How much of the picture can you label without looking at the opposite page?

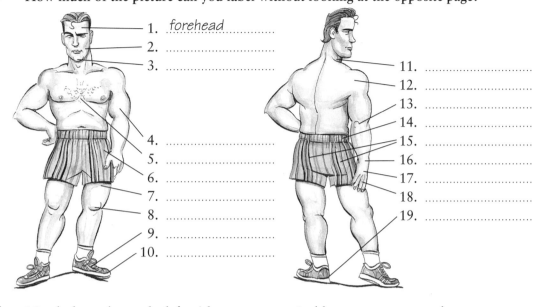

1. *forehead*
2. ....
3. ....
4. ....
5. ....
6. ....
7. ....
8. ....
9. ....
10. ....
11. ....
12. ....
13. ....
14. ....
15. ....
16. ....
17. ....
18. ....
19. ....

43.2 Match the verbs on the left with a part of the body on the right to form common expressions. Use each verb and body part only once.

1. blow   your knees
2. nod   your nose
3. comb   your nails
4. fold   your head
5. bend   your arms
6. shake   your hair
7. bite   hands

43.3 What do these actions often mean? (There may be lots of possible answers.)

1. People often smile when *they're happy or think something is funny*.
2. They often breathe quickly after ....
3. They laugh when ....
4. They may bite their nails when ....
5. They blow their nose when ....
6. They shake their head when ....
7. And nod their head when ....
8. They yawn when ....

43.4 There are fourteen words describing parts of the body, either across or down, in this word square. Can you find them?

C	E	L	B	O	W	A
H	T	I	A	E	N	R
I	O	P	C	Y	A	M
N	E	C	K	E	I	H
I	H	A	N	K	L	E
K	C	H	E	S	T	E
C	H	E	E	K	A	L

Describing people's appearance

 A   **General**

Positive: **Beautiful** is generally used to describe women; **handsome** is often used to describe men; **good-looking** and **attractive** are used for both; **pretty** is another positive word to describe a woman (often a girl) meaning "nice or pleasing to look at."

Negative: **Ugly** is a very negative word; **plain** and **homely** (for people) are more polite.

 B   **Height and build**

tall and slim   medium height and **build**   medium height and **muscular**   short and **fat**

Note: Another word for **slim** is **thin,** but **slim** has a more positive meaning, e.g., "John is nice and slim, but his brother is terribly thin." **Skinny** has the same meaning but is usually negative. It is not polite to call someone **fat; overweight** is less rude.

C   **Hair**

lightest ←————————→ *darkest*
blond   **light brown**   **dark brown**   **black**

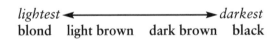

straight   wavy   curly hair

D   **Special features**

The man on the left has very **pale skin.** [very light skin] He also has **broad shoulders,** with a **scar** on his forehead. The other man has **dark skin / a dark complexion.** He also has a **beard,** a **mustache,** and a **hairy chest.**

 E   **Asking questions about a person's appearance**

Q: What does she **look like?**   A: She's fairly tall, with short blond hair.
Q: **How tall** is she?   A: About five foot nine.
Q: **How much** does she **weigh?**   A: Probably about 140 pounds.

Exercises

44.1 Complete these sentences. (More than one answer may be possible.)

1. She has blond ...hair............................
2. He has very pale ....
3. They both have curly ....
4. I would say he is medium ....
5. Her brother has very broad ....
6. She doesn't like men with hairy ....
7. Last time I saw him he had grown a ....
8. He has very muscular ....
9. Both men were very good-...................................
10. All of them have dark ....

44.2 Replace the underlined word in each sentence with a word that is either more appropriate or more polite.

1. He told me he'd met a <u>handsome</u> woman at the disco last night.
2. She's beautiful, but her younger sister is really <u>ugly</u>.
3. Peter should get some exercise; he's getting to be <u>fat</u>.
4. Most people want to stay slim, but not as <u>skinny</u> as that woman over there.
5. I think she's hoping she'll meet a few <u>beautiful</u> men at the tennis club.

44.3 You want to know about the following:

– someone's general appearance
– their height
– their weight

What questions do you need to ask? Complete these questions.

1. What ....?
2. How ....?
3. How much ....?

44.4 Now answer these questions about yourself. If possible, ask another person these questions too.

1. How tall are you?
2. How would you describe your build?
3. What color are your eyes?
4. What kind of hair do you have?
5. What color is it?
6. Would you like it to look different? If so, in what way?
7. Do you think you have any special features?
8. Are there any special features you would like to have?
9. Do you like beards?
10. Can you think of a famous woman you would describe as beautiful, and a famous man you would describe as handsome?

Describing character

A   Opposites

Positive	Negative
warm and friendly	cold and unfriendly
kind	unkind, mean
nice, pleasant	horrible, unpleasant
generous [likes to give/share]	stingy [never gives to others]
optimistic [thinks positively]	pessimistic [thinks negatively]
cheerful [happy and smiling]	miserable [always seems unhappy], grumpy
relaxed and easygoing	tense [nervous; worries a lot; not calm]
strong	weak
sensitive	insensitive [does not think about others' feelings]
honest [always tells the truth]	dishonest

Sandra is very **tense** right now because of her exams, but she's usually **relaxed** and **easygoing** about most things.

I think the weather influences me a lot: When it's sunny I feel more **cheerful** and **optimistic,** but when it's cold and rainy I feel **miserable.**

He seemed **unfriendly** at first, but later I realized that he's really very **warm** and **kind.**

The salesperson told me that the dress I tried on looked better on younger people. I thought that was very **insensitive** of her, but at least she was being **honest,** I suppose.

B   Describing character in work situations

Positive	Negative
hardworking	lazy [doesn't want to work]
punctual [always on time]	not very punctual; always late
reliable	unreliable [you cannot trust/depend on someone like this]
intelligent, smart, bright	stupid, dumb *(informal)*
flexible [willing to change]	inflexible [a very fixed way of thinking; unable to change]
ambitious	unambitious [no desire to be successful and get a better job]

Some pairs of opposites are neutral, rather than positive or negative in meaning:

He is very **shy** when you first meet him because he finds it difficult to talk to people and make conversation; but when he gets to know you, he's more **self-confident.**

People often say the British are **reserved** [do not show their feelings], but they can be very **emotional** like anyone else.

C   Nouns that describe character

One of her great qualities is that she **takes initiative.** [She can think for herself and take the necessary action; she does not always wait for orders.]

That boy has **no common sense.** [He does stupid things without thinking.] His sister, on the other hand, is very **sensible.** [has lots of common sense]

Paul is **a character** – you never know what he'll say or do next. [an unusual, humorous person]

Exercises

45.1 Arrange these words into pairs of opposites.

smart	stingy	nice	lazy	relaxed	hard working
tense	cheerful	generous	unpleasant	stupid	miserable

Positive
..smart..

....

....

....

....

....

Negative
..stupid...

....

....

....

....

....

45.2 Write the opposite of each adjective, using one of these prefixes: *un-*, *in-*, or *dis-*.

Example: kind – *unkind*

kind	flexible	friendly	honest
reliable	sensitive	ambitious	pleasant

45.3 How would you describe the person in each of these descriptions?

1. She locks the door but leaves the windows wide open. It isn't logical.
   has no common sense
2. He always promises to do things, but half the time he forgets.
3. I have to tell him what to do every minute of the day at work. He won't even open a window without someone's permission.
4. She is always here on time.
5. I don't think he's done any work since he started working here.
6. She finds it difficult to meet people and talk to strangers.
7. He could work in any of the departments, and it doesn't matter to him if he works independently or as part of a team.
8. One of the great things about her is that she is so aware of other people's feelings.

Write at least three sentences of your own to describe people's character.

45.4 What nouns can be formed from these adjectives? Use a dictionary.

Example: kind – *kindness*

punctual	optimistic	reliable	lazy
confident	generous	ambitious	stupid
sensitive	strong	flexible	shy

45.5 Choose three words from the opposite page that describe you. Is there one quality you do not have but would like to have? What, in your opinion, is the worst quality described on the opposite page? If possible, compare your answers with a friend.

Human feelings and actions

Feelings

Noun	Adjective(s)
love [≠ hate]	loving [≠ hateful]
happiness [≠ sadness]	happy [≠ sad]
anger	angry
fear	afraid (of) / frightened (of)
pride	proud (of)
jealousy	jealous (of)
embarrassment	embarrassed / embarrassing (see Unit 31)

- **Pride** has different meanings, but the most common is the feeling of satisfaction you have when you (or people you are connected with) do something well. For example, he was very **proud** when his wife became the first president of the organization.
- **Jealousy** is a feeling of anger and unhappiness you may have if (a) someone you love shows interest in others, or (b) if someone has something you want / don't have.
  a) My girlfriend gets **jealous** when I talk to other girls.
  b) He is **jealous of** his sister because she is smarter.
- A common adjective is **upset**, which means unhappy, sad, and even angry, because something unpleasant has happened, e.g., He was **upset** when we didn't invite him.

Ways of speaking, looking, and talking

whisper (v., n.) [speak very quietly]
shout (v., n.) [speak in a very loud voice]

stare (v., n.) [look at someone/something in a fixed way for a long time]
glance (at) (v., n.) [look at someone or something quickly]

stroll (v., n.) [walk in a slow and relaxed/casual way]
march (v., n.) [walk quickly and with a clear purpose/reason, as in a parade]

Things we do with our hands

clap

knock (on/at a door)

wave (good-bye)

point
(at something/someone)

press (a button)

push something

Exercises

46.1   What nouns can you make from these adjectives?

angry – *anger*   sad   happy   proud   jealous   embarrassed

46.2   Connect the two parts of each sentence.

1. He was very proud when
2. He was very jealous when
3. He was very embarrassed when
4. He was very angry when

5. He was very sad when

6. He was very frightened when

a. someone stole his money.
b. he heard that his aunt had died.
c. his father appeared on TV.
d. he saw those big dogs running toward him.
e. he gave her a birthday present on the wrong day.
f. his best friend went out with the woman he really liked.

46.3   Answer these questions. If possible, ask someone else the same questions, then compare your answers with the words on the opposite page. Are there any answers you would like to change?

1. How would you feel if you forgot your mother's birthday or your father's birthday?
2. Have you ever been a passenger in a car that was going too fast? How did you feel?
3. How do you feel when other people want you to do things that you don't want to do?
4. If you made a stupid mistake in English, how would you feel?
5. Is there any one thing that you are very proud of?
6. Are there any common situations where you sometimes feel embarrassed?

46.4   What are these people doing? Describe their actions using words from the opposite page.

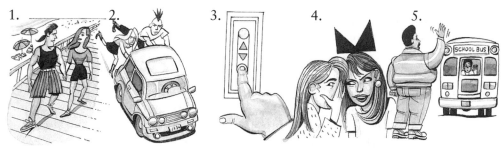

1.   2.   3.   4.   5.

46.5   Replace the underlined words with a verb with the same meaning.

1. She stopped working and <u>looked quickly</u> at the clock.   *glanced*
2. Because we were in the library, he <u>spoke very quietly</u> in my ear.
3. We <u>walked casually</u> along the street and then stopped for coffee.
4. The soldiers <u>walked quickly</u> in the parade.
5. The man <u>kept looking</u> at Susan, but she didn't seem to notice.

Family and friends

A **Relatives [members of your family]**

	Male	Female
Your parents' parents	grandfather	grandmother
Your parents' brothers and sisters	uncles	aunts
Your aunt's/uncle's children	cousins	cousins
The father and mother of the person you marry	father-in-law	mother-in-law
The brother and sister of the person you marry	brother-in-law	sister-in-law
Your brother's/sister's children	nephews	nieces
If the person you marry dies, you are a . . .	widower	widow
If your mother or father remarries, you have a . . .	stepfather	stepmother

Note: We ask "Are you **related to** him/her?" [Are you a relative / connected by a family relationship?] Also, you can say you are **related** to someone **by marriage** [not by birth].

B **Family background [family history]**

My grandfather was a farmer in Ireland. He worked hard all his life, and when he died, his son (my uncle) and daughter (my mother) **inherited** a large house and land [received this house and land from their father when he died]. They continued the **family business** together until my mother met my father. They got married and moved to Boston. I was born two years later. They didn't have any more children, so I am an **only child.**

C **Family names**

When you are born, your family gives you a **first name,** e.g., Robert or Susan. Your **last name** (also called your **family name** or **surname**) is the name that everyone in the family shares, e.g., Smith or O'Neill. Some people have a **middle name** (like a first name), but you do not usually say this name. Your **full name** is all the names you have, e.g., Susan Jean Smith.

D **Friends**

an **old** friend [someone you have known for a long time]
a **close** friend [a very good friend; someone you like and trust]
your **best** friend [the one friend you feel closest to]
The people we work with are **coworkers** or **colleagues.**

E *Ex-*

We use this for a husband/wife/boyfriend/girlfriend we had in the past, e.g., an **ex-husband** or an **ex-girlfriend.**

Exercises

47.1 Look at the family tree and complete the sentences below.

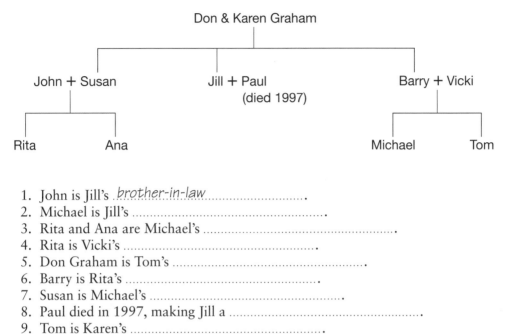

Don & Karen Graham

John + Susan   Jill + Paul   Barry + Vicki
                      (died 1997)

Rita   Ana   Michael   Tom

1. John is Jill's *brother-in-law* ....
2. Michael is Jill's ....
3. Rita and Ana are Michael's ....
4. Rita is Vicki's ....
5. Don Graham is Tom's ....
6. Barry is Rita's ....
7. Susan is Michael's ....
8. Paul died in 1997, making Jill a ....
9. Tom is Karen's ....
10. John and Vicki are related ....

47.2 Answer these questions about yourself and your country.

1. What's your first name?
2. What's your last name?
3. Is that a common name in your country?
4. Do you have a middle name?
5. Are you an only child? If not, how many brothers and sisters do you have?
6. Do you have any brothers-in-law or sisters-in-law?
7. Who is your oldest friend?
8. Who is your closest friend?
9. Do you work? If so, how many of your coworkers are also your friends?
10. Do you have any ex-boyfriends or ex-girlfriends who speak English very well?

47.3 Draw your own family tree. Are there any relationships you cannot describe in English? Write a short summary of your family background (as in B on the opposite page).

UNIT 48 Ages and stages

A Growing up and growing older

Age	Stage of life
0–1 approximately	a **baby**
1–2 years	a **toddler**
2–12 approximately	a **child** [This period is your **childhood**.]
13–19	a **teenager** [**Early teens** are 13–14.]
18+	an **adult** [In some places you are an adult at 21.]
20–29	**in your twenties** [**mid-twenties** are 24–26]
30–39	**in your thirties** [**late thirties** are 38–39]
45+	**middle-aged**, e.g., a middle-aged man
65 approximately	a **senior** / a **senior citizen**
75+	**old age** [also **elderly**, e.g., an elderly gentleman]

Note: The period from about 13 to 17, when a young person is maturing, is called **adolescence**, and the person is an **adolescent**. A person who is grown (up) is an **adult**. The time when you stop work is **retirement** [when you are **retired**], often starting at 65.

B Childhood and adolescence

Sam (on the right) **was born** in Chicago, but when he was 2, his father got a new job in Los Angeles, and he **grew up** in southern California. He **went to college** at 18, where he . . .

C Romance

. . . where he met Ann. He **went out with** her [she was his **girlfriend;** he was her **boyfriend**] for three years, but toward the end they had lots of **fights** [arguments], and they **split up** [broke up / separated]. In his **mid-twenties** he met Marie. They **fell in love** and . . .

D Marriage

. . . They **fell in love** and **got married** within six months. A year later she got **pregnant** and they had their first child, a boy. Sadly, the marriage was not a success. Sam **left** two years afterward and they **got divorced** (*also* **get a divorce**). Four years later, Marie remarried, and now she is **expecting** a second **baby** (she is pregnant).

Exercises

48.1 What stage of life are these people at? Use expressions from the opposite page.

1. Paulo isn't two yet, so he's still a _toddler_.
2. Al was a bus driver for 40 years but stopped work two years ago, so he is now ....
3. Susan is 25, so she is in her ....
4. Caroline will be 50 this year, so she is now ....
5. Ron is 32 and his wife is 31, so they are both in ....
6. Joan is 70, so she is a ....
7. Kevin was born six months ago, so he is a ....
8. Leyla will be 13 this year, so soon she will be a ....
9. In most countries, you can't vote until you're an ....
10. Fifteen is often a difficult age for boys going through ....

48.2 Are these sentences *true* or *false* about the people on the opposite page? If *false*, write the correct answer below. Try to answer first without looking at the opposite page.

1. Sam was born in Los Angeles.
   false: He was born in Chicago.
2. He grew up in southern California.
   ....
3. He went out with Ann for three years.
   ....
4. They split up because Sam went to live in Japan.
   ....
5. Sam fell in love with Marie.
   ....
6. They had a baby a year after they got married.
   ....
7. Marie is now expecting her third child.
   ....
8. Marie left Sam.
   ....

48.3 Connect the two parts of each sentence to construct Marta's life.

1. Marta was born	a. was a boy she met in high school.
2. She grew up	b. in her mid-twenties.
3. Her first boyfriend	c. in a small town.
4. She went out with him	d. after high school, when she was in her late teens.
5. She went to college	e. in a small local hospital 30 years ago.
6. She fell in love	f. for six months.
7. They got married	g. with another student, who was studying law.
8. She had a baby	h. when she graduated, in her early twenties.

Now complete the sentence parts on the left about your own life. Answer the ones you can.

UNIT 49 Daily routines

A Sleep

During the week I usually **wake up** at 6:30 a.m. Sometimes I **lie in bed** for a few minutes, but then I have to **get up** [get out of bed] and **get dressed.** Most nights, I **go to bed** [get into bed] at about 11:30 p.m. I'm usually pretty tired, so I **go to sleep / fall asleep** right away. Occasionally, though, I can't **get to sleep** [succeed in sleeping]. When that happens, I finally **fall asleep** about 3 a.m., and then I **oversleep** [sleep too long] in the morning. If I **stay up late** [go to bed very late], I try to **take a nap** [a short sleep, e.g., 30 minutes] in the afternoon. The weekends are different. On Saturday and Sunday I **sleep in** [sleep later in the morning than usual, e.g., until 10 or 10:30 a.m.].

B Food

During the week I **have breakfast** [eat breakfast] at 7:30 a.m., lunch at 1:00 p.m., and dinner around 7 p.m. I also **have** one or two **snacks** [small amounts of food], e.g., cookies or fruit, during the day at work. I live **alone / by myself** [without other people], so I have to **make my own breakfast and dinner** [prepare breakfast and dinner for myself]. I also have to **feed** [give food to] my two cats twice a day.

Note: In general, there is no definite article *(the)* with **breakfast, lunch,** and **dinner.**

C Staying clean

In the morning I **take a shower,** and I usually **wash my hair** at the same time. I usually **shave** after I **wash my face,** and then I **brush my teeth.** Sometimes I **take a bath** in the evening if I want to relax.

D Work

I **leave for work / leave home / leave the house** at about 8 a.m. and **get to work** [arrive at work] by 9 a.m. I **take a lunch break** [stop work for lunch] about 1 p.m., and I **take** a couple of **coffee breaks** [time off work for coffee or other refreshment] during the day. I **leave work / get off work** around 5 p.m. and **get home** by 6 p.m.

E Evenings

On weeknights I **stay home** [don't leave home] and relax or just **do nothing.** But on weekends I **go out** with friends [leave the house for social reasons, e.g., go to the movies] and usually **stay out late** [come home late at night]. Sometimes I **have friends over for dinner** [invite friends to my home and cook dinner for them], or friends **come over** [visit me at the house] to **watch videos** or **play cards** [play card games, e.g., poker or bridge].

F Housework

I **go shopping / do the shopping** [buy groceries] on Saturdays. I also **do the laundry** [wash clothes] and **ironing** on weekends. I **do the dishes** [wash the dishes] every evening and **take out the garbage/trash** every other day. I guess I don't **do the vacuuming** [clean carpets with a vacuum cleaner] as often as I should.

Exercises

49.1 The opposite page has some expressions with *have/take/do + noun*. Can you think of three for each verb?

have ..*breakfast*..........   take ..*a nap*............   do ..*the dishes*...........
have ....   take ....   do ....
have ....   take ....   do ....
have ....   take ....   do ....

49.2 Match the verbs on the left with the words on the right.

1. brush   home
2. do   my teeth
3. stay   the dog
4. fall   early
5. get up   the shopping
6. feed   asleep

49.3 Answer these questions about yourself. If possible, compare answers with someone else.

1. What time did you get home yesterday / last night?
2. Did you go out last night or stay home?
3. Do you have trouble getting to sleep at night?
4. How often do you have friends over for dinner?
5. Have you ever fallen asleep in class? If so, when?
6. When was the last time you overslept?

49.4 Can you find three facts from the opposite page that are the same in *your* routine and three that are different?

Same
1. *I go to bed around 11:30 p.m.*
2. ....
3. ....
4. ....

Different
I never do any ironing.
....
....
....

49.5 Describe what each person is doing in the pictures below.

Homes and buildings

A Houses

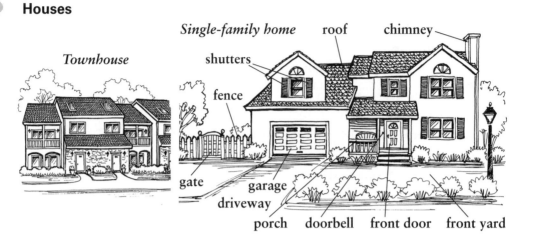

Townhouse

Single-family home   roof   chimney

shutters

fence

gate   garage   driveway

porch   doorbell   front door   front yard

B Apartments

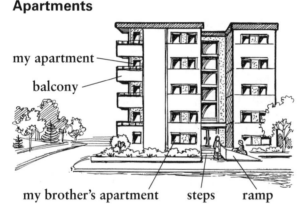

my apartment

balcony

my brother's apartment   steps   ramp

I live in an apartment building. My brother lives **on the first floor / ground floor,** and I have an apartment **on the fourth floor.** Of course, the building has an **elevator,** but I like to **climb** [go up / walk up] the three **flights of stairs** for the exercise. I have a **balcony** with a wonderful **view** of the park opposite the building.

Note: **Steps** are usually outside a building or inside a public building; they are often stone or wooden. **Stairs** *(plural)* connect floors inside a building and are often covered with a carpet.

C Buying and renting

Some people buy an apartment or a house. [They **own** it. / It **belongs to** them.] They usually borrow money from a bank to pay for the home. This money, which is called a **mortgage,** is usually paid back over a period of years.

Other people **rent** a house or an apartment. [They pay money every week or month to the owner.] The money is called **the rent,** and the person who owns the house or apartment is the **landlord/landlady.**

D Describing an apartment or a house

My home is very **bright** [≠ dark] and **sunny** because it **gets** [receives] lots of sun. But sometimes it gets **noisy** [≠ quiet] because it is near the street and the traffic. Overall, it is **in good condition** [in a good state / doesn't need to be repaired; ≠ **in bad condition**], and the rooms and closets are **huge/enormous** [very big; ≠ **tiny** / very small].

Exercises

50.1 What can you remember about the house and apartment building on the opposite page? Without looking, try to answer these questions. If an answer is false, correct it (if possible). Then check your answers by looking at the opposite page.

1. Does the house have a garage?
2. Does it have a fence around the front yard?
3. Is there any furniture on the porch?
4. Is the gate open or shut?
5. Are there any steps in front of the entrance to the apartment building?
6. Does each apartment have a balcony?
7. Does the brother live on the second floor?
8. Do the apartments have a view of the mountains?

50.2 Complete these sentences with a noun or verb.

1. I walked up to the ...*front door*....... and rang the ....
2. We had to .... six flights of stairs to get to her apartment because the .... wasn't working.
3. I've got a great .... from my balcony.
4. Do you own the apartment or do you .... it?
5. I'm living in a house now, but it actually .... to my brother. He bought it two years ago. It was in very bad .... then, but he spent a lot of money on it.
6. It took years to pay off the ...., but now we own the house and don't owe the bank any money.

50.3 Write three positive things and three negative things you could say about a house / an apartment or the rooms in it.

Positive	*Negative*
It's bright and sunny.	It's very dark.
....	....
....	....
....	....

Now think about your answers again. Which positive features are the most important for you? Which negative features do you dislike the most?

50.4 What about your home? Answer these questions.

1. Do you live in a house or an apartment?
2. If you live in an apartment, what floor is it on?
3. If you live in a house, do you have a front or back yard?
4. Does the house/apartment belong to you (or your family), or do you rent it?
5. Do you have your own garage or personal parking space?
6. Would you describe your house/apartment as dark or bright?
7. Is it noisy or quiet?
8. Are the rooms and closets big enough?

Around the house (1)

A Rooms

The **living room** [where you sit, relax, talk, and watch TV]; the **dining room** [where you eat meals]; the **kitchen**; the **bedroom(s)**; the **bathroom(s)**.

Some people also have a **study** [a room with a desk where you work]; a **spare room** [a room you don't use every day, sometimes used by guests]; a **guest room** [a room for guests]; and possibly a **playroom** for small children, sometimes located in the **basement** [a room or an area under the house, often used for storage or a play area].

B The living room

While the cat was asleep **in the armchair**, I sat **on the sofa** and **looked at/through** the newspaper. Then I **turned on the TV** and went to get a snack.

C The kitchen

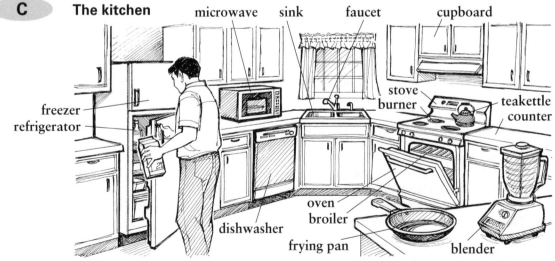

I **put** the roast **in the oven**, put the dirty dishes **in the dishwasher**, made the coffee, and **put** the milk **back** in the refrigerator.

Exercises

51.1 Complete the descriptions. (There may be more than one possible answer.)

1. The bathroom, that's where you take a ..*bath*........... or a
....
2. The bedroom, that's where you ....
3. The kitchen, that's where you do the ....
4. The living room, that's where you .... and ....
5. The dining room, that's where you ....
6. A spare room, that's often where ....
7. A study, that's usually where you ....
8. A basement, that's located ....

51.2 You are in the kitchen. Where would you put these things?

1. milk   *in the refrigerator*
2. meat that you are going to cook
3. frozen food that you want to store
4. dirty cups and saucers
5. clean cups and saucers
6. cookies and a package of spaghetti
7. vegetables that you want to chop or slice
8. different kinds of juices for a drink that you are going to mix

51.3 Complete these sentences with the correct adverb or preposition.

1. He put the plates ..*in*...... the cupboard.
2. I took the chicken .... of the refrigerator, made myself a couple of sandwiches, and then I put the rest of the chicken .... in the refrigerator.
3. I usually sit .... the sofa, and my husband sits .... an armchair.
4. I finished looking .... the newspaper, so I turned .... the television.
5. You normally bake it .... the oven for about forty minutes.
6. I took the butter .... of the refrigerator and put it .... the table.

51.4 Imagine you have just moved into a new home, and for the first six months you can have only six of the following. Which would you choose?

sofa	carpets	TV	bed	dining table
refrigerator	dishwasher	stove	stereo	blender
VCR	blinds	desk	teakettle	saucepans

51.5 Can you think of:

1. three things in the living room and kitchen you can turn on/off?   *TV, . . .*
2. three things in the kitchen you can wash?
3. three things in the living room and kitchen you can sit on?
4. two things you can use to boil water?

Around the house (2)

A **The bedroom**

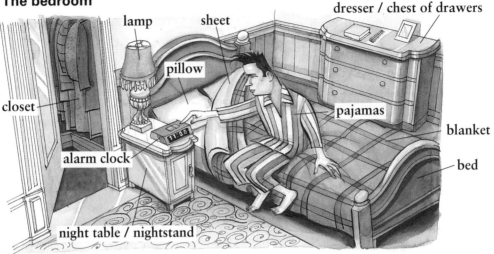

I **put on** my **pajamas**, **got into bed**, **set** the **alarm clock**, **turned out / turned off / switched off** the light, and **went to sleep**.

B **The bathroom**

I didn't have time to **take a shower**, but I **washed my face**, **brushed my teeth**, and then I **went to school**.

C **Housework (U)**

My room is very **neat and clean** [everything in order], but my brother is very **sloppy** [≠ neat]; he leaves his clothes all over the floor and never makes his bed. What's worse, he doesn't clean his room very often, so most of the time it is pretty dirty.

I **wash the dishes** every evening after dinner, and I usually **do the washing/wash/ laundry and ironing** on weekends when I have more free time. I also **vacuum** the carpets / **do the vacuuming** and **dust** the furniture once a week.

Exercises

52.1 Connect the two parts of each sentence, then put the sentences in the most logical order.

1. I brushed	the light.
2. I went	into bed.
3. I set	a bath.
4. I turned out	my teeth.
5. I took	to sleep.
6. I put on	the alarm clock.
7. I got	my pajamas.

52.2 The pictures show six things the man did this morning. Complete the sentences below.

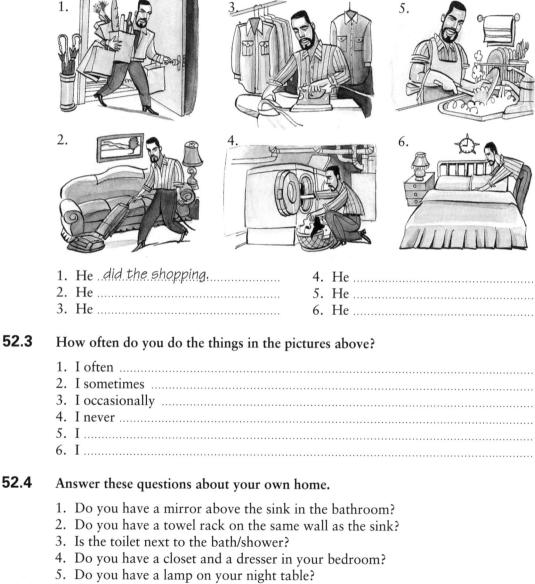

1. He *did the shopping.*
2. He ....
3. He ....
4. He ....
5. He ....
6. He ....

52.3 How often do you do the things in the pictures above?

1. I often ....
2. I sometimes ....
3. I occasionally ....
4. I never ....
5. I ....
6. I ....

52.4 Answer these questions about your own home.

1. Do you have a mirror above the sink in the bathroom?
2. Do you have a towel rack on the same wall as the sink?
3. Is the toilet next to the bath/shower?
4. Do you have a closet and a dresser in your bedroom?
5. Do you have a lamp on your night table?
6. Do you have an alarm clock?

Everyday problems

There's something wrong with . . .

If there is a problem with a machine or a thing that we use, e.g., TV, light, washing machine, computer, pen, etc., we can say:

There's something wrong with the TV. [There is a problem with it.]
The light **is not working.** [not functioning / there is no light]
The telephone is **out of order.** [not in use / not functioning]

Note: The phrase **out of order** is used when a public machine or piece of equipment isn't working, e.g., pay phone, public toilet, vending machine, etc.

In the home

Yesterday morning Paul had a lot of problems.

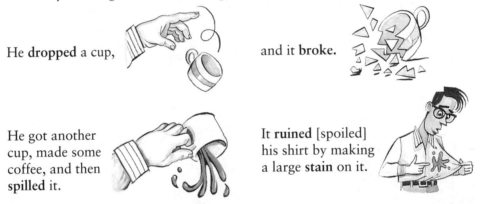

He **dropped** a cup, and it **broke.**

He got another cup, made some coffee, and then **spilled** it.

It **ruined** [spoiled] his shirt by making a large **stain** on it.

He decided to make some toast, but he **burned** the first piece [if you **burn** something, you damage it with heat or fire], then realized he had **run out of** bread [there was no more bread]. He left home **in a bad mood** [feeling very unhappy; ≠ a good mood].

Out and about

After Paul went out, things got worse. He left home with a ten-dollar bill in his pocket and walked to the bus stop. Unfortunately he was a few minutes late, so he **missed the bus.** While he waited for the next one, he got out his personal stereo, but the **batteries** had **run out.** [The batteries were dead.] When the bus arrived, he got on and put his hand in his pocket – no ten-dollar bill.  (He had **lost his money.**) The driver told him to get off. He didn't want to be late for school, so he started running. Moments later, he saw a dog, but not its leash – and he **tripped over** the leash. He got to his feet and continued on to school; then he realized he had **left** his bag on the bus.

Note: Students often mistakenly say "He forgot his bag on the bus" in this situation. In English, we use the verb **leave** if we say where something is. For example: I **forgot** my bag.   *but*   I **left** my bag <u>on the bus.</u>

Exercises

53.1 Write the past tense and past participle of these verbs.

Infinitive	Past tense	Past participle
to burn	burned	burned
to break		
to forget		
to run		
to lose		
to leave		

53.2 Match the lists to form sentences.

1. I dropped the radio on the floor,
2. The batteries have run out,
3. Unfortunately I left
4. I spilled the drink,
5. I missed the bus
6. I forgot

a. and it made a mess on the carpet.
b. and had to wait ages for another one.
c. to bring my money.
d. and now I can't get it to work.
e. my money at home.
f. so I can't listen to my personal stereo.

53.3 This is what happened when Paul had a party at his house. Write a description of the damage.

1. 2. 3.

53.4 Write logical answers for each of these questions, using vocabulary from the opposite page.

1. How did you break that glass?   *I dropped it.*
2. Why can't we watch TV?
3. What happened to the money I gave you?
4. Where's your homework?
5. Why can't you use the pay phone at the station?

53.5 How often do you do these things? Use *all the time / fairly often / occasionally / hardly ever / never.*

Example: *I drop things all the time.*

drop things?   break things?   burn things?
spill things?   lose things?   forget things?
trip over things?   leave things behind?   run out of things?

What kinds of things do you drop, burn, run out of, etc.?

Money

A   **Bills and coins**

Here are some examples of money used in the U.S. The **currency** [the type of money used in a country] is called **the dollar.**

Bills
ten dollars
a ten-dollar bill

Coins

twenty-five cents	ten cents	five cents	one cent
a **quarter**	a **dime**	a **nickel**	a **penny**

B   **Common verbs**

spend $$ on . . .	Last week I **spent** $100 **on** food and $20 **on** books.
pay for . . .	I **paid** $200 **for** my new desk. [It cost me $200.]
cost	My new desk **cost** (me) $200. [I paid $200.]
charge	The mechanic **charged** me $75 to repair my car. [asked me to pay $75 for the service]
lend/borrow	Could you **lend me** some money? [give me money that I will return] *or* Could **I borrow** some money? [receive money that I will return]
waste	Parents often think their children **waste** money on things they don't need. [use it badly]
save (up)	I'm **saving (up)** for a new bike. [keeping money when I receive it]

C   **Adjectives**

free   cheap   inexpensive   reasonable   fairly expensive   very expensive

– $ $ $ $ $

D   **Important words and phrases**

I **can't afford** to take a vacation this year. [I don't have enough money.]
How much is that watch **worth**? [What is the **value** of that watch?]
It is **worth** about $50. [**The value** is about $50.]
The **cost of living** [how much people pay for things] is high in Japan, but most people still have a good **standard of living** [the level of money and comfort people have].

Exercises

54.1 Fill in the blanks with the past tense of verbs from the box. Be careful – most of them are irregular.

buy	spend	lose	pay	cost
sell	win	waste	find	give

1. My car was five years old, so I _sold_ it and .... a new one.
2. I was very sad when I .... my watch in a store. It was a present from my wife, and it .... her a lot of money. Fortunately somebody .... it the next day and took it to a police station.
3. I .... over $2,000 for my computer, but it isn't worth very much now.
4. My father .... me $50 last week, but I .... most of it on a ticket for a concert on Friday.
5. Last week somebody .... $10 million in the lottery!
6. I .... my money on those CDs because I never play them.

54.2 Complete the sentences with words from the opposite page. Do not use the underlined words and phrases.

Example: You want to tell a friend that a restaurant wasn't cheap.
The restaurant _was fairly expensive_.

1. You want to know the value of your friend's CD player.
   How much is .... ?
2. A friend wants to go to an expensive restaurant but you don't have enough money.
   I'm sorry, but I can't ....
3. You want to borrow $5 from a friend.
   Could you .... ?
4. You want to know how much a friend paid for her dictionary.
   How much .... ?

54.3 How quickly can you answer these questions? Write down answers to all of them in one minute, then go back and check. If possible, ask someone else the same questions.

1. Is the currency in the U.S. called dollars and cents?
2. Is a quarter worth more than fifty cents?
3. If you lend something to someone, do they borrow it?
4. If you waste money, do you use it well?
5. Is "the dollar" a currency?
6. If you "can't afford" something, do you have enough money for it?
7. Does "cost of living" mean the same as "standard of living"?
8. If someone tells you a hotel is reasonable, is it very expensive?

54.4 Write down the approximate price of six things in your country, e.g., a daily newspaper, a short bus ride, a cup of coffee in a cafe, a movie ticket, a hamburger, a pair of jeans, etc. Do you think the price is expensive, reasonable, or cheap? If possible, compare your answers with someone from the same town, and someone from a different country.

Health: illness and disease

Common problems

She's sneezing. She's coughing. She has a sore throat. She's blowing her nose. She has a temperature/fever.

What's the matter?	How do you know? (the symptoms)	Cause of illness
I have **a cold.**	sneezing, a runny nose, a sore throat, a cough	a virus
I have **the flu.** (U) (more serious than a cold)	symptoms for a cold + aching muscles and a temperature/fever	a virus
I have **hay fever.** (U) / I have **allergies.**	sneezing, a runny nose, itchy eyes	allergic reaction to pollen from grass, trees, plants
I have **diarrhea.**	I have a stomachache and keep going to the bathroom.	often food, or a virus
I feel **nauseous.**	afraid I may vomit / throw up.	food, a virus

Note: For some of these **illnesses,** you can see a doctor, who may give you a **prescription** [a paper with an order for medicine] that you get from a **pharmacy,** or you can buy an **over-the-counter medication** [medicine that doesn't require a prescription].

Aches and pains

Nouns: We use **ache** with the following: I have **a toothache, a stomachache, a backache, an earache,** and **a headache.** For other parts of the body, we use **pain,** e.g., I woke up during the night with a **terrible pain** in my chest.

Verbs: You can use **ache** for some things, e.g., my back aches; but **hurt** is more common to describe real pain, and it can be used with or without a direct object:

She **hurt/injured** her foot when she jumped off the bus and fell over. *or*
She **hurt herself** when she jumped off the bus and fell over.
I hit my leg against the table, and now it **really hurts.** [gives me a terrible pain]

Adjectives: A common adjective is **painful** [≠ **painless**]:

I had **an injection / a shot** yesterday and it was very **painful.**
A: Did it hurt when you had your **filling?** [when the  dentist fills a hole/cavity in the tooth]
B: No, it was **painless.**

Serious illnesses

Doctors believe smoking is the major cause of **lung cancer.**
He had a **heart attack** and died almost immediately.
Asthma has become more common. [**chest** illness causing **breathing** problems]

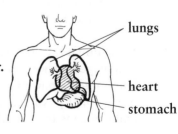

lungs

heart

stomach

Exercises

55.1 Cover the opposite page. What are the main symptoms for these conditions?

1. a cold: *..sneezing, a runny nose, a sore throat, a cough*..........................
2. flu: ....
3. hay fever / allergies: ....
4. diarrhea: ....
5. asthma: ....

55.2 Look at the underlined letters in these pairs of words. Is the pronunciation the same or different?

Examples: ache   pain   *same* /eɪ/
           shot   stomach   *different* /ɑ/, /ʌ/

1. disease   diarrhea   4. virus   illness
2. chemist   ache   5. flu   pharmacy
3. hurt   allergic   6. cough   enough

55.3 Look at the pictures and write what happened in the space below. In your description, use the words in the box.

| dentist   filling   injection   painful   painless |

I had a terrible ....
....

55.4 Fill in the blanks with an appropriate word.

1. I hit my hand on the desk, and now it really *.hurts*...........
2. They say she died of a heart ....
3. She had some apples that weren't ready to eat, and now she has a ....
4. I've got this terrible .... in my neck from sleeping in the wrong position.
5. He died of .... cancer, even though he never smoked a cigarette in his life.
6. I went to the doctor, and she gave me a .... for some medication.
7. Pollution makes his .... worse, and it's difficult for him to breathe.
8. I hurt .... when I fell off that chair.

55.5 Look at the opposite page again. Have you had any of these illnesses recently? Have you had any aches and pains recently? Are there any other illnesses you have had or still have? If so, find the name for it/them in English.

Health: injuries

A   Common injuries

An **injury** is damage to part of your body, usually caused by an accident at home, in a car, or playing sports, e.g., soccer. Here are some common **injuries:**

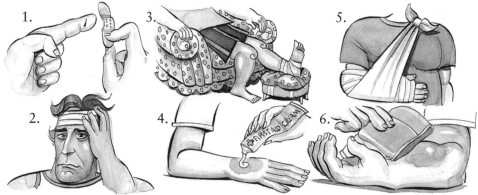

What's the problem?	How did it happen?	Result	Solution
1. I **cut** my finger.	using a knife	It's **bleeding.**	**a Band-Aid**
2. I have a **concussion.**	playing soccer	I'm confused; I don't know where I am.	rest
3. I **twisted my ankle.**	running for a bus	I can't walk on it easily.	rest + bandage
4. I **burned** my hand.	taking something out of a hot oven	It's very **painful.**	special cream
5. I **broke** my arm.	I fell off my bike.	I can't use it.	a **cast** and **sling**
6. I have a **bruise** on my arm.	I hit it on the side of my desk.	It's **swollen** and **black and blue.**	ice pack

B   Hospital treatment

Jane fell off a chair, hit her head on the floor, and **knocked herself unconscious.** Her husband called an **ambulance,** and she was still **unconscious** when it arrived. She was **rushed** to the hospital [taken very quickly], where they kept her for two days **for observation** [the hospital staff watched her to decide if anything was wrong].

I jumped for the ball and **collided** with another player. [We ran into / hit each other.] We both had **cuts** on our heads, but I had to go to the hospital for eight **stitches.**

C   Wounds and injuries

Wound (n., v.) and **injury** are both used to describe harm to the body, but a **wound** is generally caused by a **weapon** (e.g., gun or knife) and is often intentional. (Note the pronunciation of **wound** /wund/.)

He **shot** the man in the chest. [a **bullet wound,** from a gun, in the chest]
He **stabbed** the woman in the back. [a **knife wound** in the back]
He **got into a fight** and **got beaten up.** He had a **black eye** and two **broken ribs.**

Exercises

56.1 Complete the table.

Noun	Verb
cut	*cut*
bandage	....
blood	....
bruise	....

Noun	Verb
injury	....
shot	....
treatment	....
wound	....

56.2 Match the injuries and the causes.

1. He burned his finger.
2. He twisted his ankle.
3. He cut his foot.
4. He has a bullet wound in his arm.
5. He has a concussion.

a. He fell down and banged his head.
b. He was shot during a robbery.
c. He touched a hot burner on the stove.
d. He walked barefoot on some glass.
e. He missed a step walking downstairs.

56.3 Look at the pictures and write the story.

56.4 Answer these questions about yourself. If possible, ask another person the same questions.

1. Have you ever broken your arm or leg?
2. Have you ever needed stitches?
3. Have you ever had a concussion?
4. Have you ever been unconscious?
5. Have you ever had a blood test?
6. Have you ever been in an ambulance?

Clothes

A

Pockets, buttons, collar, sleeves

earrings

necklace

jacket

belt

hat

purse/
handbag

blouse
or top

V-neck

pullover /
pullover sweater

sleeve

collar

shirt

tie

scarf

pocket

jeans

skirt

pantyhose/
stockings

button

glove

overcoat

cuff

boot

suit

shoe

Note: Some of these words are plural nouns, e.g., **jeans** and **pants.** (See Unit 28.)

B

Verbs and phrases used with clothes

Try to guess the meanings of the underlined words below.

> I got up at 7:30, took a shower, got dressed, and had breakfast. It was a cold morning,
> so I put on my overcoat and left home about 8:20. When I got to work, I took off my
> coat and hung it up behind the door. It was hot in the office, so I took my jacket off
> too. During my lunch break I went shopping. I saw a nice jacket in a clothing store and
> tried it on, but it didn't fit me – it was too small and they didn't have a bigger size.

Note: Notice the different word order with the verbs *put on, take off, hang up,*
and *try on.* If you want to know the rule about this, turn to Unit 18.

C

Too small and *not long enough*

The man is wearing a suit, but it doesn't fit him
very well: The jacket **is too small** [**not big enough**]
and the pants **are too short** [**not long enough**].

Exercises

57.1 Finish this sentence with six different items of clothes.

I need a pair of ..shoes.............................

....

....

....

....

....

57.2 Find a logical order for these sentences.

1. He took off his pants.
2. He put his shoes back on.
3. He tried on the suit.
4. He went into the fitting room.
5. He took it off.
6. He paid for the suit.
7. He took off his shoes.
8. He went back to the salesperson.
9. He put his pants on again.

57.3 What's different? Find five things that the first woman has, but the second woman doesn't.

..a button..............................

....

....

....

....

1.    2.

57.4 Fill in the blanks. More than one answer may be possible.

1. She decided to wear a ..skirt........ and a .... instead of a dress.
2. I tried on a ....; the jacket was fine, but the .... were too short.
3. It was hot in the office, so he took off his jacket and ...., and rolled up the sleeves of his ....
4. I wanted to buy the jacket, but unfortunately the one I tried on wasn't big ...., and they didn't have it in a bigger ....
5. I also wanted a new sweater, but unfortunately the medium size was .... big and the small size wasn't big ....

57.5 Write down . . .

1. five things usually worn by women only; and five things worn by men and women.
2. a list of clothes you like and don't like wearing.
3. five more items of clothing you have at home in your closet and/or dresser.

Stores and shopping

A Stores and shopping

store: a place where you can buy things; a **shop** is usually a small store
salesperson: a person who helps customers in a store; also called a **salesclerk**
shop/store window: the window at the front of the shop/store
window shopping: looking at things in store windows without buying anything
shopping list: a list of things you plan to buy
shopping center: a group of stores built together and sharing a parking area
(shopping) mall: stores, restaurants, and movie theaters in a large, covered area

I **went shopping** yesterday. [I went to a store or stores to buy food or clothes, etc.]
I **did the shopping** yesterday. [I bought food and household goods.]

B Types of stores and what they sell

Name of store	What it sells
department store	almost everything – furniture, clothes, electrical appliances (e.g., TV, washing machine), toys, jewelry, etc., and sometimes food
supermarket	a large store for food and household goods (e.g., cleaning products)
office supply store	paper, pens, pencils, staplers, paper clips, files, folders, tape, stationery (e.g., writing paper, cards, envelopes)
newsstand	*(often outdoors)* newspapers and magazines, candy, lottery tickets
butcher shop	meat and poultry (*Note:* Supermarkets have meat departments too.)
grocery (store)	fruit and vegetables; other food items (smaller than a supermarket)
pharmacy/drugstore	medicine (both prescription and nonprescription), baby products, shampoo, soap, toothpaste, etc.
video (rental) store	videos to rent or buy

Note: Many stores are called by the name of the main product sold + **store**, e.g., clothing store, shoe store, record store, camera store, etc.

C Useful words and expressions

SALESPERSON: Can I help you?   CUSTOMER: I'm **looking for** a silk scarf. [I want]   *or*
                      or   No, **I'm just looking,** thanks. [I don't
                   May I help you?   need any help.]   *or*
                                                            I'm already being helped, thanks. [Another
                                                            salesperson is already helping me.]

SALESCLERK: What **size** are you looking for? (e.g., small? medium? large? 12? 14?)

CUSTOMER: Where's the **fitting room?** [the room where you try on clothes]
SALESCLERK: It's down there on the right.

CUSTOMER: **I'll take** this one. / **I'll take** these.
            [I want to buy this one / these.]

CUSTOMER: Excuse me. Where do I pay for these?
SALESCLERK: At the **cashier / checkout counter.**
CUSTOMER: And can I **pay by** check / credit card?
SALESCLERK: Yes, of course.

Exercises

58.1 Can you find a "general" word on the opposite page to describe each group of items below?

1. ..*fruit*.......................... apples, oranges, peaches
2. .... shoes, a blouse, a jacket
3. .... a sofa, an armchair, a table
4. .... a television, a washing machine, a food processor
5. .... detergent, soap, toilet paper
6. .... stuffed animals, dolls, electric train set
7. .... writing paper, envelopes, cards

58.2 Where would you buy each of the items below? Choose from the stores in the box.

butcher shop
department store
grocery store
pharmacy
office supply store

Can you think of two more things you could buy in each store?

58.3 What word or phrase is being defined in these sentences?

1. a person who works in a store   *salesperson or salesclerk*
2. the store where you rent or buy videos
3. the place where you can try on clothes in a store
4. the place where you pay for things in a store
5. a large indoor area where you can shop, eat, and go to a movie
6. looking in store windows without going inside to buy
7. the store where you buy medicine, baby products, shampoo, etc.

58.4 Complete these dialogues about shopping.

SALESCLERK: Can I help you?
CUSTOMER: Yes, I'm (1) .... a sweater like this, but in blue.
SALESCLERK: And what (2) .... are you looking for?
CUSTOMER: Extra large.
SALESCLERK: Here's an extra large one in blue.
CUSTOMER: Great! I'll (3) .... it. Can I (4) .... check?
SALESCLERK: Yes, of course.

SALESCLERK: Can I help you?
CUSTOMER: No, it's OK, I'm just (5) ...., thanks.

Food

A Fruit

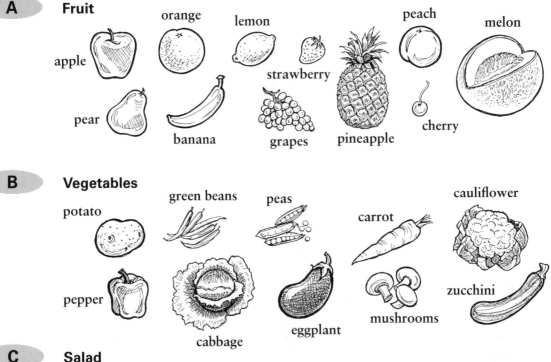

apple
orange
lemon
peach
melon
pear
strawberry
banana
grapes
pineapple
cherry

B Vegetables

potato
green beans
peas
carrot
cauliflower
pepper
cabbage
eggplant
mushrooms
zucchini

C Salad

A green salad is a mixture of uncooked vegetables. The main ingredient in a salad is usually **lettuce**, but it may also contain **tomatoes, cucumbers, onions,** and other things.

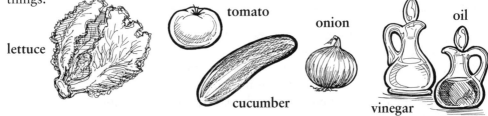

lettuce
tomato
onion
oil
cucumber
vinegar

D Animals (meat), fish, and shellfish

| *Animal:* | cow | calf (a young cow) | lamb (a young sheep) | pig |
| *Meat:* | beef | veal | lamb | pork |

Note: A person who does not eat meat is a **vegetarian.**

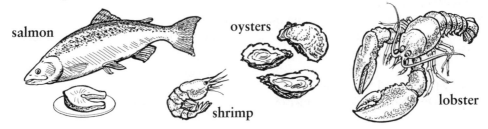

salmon
oysters
shrimp
lobster

Exercises

59.1 Can you write the name of a vegetable and fruit . . .

		Vegetable	Fruit
1.	beginning with the letter **p**:	potato	
2.	beginning with the letter **b**:		
3.	beginning with the letter **m**:		
4.	beginning with the letter **c**:		
5.	beginning with the letter **l**:		

59.2 Match the words in the right-hand box and the left-hand box where the underlined letters are pronounced the same way.

Example: banana - melon /ə/

banana	onion
peach	salmon
pepper	oysters

lemon	lamb
oil	mushroom
zucchini	melon

59.3 Which is the odd one out in each group, and why?

1. pork   veal   salmon   beef
   Salmon is the only fish; the others are types of meat.
2. salmon   shrimp   oyster   lobster
3. lettuce   eggplant   tomato   cucumber
4. peach   onion   mushroom   zucchini
5. pork   lamb   oysters   beef

59.4 Do you eat the skin [the outer covering] of these fruits *always, sometimes,* or *never?* Make three lists.

apples	pineapples	cherries	grapes
pears	bananas	peaches	mangoes
oranges	lemons	melons	strawberries

59.5 Using words from the opposite page, complete these sentences about yourself and your country. If possible, compare your answers with someone else.

1. In my country, ... is/are more common than ....
2. In my country, ... is/are more expensive than ....
3. In my country, a mixed salad usually contains ....
   ....
4. In my country, we don't grow ....
5. And we don't often eat ....
6. Personally, I prefer .... to ....
7. I love ...., but I don't really like ....
8. My favorite meat (or fish or vegetable or fruit) is ....

Cooking and restaurants

A Ways of cooking food

boil: in water, e.g., potatoes
fry: in oil or butter above the heat, e.g., eggs
broil: under the heat, one side at a time, e.g., chicken
grill: on a metal frame, over the heat, e.g., steak
bake: in the oven, e.g., cake, potatoes
roast: in the oven, often with liquid spooned over it,
   e.g., meat, chicken

Note: Food that is not cooked is **raw.**

B Cooking meat

If you have meat (e.g., steak, roast beef), you can eat it **rare** [cooked very quickly and still red on the inside]; **medium-rare** [cooked a bit longer and a little red in the middle]; **medium** [cooked a bit more and pink in the middle]; or **well-done** [cooked even longer and not pink at all].

C Describing food

tasty: has lots of flavor (a positive word); ≠ **tasteless:** has no taste (a negative word)
bland: without a strong taste; neutral in flavor, e.g., boiled rice (sometimes negative)
sweet: lots of sugar; ≠ **bitter** (like strong coffee); ≠ **sour** (like lemons)
salty: lots of salt
hot/spicy: lots of spice, e.g., curry, salsa
fresh: recently produced or picked, e.g., fresh bread, fresh fruit
tender: easy to cut; a positive word used to describe meat; ≠ **tough**
fatty: has a lot of fat, especially meat; ≠ **lean**
fattening: food that makes you **put on weight**, e.g., cream, cake, etc.

D Eating in restaurants

In many restaurants, you often have three **courses: an appetizer** (e.g., soup), **a main course** (e.g., steak or chicken), and **a dessert** (e.g., fruit or ice cream). When you **pay the check** [money for the meal], you also **leave a tip** [money] for the server. (15% is a normal tip.) If it is a popular restaurant, you may also need to **make a reservation** [call to reserve a table] **in advance** [before you go].

E A menu

APPETIZERS
Broccoli soup
Homemade chicken liver paté
Buttered noodles with zucchini and bacon

MAIN COURSES
Baked salmon with spinach
Breast of chicken in a white sauce with mushrooms
Grilled steak in a pepper sauce

DESSERTS
Chocolate mousse   *Fruit salad*   *Ice cream*

Exercises

60.1 Do you often eat the following foods in your country? If so, do you eat them the same way?

Example: *People in my county often eat "fish," but not usually "raw fish."*

raw fish	fried rice
fried eggs	fried chicken
baked potatoes	roast beef
raw spinach	roast peppers
fried bread	boiled eggs
grilled cheese	baked bananas

60.2 Answer these questions about the menu on the opposite page.

1. Which appetizer doesn't contain vegetables?   *homemade chicken liver paté*
2. Which dish contains pasta?
3. Which dish may be rare or well-done?
4. Which dish is definitely cooked in the oven?
5. Which dish will probably be spicy?
6. Which main dishes do not contain beef?
7. Which meat may be fatty or tough if you are unlucky?
8. Which dessert(s) will be very sweet?
9. Which dessert should be very fresh?
10. Imagine you are **on a diet** [trying to lose weight] and you do not want to have a fattening meal. Which would probably be the best dish to choose for each course?

60.3 Choose a possible adjective from the opposite page to describe each of these foods.

	Adjective		Adjective
lemon	*sour*	ice cream	
chicken		steak	
honey		chili peppers	
bacon		avocado	

60.4 Answer these questions about restaurants in your country, and your own taste in food. If possible, ask another person the same questions.

1. Do you usually make a reservation at a restaurant in advance?
2. Is it common to give the server a tip? If so, how much?
3. Do you normally eat three courses in a restaurant? If not, how many courses do you usually have?
4. What is your favorite food in a restaurant?
5. Do you like steak? If so, how do you like it cooked?
6. Would you say that food in your country is very spicy?
7. Would you say that food in your country is generally fattening?

Town and country

A   **Towns**

Here are some of the things you will find in or near most big towns or small cities.

business district / downtown area: an area with lots of banks, stores, and offices
shopping centers: places with many stores, either indoors or outdoors
(shopping) malls: stores, restaurants, and movie theaters in a large, covered area
parking lots / parking garages: places to leave cars
factories: buildings where people make/manufacture things, e.g., cars
suburbs: areas outside the center of town where people live
libraries: places where you can borrow books
air pollution: dirty air because of smoke and gas fumes from cars, trucks, and
    factories
nightlife: places to go at night for entertainment, e.g., theaters, discos, etc.

B   **The country**

Here are some of the things you will find **in the country/countryside.**

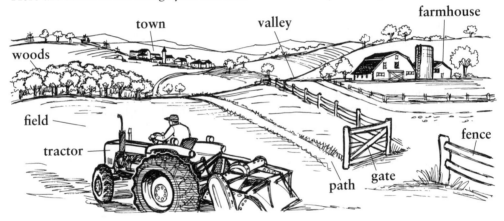

C   **Advantages and disadvantages**

People who prefer the country to big towns often say this:

Towns:
are noisy and stressful.
are dirty, with polluted air.
are **crowded.** [full of people]
are dangerous.

The country:
is quiet, peaceful, and relaxing.
is clean, with fresh air.
has lots of open space.
is safe.

People who prefer big towns have a different point of view:

In towns:
there are **plenty/lots** of things to do.
it's exciting.
there's a **variety of stores.** [many different stores]
there's lots of **nightlife,** e.g., theaters, discos.

In the country:
there's nothing to do.
it's boring.
there aren't many stores.
there's no nightlife.

Exercises

61.1 Cover the opposite page, then complete this list of opposites.

Big towns and cities
..noisy and stressful.........................

....

exciting

....

....

dangerous

The country
quiet, peaceful, and relaxing
clean, with fresh air

....

lots of open space
nothing to do in the evening

....

Do you agree with everything in the list above? Put a check (✓) beside each
answer you do, and an (✗) beside each answer you don't. If possible, compare
and discuss your answers with someone else.

61.2 Organize the words in the box into three groups: things that you usually find in
towns (in your country), things you usually find in the countryside, and things
you often find in both town and country.

fields	factories	fences	parking lots	hills
libraries	tractors	suburbs	farmhouses	paths
traffic	town hall	shopping malls	rivers	
pollution	valleys	nightlife	woods	

Town
traffic

Country

Town and country

61.3 Look at the picture on the opposite page for one minute, then cover it and
complete this paragraph based on the picture.

We opened the (1) ..gate.............., said hello to the man on the
(2) ...., and then walked along the (3) .... across
the (4) .... and down into the (5) ....We
stopped and had a picnic by the river, and then walked through the
(6) ...., where it was much cooler. A little later we came to a
small (7) ...., where we stopped and bought some cheese.

61.4 Think of your trip to work or school. How many of these things do you see or
pass by? Can you think of two more things to add?

a public parking lot	factories	woods	a library
a museum	parking meters	lots of traffic	fields
a shopping mall	a theater	suburbs	a train station

On the road

A **Road features**

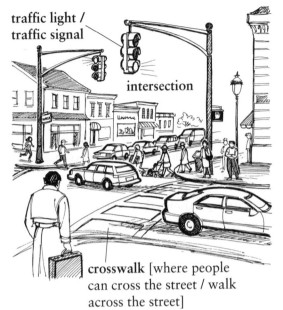

traffic light /
traffic signal

intersection

crosswalk [where people
can cross the street / walk
across the street]

fast lane [for higher speeds
or passing other cars]

overpass

passing

highway/freeway/expressway
[a wide road where cars travel
at high speed]

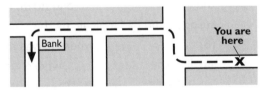

road signs   construction

B **An accident**

There was a serious car **accident** this morning. A **truck
broke down** in the middle of the road, and the driver
couldn't move it. It was 8:00, the height of the **rush hour,**
so it quickly caused a major **traffic jam. Motorists** got
very angry, and a driver in a Mercedes tried to go around
the truck. Unfortunately another car **was coming in the
opposite direction.** The driver **braked** hard and tried to
stop but couldn't **prevent** the accident – the Mercedes
crashed into the front of the other car. Both drivers were
badly injured, and both cars were very **badly damaged.**

Note: People are **injured;** things are **damaged.**

C **Giving directions**

Go **straight, turn** right **onto** the main
road, then **take the first left. Keep going,**
and you'll see a bank **on your left.** When
you **get to** the bank, **turn left** again.

Bank

You are
here

X

D **Important words and phrases**

Taxis and cars use the road; **pedestrians** use the **sidewalk.**
The **speed limit** on this road is 55 mph. (mph = miles per hour; 55 mph = 88 kph)
This **gas station** has both **self-service** and **full-service.**
Get in the car and remember to **fasten/buckle your seat belt.**

Exercises

62.1 Complete the directions to the bank, using the map.

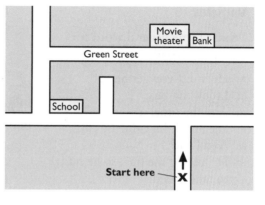

Go ..*straight*.. and ....
.... at the intersection. Then
you keep .... and ....
right when you .... to the
.... Then ....
.... again at ....
Street, and the bank is ....
.... left, just after the
....

62.2 Fill in the blanks.

1. Don't forget to ..*fasten/buckle*.. your ..*seat*...... belt when you
   ..*get*.......... ..*in*............. the car.
2. There was a bad accident last night. One driver was killed, the other driver
   was badly ...., and both cars were badly ....
3. In the morning, ... starts at about 7:30 and goes on
   until at least 9:00. Then it starts again about 4:30 in the afternoon.
4. It was raining, so when I ...., the car didn't stop quickly enough,
   and I .... into the rear of the car ahead.
5. The bicycle hit me just as I stepped into the .... to cross the street.
6. The car .... on the highway, so I called a garage and
   they sent someone to repair it.
7. There was a terrible ...., and that's why it took me
   two hours to drive home.
8. I was doing about 55 mph on the freeway, and suddenly a car ....
   me in the fast ...., doing about 90 mph.

62.3 Do you know or can you guess what these road signs mean?

1. You can't ..*turn left*.. 3. .... road 5. traffic .... ahead

2. 55 mph is the .... 4. .... ahead 6. ....

(See also Unit 98.)

Transportation

A Vehicles

Vehicle is the general word for all types of road transportation.

A: How did you get here?
B: I took the bus.
A: And the others?
B: Sue and John came by car.
A: And Paul?
B: He missed the bus, so he had to take a taxi.

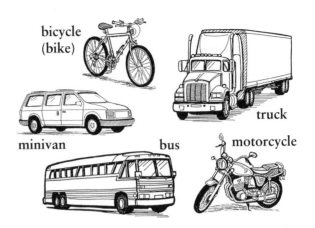

bicycle (bike)

truck

minivan   bus   motorcycle

B Catch a bus, take a taxi

Bus	Train	Plane	Taxi	Bicycle	Car
driver	engineer	pilot	driver	cyclist/rider	driver
drives	drives	flies	drives	rides	drives
fare ($)	fare ($)	airfare ($)	fare ($)	–	–
catch/take	catch/take	take	take	ride/go on (my)	go by
get on/off	get on/off	get on/off	get in/out	get on/off	get in/out
bus station / bus stop	train station	airport	taxi stand	–	–

C Buses

Sometimes buses are not very **punctual** [they don't arrive at the right time]. Where I live, buses should **run** [come] every ten minutes, but sometimes I wait at the **bus stop** [a place on the side of the road where buses stop for passengers] for half an hour with a long **line** of people. Finally three buses come together, but they're all **full** [full of people, so no more people can get on]. Other times the bus is early and I **miss** it [I don't catch it; *not* I lost the bus].

D Announcements at a train station

The 7:30 train **to** Washington, D.C., is now **boarding** [passengers are getting on] on **track** number 10. This is the **final call** [last announcement] for the 7:30 train to Washington, D.C., **making stops** at Newark, Philadelphia, Wilmington, and Baltimore. Now **arriving**, the 7:25 train **from** Toronto, on track number 4. The 7:45 train from Chicago is **running** [operating or going] ten minutes late **due to** [because of] operating difficulties. We apologize for the **late arrival**.

Exercises

63.1 Circle the best word in each sentence.

1. It's against the law to (ride)/ drive a motorcycle without a helmet.
2. She told him to get in / get on the car and fasten his seat belt.
3. Buses to the airport travel / run every half hour.
4. The pilot couldn't drive / fly the plane in such bad weather.
5. We were late, so we had to take / catch a taxi.
6. I left my house a little late and I lost / missed the bus.

63.2 Write two different words or phrases that combine with the words below.

1. miss _the bus_ .... 3. .... station 5. get in ....
 ....

2. _taxi_ .... driver 4. get on .... 6. .... fare
 ....

63.3 Identify these vehicles without looking at the opposite page.

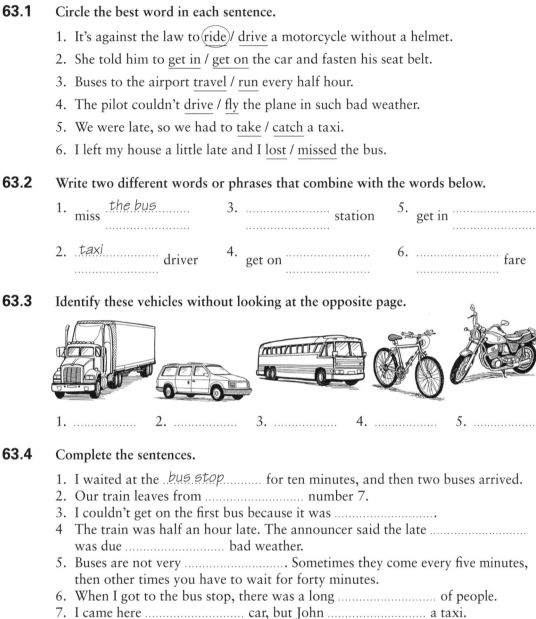

1. .... 2. .... 3. .... 4. .... 5. ....

63.4 Complete the sentences.

1. I waited at the _bus stop_ .... for ten minutes, and then two buses arrived.
2. Our train leaves from .... number 7.
3. I couldn't get on the first bus because it was ....
4. The train was half an hour late. The announcer said the late .... was due .... bad weather.
5. Buses are not very .... Sometimes they come every five minutes, then other times you have to wait for forty minutes.
6. When I got to the bus stop, there was a long .... of people.
7. I came here .... car, but John .... a taxi.
8. The train .... Chicago makes a few .... before arriving in Chicago.

63.5 Are these statements *true* or *false* in your experience? Why?

1. Trains are more reliable than buses.
2. Train fares are more expensive than bus fares.
3. Train stations are nicer places than bus stations.
4. You get to the place you are going faster by taxi than by bus.

Work: responsibilities, conditions, and pay

A   What do you do?

What do you do?   I'm **a** banker / **an** engineer / **a** teacher. (**be** + **a/an** + name of job)
What's your job?   I **work in** marketing / a bank. (**work in** + place or general area)
What do you do   I **work for** IBM/Toyota. (**work for** + name of company)
  for a living?

Note: **Work** (n. when it means employment) is usually uncountable, so you cannot say "I have a work." However, you can say "a job," e.g., "She doesn't have a job."

B   What does that involve?

When people ask you to explain your work/job, they want to know your **responsibilities** [your duties / what you have to do], or something about your daily **routine** [what you do every day/week]. They may ask: "What does that **involve?**" ["What do you do in your job?"]

Main responsibilities
I'm **in charge of** all the shipments out of the factory. [**responsible for**]
I have to **deal with** any complaints. [take all necessary action if there are complaints]
I **run** the restaurant in the museum. [I manage it.]

Daily duties/routines
I have to **go to** / **attend** *(formal)* a lot of meetings.
I meet with / visit / see **clients.** [people I do business with, who pay for my service]
It involves **doing** a lot of **paperwork.** [routine work that involves paper, e.g., writing letters, filling in forms, etc.] Note the **-ing** form after **involve.**

C   Pay

Most workers are **paid** regularly, e.g., every week or month. [They receive money.] This **pay** is called a **salary.** We also use the verbs **to earn** or **to make** (money), e.g., "I **earn/make** $40,000 a year." ["My **salary** is $40,000 a year."] Some people are paid for the hours they work; the lowest hourly pay in the U.S. (set by the government) is called the **minimum wage.**

With many jobs, you **get** [receive] **vacation pay** and **sick days** [days you can take off work, with pay, when you are sick]. If you want to ask about vacation time, you can say: "How **much vacation** do you get?" *or* "How **many weeks' vacation** do you get?" The total amount of money you receive from your job(s) is called your **income.** You usually have to **pay** part of your income to the government – called **income tax.**

D   Working hours

For many people in the United States and Canada, working hours are 9:00 a.m. to 5:00 p.m. Consequently people often talk about a **nine-to-five job** [regular working hours]. Some people have **flextime** [they can start work earlier or finish later]; and some people work different **shifts** [periods of time when people are scheduled to work, e.g., **night shift, day shift**]. Some people also **work/do overtime** [work extra hours].

Exercises

64.1 Match the verbs on the left with the words on the right. Use each word or phrase only once.

1. earn   overtime
2. work   meetings
3. pay   a store
4. attend   clients
5. see   a salary
6. run   income tax

64.2 Rewrite each sentence using vocabulary from the opposite page. Keep the basic meaning the same.

1. I'm a banker.
   I work .in banking / in a bank... .
2. What do you do?
   What's .... ?
3. I earn $35,000 dollars a year at my job.
   My ....
4. I make $40,000 from my teaching job and another $10,000 from writing.
   My .... is $50,000.
5. I'm an engineer.
   I work for ....
6. I'm responsible for one of the smaller departments.
   I'm in ....

64.3 This is part of a conversation with a teacher about her job. Can you supply the missing questions?

A: *What are your working hours? /*
   What hours do you work?
B: I usually start at nine and finish at four.

A: .... ?
B: Yes, sometimes. With certain courses I work evenings, and then I get paid extra.
A: .... ?
B: Two months. That's one of the good things about being a teacher.
A: .... ?
B: No, they don't, unfortunately. That's one of the disadvantages of being a teacher. But I suppose money isn't everything.

64.4 Can you answer these general knowledge questions about work?

1. What are normal working hours for most office jobs in your country?
2. Can you name three jobs that are paid very high salaries in your country?
3. When you start paying income tax in your country, what is the minimum amount or minimum percentage you have to pay?
4. What jobs often involve working in shifts? (Give at least two examples.)
5. Is flextime common in your company or your country?

UNIT 65 Jobs

A The medical profession

These people **treat** [give medical help] and **take care of** [care for] others:
doctor, nurse, surgeon [a specialist doctor who **operates on** people in a hospital], **dentist**, and **veterinarian** [animal doctor; **vet** for short].

B Manual jobs

These are jobs where you work with your hands, and all the examples below are **skilled** jobs [they need a lot of training].

bricklayer
[builds walls
with bricks]

carpenter
[makes things
using wood]

plumber
[installs and
repairs water
pipes, etc.]

electrician
[installs and
repairs electrical
things]

mechanic
[repairs cars]

C Professions

Job	Definition
architect	designs buildings
lawyer	advises people on legal problems
engineer	plans the building of roads, bridges, machines, etc.
accountant	keeps and examines financial records of people and companies
professor	teaches in a university
broker (stock market)	buys and sells stocks and bonds

D The armed forces and emergency services

soldier
(in the army)

sailor
(in the navy)

pilot
(in the air
force)

police officer
(in the police
force)

firefighter
(in the fire
department)

Exercises

65.1 Write down at least one job from the opposite page that would probably be
impossible for these people.

1. Someone who doesn't have a college education.
2. Someone with very bad eyesight [cannot see very well].
3. Someone who is always seasick on a boat.
4. Someone who understands nothing about cars.
5. Someone who will not work in the evening or on weekends.
6. Someone who is afraid of dogs.
7. Someone who is afraid of heights and high places.
8. Someone who is terrible at numbers and math.
9. Someone who can't stand the sight of blood.
10. Someone who is a pacifist, who is antiwar.

65.2 Complete these definitions without looking at the opposite page.

1. An architect *designs buildings* .
2. A professor ....
3. An accountant ....
4. A vet ....
5. A lawyer ....
6. An engineer ....
7. A bricklayer ....
8. A stockbroker ....
9. A mechanic ....
10. A surgeon ....

65.3 Respond to the statements below, as in the example.

1. A: He's a police officer.
   B: *Really? When did he join the police force?*
2. A: She's a soldier.
   B: .... ?
3. A: He's a sailor.
   B: .... ?
4. A: He's a fighter pilot.
   B: .... ?
5. A: She's a firefighter.
   B: .... ?

65.4 Imagine you just bought a piece of land and you are planning to build a house on
it. Write down at least six people from the opposite page that you may need to
help you. What would you need their help for?

Example: a bricklayer to build the walls

65.5 Write a list of at least four friends, relatives, and neighbors who have jobs. What
does each person do?

Example: My uncle Jim is an engineer. His wife is an accountant.

The career ladder

A

Getting a job

While Ray was in his last year of college, he became **an intern** [an unpaid job for a short time] to gain **experience** [skill or knowledge you get from doing a job] at a local company. Before he graduated, he **applied for** [wrote an official request for] a job in the accounting department of the same company. He got a job as a **trainee** [a very junior person in a company]. He didn't earn much money, but they gave him a lot of **training** [help and advice in learning the job].

Note: **Training** is an uncountable noun, so you cannot say "a training." **Experience** is uncountable when it means skill or knowledge.

B

Moving up

Ray worked hard and his **prospects** [future possibilities in the job] looked good. After his first year he got a **raise** [more money], and after two years he was **promoted** [given a higher position with a higher salary and more responsibility]. After five years he was **in charge of** [**responsible for** / the boss of] the accounting department with five other **employees** [workers] **under him** [under his responsibility/authority].

C

Leaving the company

By the time Ray was 30, however, he decided he wanted a **new challenge** [a new, exciting situation]. He was interested in working **abroad** [in foreign countries], so he **resigned** from the company [officially told the company he was leaving his job; you can also say "he **quit** his job"] and started looking for a new job with a bigger company. He found a job with an international company, which **involved** [included] a lot of foreign travel. He was excited about the new job and at first he really enjoyed the traveling, but . . .

D

Hard times

After about six months, Ray started to dislike moving around constantly, and after a year he hated it; he hated living in hotels, and he never really made any friends in the new company. Unfortunately his **job performance** [how well he did his work/job] was not satisfactory either, and he was **fired** [told to leave the company / **dismissed**] a year later.

After that, Ray was **unemployed** [**out of work** / without a job] for over a year. He had to sell his car and move out of his new house. Things were looking bad, and finally Ray had to accept a **part-time** job [working only part of the day or part of the week] as a chef's assistant at a restaurant.

E

Happier times

To his surprise, Ray loved working at the restaurant. He made lots of friends and enjoyed learning to cook. After two years he became chef, and two years later he **took over** [took control of] the restaurant. Later he opened a second restaurant, and after ten years he had five restaurants. Ray **retired** [stopped working completely] at the age of 60, a rich man.

Exercises

66.1   Write a one-word synonym for each of these words/phrases.

1.   dismissed   _fired_
2.   someone who does an unpaid job to gain experience
3.   out of work
4.   left the company
5.   given a better position in the company
6.   future possibilities in a job
7.   stopped working forever
8.   workers in a company
9.   an increase in salary
10. in a foreign country

66.2   Find the logical answer on the right for each question on the left.

1.   Why did they fire him?   a.   Because he was nearly 65.
2.   Why did they promote him?   b.   Because he was late for work every day.
3.   Why did he apply for the job?   c.   Because he didn't like his boss.
4.   Why did he retire?   d.   Because he was out of work.
5.   Why did he resign?   e.   Because he was the best person in the
                                              department.

66.3   Complete these sentences with a logical word or phrase.

1.   I don't want a full-time job. I'd prefer to work _part-time_ .
2.   She just started her first job and needs a lot of
3.   I'm bored with my job. I need a new
4.   She has more than a hundred workers under
5.   I didn't know he was the new manager. When did he take   ?

66.4   Complete this word-building table. Use a dictionary to help you.

Verb	General noun	Person noun(s)
retire	_retirement_	_retiree_
promote		–
employ		
resign		–
train		

66.5   Do you have a job in a company? If so, answer these questions. If possible, ask
another person the same questions.

1.   What does your job involve?
2.   Are you responsible for anything or anyone?
3.   Have you had much training from the company?
4.   Have you been promoted since you started in the company?
5.   Do you usually get a good pay raise at the end of each year?
6.   How do you feel about your future prospects in the company?

The office and the factory

A **The office**

briefcase · monitor · calendar · computer · files · keyboard · bulletin board · appointment book · desk · calculator · wastebasket · drawer · filing cabinet

B **Office work**

Laura works for a company that produces furniture. She works in an office, which is next to the factory where the furniture is made. This is how she spends her time:

She **works at a computer,** writing letters and reports.
She **answers phone calls,** often from **retailers** [stores that sell the factory's furniture].
She **makes phone calls** to retailers and to the factory.
She **does general paperwork,** e.g., filing reports, writing memos, answering letters.
She **sends invoices** to customers. [paperwork showing the cost of the products sold]
She **arranges/schedules meetings** for her boss and for other managers.

C **The factory**

This is where products are **manufactured** [made by machine]. Most factories have fewer workers than in the past because of **automation** [machines do most of the work]. Most factories use an **assembly line** [each worker makes a part of the product and then passes it on to the next person or

machine]. On an assembly line, workers **assemble** [put together] the different parts, and **supervisors** [people in charge] **check/inspect/examine** each stage to make sure the product **meets the required standards** [is good enough].

D **Finished goods**

Goods *(plural)* is the general word used for "products that are made to be sold." When the product, e.g., a radio, is finished, it is **packaged** [put in plastic and then in a box] and **stored** [kept] in a **warehouse.** When a customer, e.g., an electronics store, **orders** some of **these** goods, they are **delivered** [taken to the store] by plane, ship, train, or truck.

Exercises

67.1 Write three nouns that can follow each verb. You can use the same noun more than once. Not all of them are on the left-hand page.

1. write   ..*a letter*.............................

2. send   ....

3. make   ....

4. answer   ....

67.2 Fill in the blanks to form compound nouns.

1. I told him to put the notice on the bulletin ..*board*.................... .
2. She has to check the goods when they come off the assembly ....
3. I'm sure I took the reports out of the filing .... and put them in my brief........................... .
4. It's a very boring job and I spend most of my time doing general paper............................... .
5. I threw all that stuff in the waste........................... .

67.3 Which words from the opposite page are being defined here?

1. The place where you store finished products before they are sold.   *warehouse*
2. The process of using machines to do work that used to be done by people.
3. A plural noun for things that are made to be sold.
4. A thing you often hang on the wall, which tells you the date.
5. A book where you write down the meetings you have planned and other things you have to do.
6. A piece of paper that shows the products a customer bought and the price.
7. A store that sells goods to the public.

67.4 Replace the underlined verb with a verb that has the same meaning.

1. This machine is <u>made</u> in Japan.   *manufactured*
2. I help them <u>assemble</u> the different parts.
3. The supervisor always <u>inspects</u> our work carefully.
4. After the books are printed, they are <u>kept</u> in the warehouse.
5. The factory said they'll be able to <u>take</u> the furniture to the store next Monday.

67.5 Do you have a job? If so, how many of these statements are true for you in your job?

1. I work at a computer a lot of the time.
2. I do a lot of paperwork.
3. I make a lot of phone calls.
4. I send faxes and e-mail.
5. I attend [go to] a lot of meetings.
6. I have to write letters and reports.

Business and finance

A   Banks and businesses

Businesses sometimes need to borrow money in order to **finance** [pay for] **investments** [things they need for the company, e.g., machines]. The money they borrow from the bank is called **a loan**, and they have to **pay interest** on the loan. For example, if you borrow $1,000 and the **interest rate** is 10%, then you have to **pay back** $1,000, plus $100 in interest.

B   Businesses and profit

One of the main **aims/objectives/goals** [the things that you hope to do/achieve] of a company is to **make a profit** [earn/receive more money than it spends ≠ **a loss**]. If a company does not make a profit or have a loss, it **breaks even.**

Companies receive money from selling their products – this money is called **income** or **revenue.** The money that they spend is called the **expenditure(s)** *(formal).* They spend money on these things: **raw materials** [materials in their natural state used to make something else, e.g., coal and oil are **raw materials** used to make plastics]; **labor** [employees]; **overhead / overhead costs** [operating costs, e.g., rent and electricity].

C   Rise and fall

Businesspeople often need to talk about the movement of sales, prices, interest rates, profit and loss, etc. Here are some of the words used to describe these **trends** [movements]:

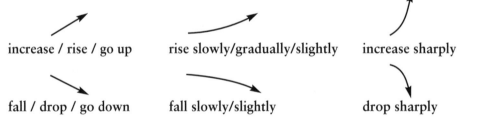

increase / rise / go up   rise slowly/gradually/slightly   increase sharply

fall / drop / go down   fall slowly/slightly   drop sharply

Note: **Increase, drop, fall,** and **rise** are also used as nouns: a **steady increase** in sales, a **dramatic** [sharp] **drop** in inflation, a **sharp fall** in profits, a **slow rise** in interest rates. We can also use **be up/down:** Prices **are up** by 10%; profits **are down.** **Decrease** is less common as a verb.

D   Businesses and the economy

In order to **grow/expand** [get bigger] and **thrive/prosper** [do well / be successful], many companies want or need the following:

low inflation, so prices do not go up very much
low interest rates, so the company can borrow money without paying a lot of
    interest
economic and **political stability** [things remain steady and stable and there are no
    sudden changes in the economic and political situation]
a **healthy/strong economy** [in good condition], and not an economy **in recession**
    [in a period of reduced and slow business activity]

Exercises

68.1 **What word or phrase is being defined?**

1. Money you borrow from a bank for your business. *a loan*
2. What you have to pay the bank if you borrow money.
3. The continuous increase in the price of things.
4. The things you hope to do/achieve within a period of time.
5. When a company does not make a profit or have a loss.
6. When an economy is in a period of reduced and slow business activity.

68.2 **Replace the underlined word(s) with another word that has a similar meaning.**

1. There has been a <u>slow</u> rise in sales. *gradual*
2. This comes after a <u>dramatic</u> fall last year.
3. Fortunately the company <u>is doing well</u> now.
4. And it's <u>growing</u> very quickly.
5. This is one of their main <u>objectives</u>.
6. Profits have <u>risen</u> considerably.

68.3 **Look at the graph and complete the sentences with one word for each blank.**

1. In 1994 sales *increased/rose* .
2. The following year they

   ....
3. In 1996 there was a ....
   .... in sales.
4. In 1997 business improved, and there
   was a ....
   ....
5. And in 1998 sales ....
   ....
6. In the five-year period, sales
   .... by 40,000.

Graph y-axis values: 160,000 / 140,000 / 120,000 / 100,000 / 80,000 / 60,000

Graph x-axis values: 94 95 96 97 98

68.4 **Fill in the blanks to form compound words or common phrases.**

1. *break*........... even
2. .... stability
3. .... a profit
4. .... rate
5. raw ....
6. profit and ....

68.5 **Can you answer these questions about your own country?**

1. What is the current inflation rate?
2. If you borrowed $10,000 from your bank, what would the interest rate be
   approximately?
3. What is the state of the economy right now? Is it strong? Is it in recession?
4. Are labor costs high, low, or about right?
5. Do you think businesses are optimistic about the future?

Sales and marketing

A What is marketing?

People talk about the **marketing mix.** This **consists of** [it is formed from and includes]:

having the right **product** [what a company produces/makes or offers]
selling it at the right **price** [what it costs the buyer/consumer]
using the right kind of **promotion** [the ways to make the product popular and
    well known; this includes **advertising**]
making it available in the right **place** [where you sell the product and how it
    reaches the **consumer**; also known as **distribution**]

Marketing people have the job of matching these things to the needs of
consumers [the people who buy and use products]. People who buy the products
or services of a company are that company's **customers/clients.**

B *Sales* and *market:* some compounds and word partners

sales figures: the number of items or amount you have sold
sales forecast: the amount you *think you will sell* in a future period, e.g., next year
sales representative (or **rep**): a person who sells a company's products
sales manager: the person in charge of the **sales department** and the sales reps
sales force: all the sales representatives as a group
marketing manager: the person in charge of the **marketing department,** which
    handles advertising, etc.
market research: collecting and studying information about what people want
    and need
market share: the percentage of a market that a company has, e.g., a 20% market
    share
market leader: the company or product with the biggest market share

C Competition and a company's image

Companies have to be aware of their **competitors** [the most important companies
in the same market; also called **the competition**]. Competitors constantly try to
take away market share from each other with new products.

The **image** of a product/company [the picture or idea that people have of the
product/company] is very important in sales and marketing. Some companies
want a **fashionable** image [modern and up-to-date]; others do not. For example:

mass-produced [made
in large numbers];
reliable [you can trust
it]; **affordable** [not
expensive]; functional
but boring

young; **exciting** and
glamorous [exciting
+ attractive]; often
fashionable and
dangerous; not very
practical

high quality [high standard
/ very good]; **luxury**
[expensive and giving great
comfort]; **upmarket/upscale**
[important; driven by
people with money]

Exercises

69.1   The "marketing mix" consists of four words, each starting with *p*. Can you remember them? Write them down and then check A opposite.

69.2   How many different compounds and word partnerships can you form with the words in the box? (You can use a word more than once.)

Example: sales force

sales	market	manager	share	figures	force
marketing	leader	research	department	forecast	

69.3   Complete the definitions below using compounds from 69.2.

1. A sales *forecast* is what you think you are going to sell during a future period.
2. The marketing .... is responsible for all the activities in the marketing ....
3. Sales .... tell you how much you have sold of a product.
4. The market .... is the company with the largest market .... in a particular market.
5. The sales .... consists of all the sales reps in the company.

69.4   What knowledge is necessary to be a good sales rep? Complete this paragraph and then try to add an additional sentence of your own.

First of all, good sales (1) *representatives/reps* need to have an excellent knowledge of the company's (2) .... Second, they need to know all about the (3) .... of their main (4) .... Third, sales representatives should be familiar with the needs of (5) .... in their particular market, and should obviously be very familiar with the needs of the company's most important (6) ....

69.5   Complete this word-building table. Use a dictionary to help you.

Noun	Adjective	Noun	Adjective
competition	*competitive*	....	glamorous
....	dangerous	luxury	....
....	exciting	mass production	....
fashion	....	....	reliable

69.6   Can you answer these questions about your own country? If possible, compare your answers with someone else.

1. Think of an important industry or business in your country, e.g., cars, computers, athletic shoes, watches, etc. Who is the market leader in that industry in your country?
2. Do you know its approximate market share? its main competitors?
3. What kind of image do the company's products have?

Hobbies

Hobbies are activities that we do in our **spare time.** [free time]

A **Things people play**

musical instruments

cards   board games   chess   guitar   saxophone

Note: Some people **join clubs** [become members] where they can **play** cards and chess.

B **Things people collect**

stamps   coins   antiques   matchbooks

C **Outdoor activities**

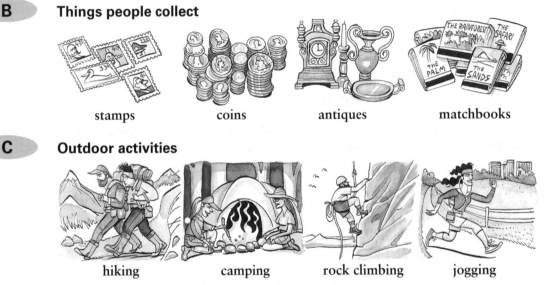

hiking   camping   rock climbing   jogging

With these hobbies we often use the verb **go,** e.g., **I go camping** in the summer. *or* **I go jogging** every morning.

D **Creative hobbies**

Caroline **makes her own clothes.** [She makes clothes for herself.]

Barbara likes **photography.**

Maria loves **carpentry.**

Note: When we start a hobby for the first time we often use the phrasal verb **take up,** and if we stop doing the hobby, we often use the phrasal verb **give up,** e.g., I **took up** golf when I was fifteen, but I **gave** it **up** last year.

Exercises

70.1 Without looking at the opposite page, write down . . .

1. three things that people often play.
2. three things that people often collect.
3. four outdoor activities that include some physical exercise.

70.2 Here are some people talking about their hobbies. Can you guess what each hobby is?

1. I usually use color, but sometimes you get a better effect with black and white. It really depends on the subject.   *photography*
2. I really enjoy going to stores and markets looking for a bargain.
3. I try to practice every day, but sometimes it's difficult because I don't like to disturb my neighbors too much. And one neighbor gets very angry if I play the same thing over and over again.
4. The great thing is you can do it whenever you like. I usually do it three or four times a week – either early in the morning, or after school. I only go for about 25 minutes but it really keeps me in good shape.
5. Obviously it saves me a lot of money. Besides, I hate shopping in clothing stores, because so many things are badly made.
6. I joined a club because I wanted to get better, and now I play twice a week in the evenings. It has helped me a lot, and I have a much better memory for all the different moves and strategies.
7. I love to work with wood, especially around the house. That's why I started, but now I think I do a better job than many professionals.

70.3 Complete these sentences with a verb from the opposite page.

1. How often do you ...*go*........... jogging?
2. She .... hiking because she wanted to get more exercise. Unfortunately she didn't like it, and she .... it .... about six months later.
3. She has always .... her own clothes; it's much cheaper than buying them.
4. He .... old coins.
5. I like to .... rock climbing when I'm on vacation.
6. I learned to .... the piano when I was in school.
7. I wanted to improve my chess, so I .... a chess club.
8. I don't really .... anything in my spare time.

70.4 Answer these questions. If possible, ask another person the same questions.

1. Do you have a hobby? If so, what is it?
2. How long have you had this hobby?
3. Is it an expensive hobby?
4. Why do you like it?
5. How much time do you spend on your hobby?
6. Is it a common hobby in your country?
7. Write down three other common hobbies in your country.

Sports

In English you **play games / play sports**, but we also say **do a lot of / do a little +** sport, e.g., In the winter I **do** a lot of **skiing,** but in the summer I **play tennis** and **golf.**

A   Ball games and racquet sports

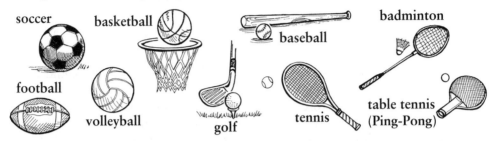

soccer   basketball   badminton   baseball

football   volleyball   golf   tennis   table tennis (Ping-Pong)

For most ball games you need **athletic shoes.**
For tennis and badminton you need a **racquet,** for table tennis a **paddle.**
For baseball you need a **bat.** For golf you need **golf clubs.**
In tennis, volleyball, and badminton there is a **net** across the middle of the **court.**
    There is also a **net** around each **goal** in soccer.

B   Things you can do with a ball

throw it   head it   pass it   hit it   catch it   kick it

C   Places and people

The playing area for soccer, football, and baseball is called a **field;** for tennis, volleyball, basketball, and badminton it is a **court;** for golf it is a **course.** The playing area for football and the area around for the **crowd** [the people who watch, also called **spectators**] is called a **stadium.**

Some games are played by individuals, others are **team** games. In professional sports the team usually has a **manager** (e.g., in baseball) or a **coach** (e.g., in basketball). Some sports (soccer, basketball) have a **referee,** and others (baseball, tennis) have an **umpire.** The referee or umpire makes sure the rules are followed.

D   Winning and losing

Mexico **beat** Switzerland 3–2. [Switzerland **lost to** Mexico 3 to 2.] In other words: Mexico **won** the game. [Switzerland **lost** the game.]
Mexico **defeated** Switzerland. [Switzerland **was defeated** by Mexico.]
Mexico was **the winner.** [Switzerland was **the loser.**]

If both teams have the same **score** [number of goals or points], e.g., 2–2, at the end of the game, we say it is a **tie** or a **draw.** When the game is in progress, we often use the verbs **lead** or **tie** to describe the score: *Brazil is leading Italy 2–1 / 2 to 1; the teams are tied 2–2 / 2 to 2* [*not* are tying].

Exercises

71.1 Cover the opposite page and then write six things you can do with a ball.

..*throw*.............. it .... it .... it

.... it .... it .... it

71.2 Write at least:

1. three games where you can hit the ball (with various kinds of equipment).
   baseball, . . .
2. three games where you can pass the ball.
3. three games where you can catch the ball.
4. two games where you can kick the ball.
5. one game where you can head the ball.

71.3 *True* or *false*? If *false,* correct the sentence to make it *true.*

1. The people who watch a football game are the audience.
   False. They are the crowd/spectators.
2. The official who makes sure the rules are followed in tennis is the umpire.
3. Most players wear athletic shoes.
4. Basketball has an umpire.
5. If the current score is Red Team 4, Blue Team 2, then the Blue Team is leading.
6. Tennis is played on a field.
7. You need clubs to play golf.
8. If both teams have the same score at the end of the game, it is a draw.

71.4 Fill in the blanks in this radio broadcast about baseball.

Here is a major league baseball update from your 24-hour news
station: At the end of a long game in San Diego, the Padres finally
(1) *beat/defeated*.. the Atlanta Braves 6 to 3 – the first time
Atlanta has (2) .... this season. The Padres are (3) ....
at last, and their fans are thrilled! Meanwhile, in Montreal, the Expos are
(4) .... the Chicago Cubs 4 to 0, and it's only the beginning of the
first inning! Poor Cubbies. And finally, news has just come in that the Toronto
Blue Jays and the New York Yankees are still (5) ...., with a
(6) .... of 3 to 3 in extra innings. More scores next hour.

71.5 Answer these questions. If possible, ask a friend the same questions.

1. Are there any games or sports on the opposite page that you watch but don't play? If so, what are they and where do you watch them?
2. Are there any games or sports on the opposite page that you play/do yourself?
3. Are there any that are not played much in your country?
4. Which game or sport is the most popular in your country?
5. Which sport on the opposite page is the most dangerous, in your opinion?
6. Which game or sport requires the most strength?
7. Which one has the biggest crowds?
8. Can you think of at least three more games/sports not included on page 144?

Movies and theater

curtain
stage
orchestra
box
rows
balcony
aisle

A Theater

At **the theater** you can see **plays**, e.g., *Hamlet* by Shakespeare, or **musicals**, e.g., *Phantom of the Opera* or *West Side Story*. In a musical the **cast** [all the actors] is usually fairly large, but plays often have a smaller cast.

One difference between the theater and movies is that you usually **reserve** [arrange to buy] tickets **in advance** [at some time before the actual performance] if you are going to the theater. Another difference is that the **audience** [the people watching the play/musical] **claps/applauds** [hits open hands together to show they have enjoyed it] at the end of the **performance**. This does not usually happen at the end of a movie.

B Movies

Plays are **performed** on a **stage**; movies/films are **shown** on a **screen**. In your country, movies in English might be shown with **subtitles** [with a translation across the bottom of the screen], or they might be **dubbed** [the English speech is removed and replaced by actors speaking in your own language]. When people talk about movies, they often talk about the **director** (e.g., Spielberg, Bertolucci) and the **stars** [the most important actors and actresses] (e.g., Harrison Ford, Jodie Foster).

C Types of movies

western: about the American West in the 19th century; often with cowboys and Indians
horror movie: scares you with monsters, etc.
science fiction movie: about imaginary scientific developments, often in the future
thriller: an exciting story, often about a crime

war movie: about war
action movie: has a lot of excitement
comedy: funny; makes you laugh
animation: cartoon

D Describing plays and movies

Critics/reviewers are journalists who write or give **reviews** [opinions about the quality] of new movies and plays, on TV and in newspapers. These are some words they may use:

moving: producing strong emotions, often of sadness; a positive word
violent: includes lots of scenes with fighting and death
powerful: has a big effect on our emotions
gripping: exciting and very interesting   **slow:** boring

Exercises

72.1 Look at the picture of your trip to the theater and answer these questions.

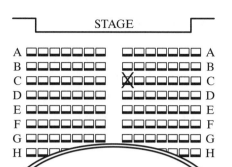

1. Did you sit in the orchestra or the balcony?
2. Which row were you in?
3. Were you next to an aisle?
4. Did you have a good view of the stage?

72.2 What word or phrase is being defined?

1. A play or movie with singing.   *musical*
2. All the actors in a play or movie.
3. The people who watch a play at the theater.
4. What these people do with their hands at the end of a play.
5. The person who directs a movie.
6. Journalists who talk on TV or write articles about movies and plays.
7. The name of the articles they write or the opinions they give on TV.
8. The translation of the story of a movie across the bottom of the screen.
9. To arrange to buy tickets before the performance.
10. The most important actors or actresses in a movie.

72.3 Read the examples of well-known movies below. Then think of at least three of your favorite movies and complete the table.

Movie	Type of movie	Subtitles or dubbed?	Description of movie (adjectives)
1. *The Godfather* with Marlon Brando	action, thriller	?	violent, gripping, exciting, fast-moving
2. *Schindler's List* by Steven Spielberg	war, thriller	?	moving, powerful, heartbreaking
3. *Beauty and the Beast* by Walt Disney Pictures	animation, musical	?	delightful, funny, visually breathtaking
4. *Titanic* with Leonardo DiCaprio and Kate Winslet	action	?	gripping, moving, exciting
5.			
6.			
7.			

Music, art, and literature

A Forms and people

	Forms/Types	*Person who creates*
music	classical	composer
	pop/rock	songwriter
art	painting	painter ⎫
	sculpture	sculptor ⎭ artist *(general)*
literature	novels	novelist ⎫
	short stories	short story writer ⎬ writer *(general)*
	poetry	poet
	plays	playwright ⎭

Seiji Ozawa, conductor

B Music

classical music: e.g., music by Beethoven, Tchaikovsky, and Mozart, who were
  composers [people who write music]. Most of their music is played by an
  orchestra [large group of musicians including violins, cellos, etc.], which is led
  by a **conductor.**
opera [a play in which the words are sung]: e.g., *Madame Butterfly* by Puccini
rock and **pop (popular) music:** This music is played by **groups/bands** (e.g., the
  Spice Girls) or **solo artists** [singers/musicians who perform alone; e.g., Whitney
  Houston]. Many solo artists are **singer-songwriters.** [They **write** and
  perform/play their own songs; e.g., Elton John.]
jazz: e.g., music by Duke Ellington, Miles Davis, Wynton Marsalis

C Musical instruments and musicians

cellist   violinist   pianist   guitarist   saxophonist   drummer

cello   violin   piano   guitar   saxophone   drums

D Art

You can see the paintings of famous artists at an **art gallery** or a **museum,** where
they show individual paintings and sometimes an **exhibit/exhibition** [a collection
of paintings by one painter or **school of painters,** e.g., the Impressionists]. For
example: There's a Picasso **exhibit** at the National **Gallery** next week.

There are many different types and styles of painting:

a **portrait** [a painting of a person]
a **self-portrait** [a painting of the artist by himself/herself]
a **landscape** [a painting of part of the countryside]
an **abstract painting** [a painting that is not realistic]

Exercises

73.1   **What do you call the people who play the following instruments?**

Example: piano – *pianist*

piano   saxophone   guitar   drums   violin   cello

73.2   **What types of painting are these?**

1.   2.   3.

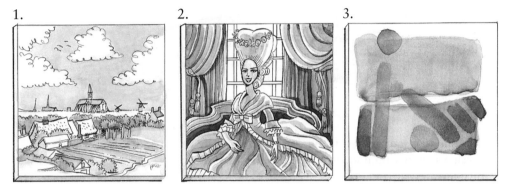

73.3   **Use the context and your own knowledge to fill in the blanks.**

1. Seiji Ozawa is the ...*conductor*......... of the Boston Symphony Orchestra.
2. A: Do you like .... music?
   B: Yes, very much.
   A: Who is your favorite ....?
   B: It's hard to say, but I love Bach and Chopin.
3. He's a .... His first .... was performed in a very small theater.
4. There's going to be an .... of her paintings at the new art ....
5. She used to .... her own songs, but now she mainly .... material written by other people.
6. I haven't been to the .... since I saw *Madame Butterfly* last year.
7. *A Farewell to Arms* is one of Hemingway's best .... Have you read it?
8. Picasso, Gauguin, and Cézanne were all great ....

73.4   **Name your favorites in each category. (The people you name can be living or dead.) Some of them may fit into more than one category. You may want to add more categories to the list.**

Example: Leonard Bernstein is my favorite composer. His most famous work is "West Side Story."

1. composer   6. pop or rock singer
2. song   7. play
3. orchestra   8. novel
4. band/group   9. poem
5. songwriter   10. novelist

Newspapers

A Background

In the U.S. and Canada, most newspapers/papers are **daily** [they **come out / are published** every day] with a special, larger **Sunday edition**; a few come out only on Sundays. Magazines are usually **weekly** [they come out once a week] or **monthly** [published once a month]. **Tabloid newspapers / Tabloids** have short articles and lots of pictures about famous people, crime, the supernatural, etc., rather than more serious news.

B Contents

national news: news about the country where the newspaper is published
foreign/international news: news about other countries
business news
sports news
features: longer articles about special subjects, e.g., a political issue or a health subject
radio and TV listings: schedules for radio and TV programs
weather forecast: tells you what the weather will be like
reviews: Movie, theater, music, and restaurant **critics/reviewers** write their opinions about new movies, plays, recordings, and restaurants.

C People

editor: the person in control of the daily production
reporters/journalists: people who report news and write articles; many journalists are **freelance** [they work for themselves and are not employees of the newspaper]
photographers: people who take photographs published in the newspapers

D Headlines

Certain words (usually very short) are often used in newspaper headlines. Here are some:

link (v., n.): to make a connection	**back:** to support
quit: to leave a job / resign	**probe** (n., v.): an investigation
bid (n., v.): an effort / a try / an attempt	**talks:** discussions
cut (v., n.): to reduce / make less / lower	**key:** very important

E "It said in the paper that . . ."

When we talk about something in a newspaper, we can use the verb **say** (*not* write], or the expression **according to**:

It **says** in *The Times* that they've found the missing girl.
According to *The Star*, the missing girl was found last night.

Exercises

74.1 Answer these questions about newspapers in your country.

1. How many daily national newspapers are there?
2. How many tabloid newspapers are there?
3. How many newspapers come out *only* on Sunday in your country?
4. Can you name two or three famous journalists who write for daily or weekly papers?
5. Can you name any famous critics? What do they usually review?
6. How often do you read the newspaper? How often do you buy a newspaper?

74.2 Explain these headlines in your own words. Do not use the underlined words.

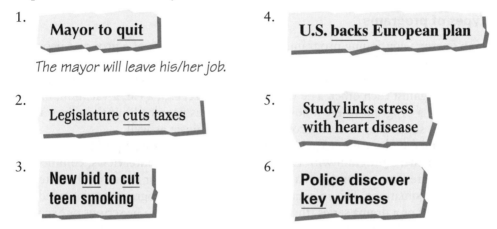

1.

Mayor to quit

The mayor will leave his/her job.

2.

Legislature cuts taxes

3.

New bid to cut teen smoking

4.

U.S. backs European plan

5.

Study links stress with heart disease

6.

Police discover key witness

74.3 Buy two different newspapers (in English or your own language) and complete these two tables.

	Paper 1 (number of pages)	*Paper 2* (number of pages)
national news	……….	……….
foreign/international news	……….	……….
feature articles	……….	……….
business news	……….	……….
sports news	……….	……….

	Paper 1 (yes/no)	*Paper 2* (yes/no)
weather forecast	……….	……….
cartoons	……….	……….
crossword puzzle	……….	……….
radio and TV listings	……….	……….
reviews	……….	……….

How many pages are left? What are they about? If possible, compare answers with a friend.

Television

A Watching TV

plug it in   turn it on [≠ turn it off]   remote control

You can also **turn it up** [increase the volume / make it louder] [≠ **turn it down**], or **switch channels** [**change** to a different channel, e.g., from channel 2 to 4].

Note: You can also say **switch** it **on/off** [turn it on/off], but *not* switch it up/down.

B Types of programs

soap opera: a continuing program, which follows the lives of a group of people; the stories are often romantic, exciting, dramatic, and hard to believe.

quiz show or **game show:** individuals, families, or teams answer questions or play games against each other. The winner gets a **prize**, e.g., a car, a vacation, money.

talk show: a program where a host talks to famous people about their lives and careers; sometimes there are comedy acts and music as well.

documentary: a film with factual information, often analyzing a problem in society.

newsmagazine: a program with brief informational films, interviews, commentary

a series: more than one program about the same situation or the same characters in different situations. This may be a **comedy** series (the programs are intended to be funny) or a **drama** series (the programs are intended to be serious or exciting).

current affairs / current events program: a program about a current social/political issue or problem. **Current** means "happening now / at the present time."

TV movie: a movie made for television, not shown in theaters.

cartoons: animated programs or movies, often for children, sometimes for adults too.

rerun/repeat: a program that is being shown again (i.e., not for the first time).

C Network TV, satellite TV, cable TV

Network TV refers to groups of TV stations that broadcast many of the same programs all over the country through radio waves in the air. You don't have to pay to watch network TV stations. If you pay extra, you can have a **satellite dish** and receive **satellite TV,** or you can **subscribe to** [pay for] **cable TV** [TV sent through wire cables underground] – there are many channels available.

D Talking about TV

What's **on** TV tonight? [What programs are showing on TV tonight?]

What time is the movie **on?** [What time does it start?]

How long do the **commercials last?** [advertisements between and during programs]

a satellite dish

What's your **favorite program/show?** [the program you like most/best]

Are they showing the game **live** [as it happens] or just **recorded highlights?** [parts of the game after it has been played, e.g., later in the day/evening]

Exercises

75.1 Imagine you are watching TV with a friend. What could you say in each situation below?

1. You want to watch a program on TV.
   Could you *turn the TV on / turn on the TV?*
2. You can't hear the program very well.
   Could you ....?
3. You want to watch a different program.
   Could you ....?
4. Now it's too loud for you.
   Could you ....?
5. You don't want to watch anymore.
   Could you ....?

75.2 Here is part of a TV guide for several TV channels in the U.S. Can you find at least one example of: a drama series, a newsmagazine, a game show, a sports program, a talk show, a cartoon show, and a current affairs program? There is also a soap opera and two comedy series. Can you guess which ones they are? (Some programs fit into more than one category.)

THE LIGHT OF OUR LIVES. Ellen finds out she has an evil twin; Sandy can't hide her fatal attraction for David; Stuart finds happiness.

SEINFELD. A librarian says that Jerry has a book that's 20 years overdue.

THE SIMPSONS — *animated.* Bart visits the school psychologist and drives her crazy.

60 MINUTES. The price of terrorism; lottery winners who go broke; charities that make a difference.

JEOPARDY! Contestants vie for cash prizes.

THE X-FILES. The probe of two deaths unearths a frightening discovery.

NASCAR RACING. Live auto racing.

WASHINGTON WEEK IN REVIEW. Discussion of political issues.

LAW & ORDER. The murder of an actress leads to an investigation of her ex-husband and the child they'd given up for adoption.

THE TONIGHT SHOW. Jay's guests are Tom Hanks and Madonna.

75.3 Answer these questions about TV in your own country.

1. How many network channels are there?
2. Do you watch satellite TV and/or cable TV?
3. In total, how much TV do you watch every week? (i.e., how many hours?)
4. What are your favorite TV programs? Do they fit in the categories in B opposite?
5. What day(s) or night(s) are they on?
6. Do you enjoy watching commercials?
7. Do you often watch sports live on TV? If not, do you watch the highlights?
8. Do you ever watch reruns of TV shows? Which ones?

On the phone

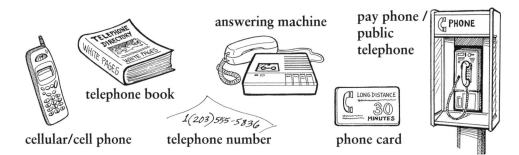

answering machine

pay phone /
public
telephone

telephone book

cellular/cell phone   telephone number   phone card

A   **Starting a phone conversation**

A: Hello?

B: Hi. (**Is this**) Mary? [*not* Are you Mary? / Is it Mary?]

A: Yeah.

B: **It's** Ruth. / **This is** Ruth. [*not* I am Ruth. / Here is Ruth.]

Note: When people in the U.S. and Canada answer the phone at home, they usually say "hello." They do not give their name or telephone number.

C: **Thank you for calling** Hayes Electronics. **How may I direct your call?** [Which department or person do you want to speak to?]

D: Yes, **can I speak** to Ms. Gold, please? [We also say "Could I . . ." or "May I . . ."]

C: I'm sorry, but **her line is busy.** [Her phone is in use, i.e., someone is **on the phone.**] Do you want to **hold?** [wait]

D: Yes, OK.

B   **Telephone problems**

4:30 p.m.   You try to **call** [telephone] your sister Susan, but you get a **wrong number.** [You have **dialed** the number incorrectly and a stranger answers.]

4:35 p.m.   You **get through to** Susan's number [make contact], but she's **out** [not at home]. Her husband, Bill, answers and says that Susan **won't be back** [will not return] for two hours, so you **leave a message:** "Could you ask her to call me when she gets back?" Bill **takes the message.** [writes it down]

7:30 p.m.   Susan **calls** you **back,** but now *you* are out. She leaves a message on your answering machine. Her message is: "This is Susan. I'm just returning your **call** [phone/telephone call]. I'll **give you a call** [call you] tomorrow."

C   **Useful telephone vocabulary**

A **collect call:** This is when the person you call agrees to pay for the phone call. If you **make a collect call,** you may have to go through the **operator.** If you don't know someone's phone number, you can call **Information / Directory Assistance** to get the number. If you call another town or city, you need to dial the **area code** first. For example, the area code for parts of New York City is 212. This type of call is usually a **toll call** or a **long distance call** [≠ a **local call**], and it may cost extra.

Exercises

76.1 Write down five words or expressions that include the word *phone* or *telephone*.

Example: telephone call / phone call

76.2 Fill in the blanks in these phone conversations with logical words or phrases.

A A: Classic Computers. May I help you?
   B: Yes. (1) ..*This is*........... Kevin Lee at Offices Unlimited. I'm trying to reach Mr. Patterson. He left a (2) .... on my answering machine.
   A: I'm sorry, but Mr. Patterson is (3) .... Can I ask him to (4) .... later?
   B: Yes. My (5) .... is 555-7267, and I'll be here until noon.

B A: Hello?
   B: Hi. Debbie?
   A: No, (6) .... Diane. Debbie's not here.
   B: Oh. Do you know when she'll (7) ....?
   A: I'm sorry, but I have no idea.
   B: Well, could I (8) .... a .... for her?
   A: Sure.
   B: Could you ask her to (9) .... this evening, please?
   A: OK. What's your name?
   B: Catherine. I'm a friend from work. She's got my number.
   A: OK, I'll tell her.
   B: Thanks. Bye.

C A: Hello?
   B: (10) .... Carlos?
   A: Yeah, speaking.
   B: Hi, Carlos. (11) .... Selena.
   A: Oh, hi. I was expecting you to call yesterday.
   B: I did – or at least I tried. I (12) .... your number about six times last night but I couldn't (13) .... It was always (14) ....
   A: Oh, sorry about that. I was (15) .... the phone with my brother for about an hour, and then someone from school called.
   B: Oh, OK. Anyway, I'm calling about . . .

76.3 Can you answer these questions?

1. What is the emergency number for the police, fire department, or ambulance where you live?
2. Is there a Directory Assistance or Information number? What is the number?
3. How much does it cost to make a local call from a pay phone?
4. How often do you have to pay your phone bill?
5. Is it cheaper to make calls at night? on weekends?
6. Have you ever made a collect call? When?

Computers

A Hardware and software

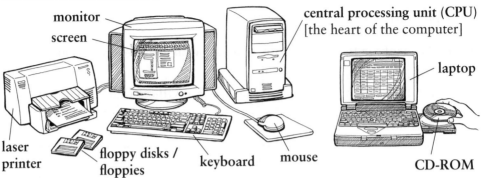

monitor
screen
central processing unit (CPU)
[the heart of the computer]
laptop
laser printer
floppy disks / floppies
keyboard
mouse
CD-ROM

You need **hardware** [computer machines and equipment] and **software** [the computer programs needed to work the machines]. These computer programs are on **disks**: e.g., the **hard disk** inside the CPU, or **floppy disks** [small plastic disks], or **CD-ROMs** [Compact Disc Read Only Memory, a CD on which you can put a large amount of information].

B Operating a computer

Using the **mouse**, you can do many different things by **clicking on** different icons [moving the mouse to point at, or to select, different pictures on the screen]. Here are examples of icons from a popular word processing program:

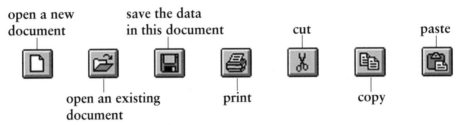

open a new document
save the data in this document
cut
paste
open an existing document
print
copy

C What do people use computers for?

Many people use their computers for **word processing**, e.g., writing letters and reports. Some businesspeople use **spreadsheets** [programs used to enter and arrange numbers and financial information] and **databases** [programs that allow you to store, look at, or change a large amount of information quickly]. Some people also use **graphics** [the pictures and symbols a computer program can produce].

D Important vocabulary

More and more people are becoming **computer-literate** [have experience working with computers and know how to use them], since many programs and machines are so **user-friendly** [easy to use]. If a computer works slowly, it may need more **memory** [space to store information]. It might **crash** [stop working] if there is not enough memory or if it has a **bug** [a software problem; also a **virus**]. Always make a **back-up copy** of your work [a copy on a separate disk].

Exercises

77.1 Add another word, abbreviation, or part of a word to complete common "computer" words and phrases.

1. word *processing*
2. soft..................................
3. floppy ....
4. ....-friendly
5. ....-literate
6. key....................................

7. a computer ....
8. ....-ROM
9. laser ....
10. lap..................................
11. spread..........................
12. back-.......................... copy

77.2 Match these symbols with the computer commands.

cut   copy   print   paste   save

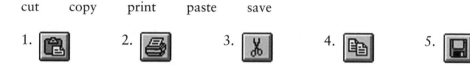

1. [icon]   2. [icon]   3. [icon]   4. [icon]   5. [icon]

77.3 Complete this description of using a computer for word processing.

I wrote a report on the (1) ..*computer*.......... this morning. When I finished, I (2) .... out two copies – one for me and one for my boss. Then, without any warning, the computer (3) ...., and unfortunately I lost the whole document. This is very unusual, because I almost always (4) .... the data while I'm writing and then make a (5) .... copy when I'm finished; this morning I forgot.

Anyway, I gave the report to my boss, hoping she would not ask me to make any changes. She did. She thought it was too long and said it would be better if I used more (6) .... to illustrate some of the written information. She also thought it would make the report look more attractive.

I went back and rewrote most of the report when the computer was OK, only I (7) .... part of the middle section, which was fairly repetitive, and I added extra (8) .... as my boss advised. It did look better by the time I'd finished, and this time I remembered to (9) .... it and make a (10) .... copy.

77.4 Answer these questions. If possible, ask someone else the same questions.

1. Do you have a computer at home? If so, what kind is it?
2. Do you use computers at school/college/university/work? If so, what type?
3. What do you use them for?
4. Are you computer-literate?
5. Do you find most computers user-friendly?
6. Which software programs are you familiar with?
7. Have you ever used a CD-ROM? If so, what kinds have you used and why?

The Internet

What is the Internet?

The Internet / the Net is a system connecting millions of computers worldwide. In order to **go/get online** [become connected], you must connect your computer to a **modem** [equipment that sends information along telephone lines to other computers]. A popular use of the Internet is sending and receiving **e-mail /**

electronic mail [letters or documents sent electronically] to or from people who are also connected to the Internet. Here is an **e-mail address:** billc@abcindustries.com

Note: The @ is pronounced "at," and the period is pronounced "dot."

You can **download** documents and software programs on the Internet. [move information from another computer to your computer] You may be able to download **shareware**. [software programs to try for free and pay for later if you keep them]

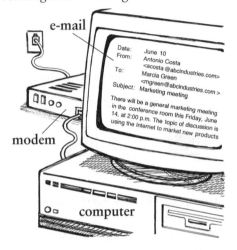

The World Wide Web

The World Wide Web / the Web (WWW) is a large part of the Internet; it is a system of electronic documents **linked** [connected] to one another. If you are not sure where to find something on the Web, you can use a **browser / search engine**, a program that finds information on the WWW or helps you **surf the Net / surf the Web** [look at a lot of information quickly]. Many businesses, and some people, have **Web pages / Web sites** [documents you can view on the WWW]. The **home page** [the main page, which gives general information] is usually the first Web page you connect to at a Web site. You can **click on** [select] **hypertext** [special, highlighted words on a Web page] to link your computer to other pages or documents. Here is Cambridge University Press's home page.

URL (uniform resource locator), the "address" of the Web site

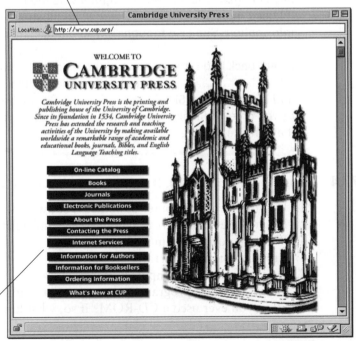

hypertext links

Exercises

78.1 Write each word or phrase a different way.

1. WWW   *the World Wide Web*
2. the Net
3. search engine
4. electronic mail
5. the Web

78.2 Match the words on the left with the explanations on the right.

1. Web pages
2. maryv@cal.edu
3. http://www.cup.org
4. hypertext
5. home page
6. to download
7. to surf the Net
8. modem

a. to transfer information from one computer to another
b. documents you can view on the World Wide Web
c. equipment that sends information along telephone lines
d. the main page within a Web site
e. a URL, the address for a Web site
f. an e-mail address
g. special words linked to documents on the Web
h. to browse or look around the Internet

78.3 Complete this e-mail message.

MESSAGE TEXT	FOLDER INBOX	MESSAGE 1 OF 5	NEW

Date: May 1
From: Nancy Kim <nkim@netsource.com>
To: Bob Sanchez <bobs@stateu.edu>
Subject: Getting on line

Hi. I finally got (1) ...*online*........... this morning, and this is my first
(2) .... message. I'm really excited! As you know, I've had a
computer for ages, but I didn't have a (3) .... to connect to the
telephone line. Now that I've got one, I'll be able to surf the (4) ....,
send and receive (5) ...., (6) .... software, and do all
kinds of fun things. A friend of mine has her own Web (7) ...., so
now I have to figure out how to get on the (8) .... and find it!

Best,
Nancy

78.4 Answer these questions. If possible, ask someone else the same questions.

1. Are you connected to the Internet? If so, how often do you use it?
2. Have you ever sent or received e-mail? If so, what is your e-mail address?
3. If you've never used e-mail, would you like to? Who would you write to?
4. What are some advantages and disadvantages of using e-mail?
5. Do you think the Internet will have an important influence on your daily life in future?
6. Can the Internet help people in different countries learn English? How?

UNIT 79   Education: school

A

K–12

In the U.S., **K–12** means "kindergarten through twelfth grade (the last year of high school)" for **public schools** [free education]. In most states, school is **compulsory** [you have to go] from age 6 to 16, and most children follow this route in school:

Approximate age	Kind of school
3 or 4	Some go to **nursery school** (not compulsory).
5	Most children start **kindergarten** (compulsory in some states, optional in others), which is the first year of **elementary school** (usually kindergarten and grades 1–6). At age 6, all children must attend first grade.
10, 11, or 12	Some children go to **middle school,** grades 5–8 or 6–8. Those who don't **attend** [go to] middle school go to **junior high school,** grades 7–9.
15	Students go to **high school / secondary school** (grades 9–12 or 10–12). Regular high schools offer academic and vocational programs. **Vocational high schools** offer training for a job, e.g., auto mechanic, beautician. **Specialized high schools** are for students with special interests, e.g., music, business.
18	They **graduate** [finish school successfully] and get a job or **go to college** for higher education. Those who leave school without graduating are called **dropouts**. [They **drop out** of school.]

Note:
- Students **go to school** and **go to college** to study (*not* go to the school / the college). In the U.S., **go to college** can mean university, college, or community college.
- There are also **private schools** and **parochial** [religious] **schools.** Neither is free, and some can be expensive.
- Some states now have **charter schools** [public schools that parents can choose to send their children to] as an alternative to traditional public schools. Parents and teachers in charter schools have more freedom to choose the curriculum.

B

A school schedule

Class schedules and courses can be very different from state to state, and even from school to school. However, certain **core subjects** [most important areas of study] are taught in most schools, e.g., **reading/English, writing, math** [an abbreviation of mathematics], **science,** and **social studies** [the study of society, including history, politics, and economics]. A schedule for one day in a typical high school might look like this:

8:00	Science	11:40	Lunch
8:55	Math	12:30	History
9:50	English	1:25	PE [physical education] / Computers
10:45	Elective (music, art, etc.)	2:20	Foreign language

Note: Some words in English that end in -s look plural, but in fact they are singular, e.g., mathematics, politics, physics: "Physics is my favorite subject."

Exercises

79.1 Here are some school subjects, but the letters are mixed up. What are the subjects?

Example: TREPCUMOS ....*computers*............

1. TAHM ....
2. IRTHOSY ....
3. CNECSEI ....
4. NISGEHL ....
5. RAT ....
6. SIMCU ....

79.2 How much can you remember? Try to answer these questions or complete the sentences without looking at the opposite page.

1. What does K–12 mean? *kindergarten through twelfth grade*
2. At what age do children go to nursery school?
3. At what age do they start elementary school?
4. Which year of elementary school is compulsory in some states but optional in others?
5. When students go to high school, it could be a regular school or a .... school or a .... school.
6. Can you name at least four core subjects taught in schools?
7. Which of these schools is free: parochial, private, public?
8. What type of school comes between elementary school and high school?

79.3 What about you and your country? Answer these questions.

1. Did you go to nursery school? kindergarten?
2. Do most children start elementary school / primary school at the age of 5?
3. Is the high school system similar to or different from the system in the U.S.?
4. How many subjects did/do you study in high school?
5. Did/do you study any subjects that are not included on the opposite page? Which ones?
6. What was/is your favorite subject? your worst subject?
7. How many classes did/do you have every day?
8. Did/do you attend public school or private school?
9. Until what age do students have to stay in school?
10. Are there a lot of high school dropouts?

79.4 Complete these sentences with the correct word or expression.

1. When she was a child, she lived in a small town and went .... with only fifty other students.
2. After I .... from high school, I went .... and studied art history.
3. He wanted to finish school, but he needed to get a job and support his family. That's why he .... of school at 16.
4. They didn't have to send their children to kindergarten because it wasn't .... in their state.

79.5 The next unit is about college and higher education. Can you think of six subjects you can study at a university that you do not usually study at school (K–12)? Write down your answers, then turn to the next page.

Education: university/college

A Higher education in the U.S.

Higher education refers to education at a university or college. A **college** may be an independent institution or a part of a university; e.g., some universities have a college of engineering, college of liberal arts, etc. Some students attend a **community college / junior college** [a two-year government-supported college that usually offers technical and vocational studies]. **School** usually means K–12 (kindergarten through high school), but it can also mean university or college, e.g., "Where did you go to school?" "Harvard." We also say **graduate school. College** frequently means either university or college, e.g., "My son is in college."

If you go to a state college or a community college, the **tuition** [the money you pay for courses] is lower than at a private institution. Some students **get** [receive] a **scholarship** [money to pay all or part of the tuition]. Students at a university are called **undergraduates** while they are studying for their first **degree** [the qualification when you complete university/college requirements successfully]. It can be a **B.A.** [Bachelor of Arts] or a **B.S.** [Bachelor of Science] at four-year institutions, or an **associate degree** after two years at a community/junior college.

B Subjects

You usually **take/study** these **subjects** at a university or college but not usually in high school or in the lower grades. (*Note:* The underlined letters show the syllable with the main stress.)

agriculture	business	history of art / art history	political science
anthropology	education	hotel administration	psychology
architecture	engineering	philosophy	sociology

The main subject that a student takes at college is his/her **major.** We can also say: "Chris **is majoring in** psychology."

C Postgraduate courses

When you complete your first degree, you are a **graduate.** Some students then go on to do/take a second degree (**postgraduate degree**). They are then **postgraduates / graduate students.** Some of the possible postgraduate degrees include **M.A.** (Master of Arts) or **M.S.** (Master of Science), and **Ph.D.** (Doctor of Philosophy), the most advanced degree. When people study one subject in great detail (often to find new information), we say they are **conducting/doing research** (U); e.g., "I'm **doing research into/on** the languages of African tribes." [*not* "I'm doing a research."]

D School vs. university/college

At school (K–12), you have **teachers** and **lessons;** at university or college, you have **professors** and **instructors,** and **lectures, discussion classes,** and **seminars.** When a professor **gives** a lecture, the students listen and **take notes** [write down the important information] but do not usually say much. In a discussion class, students discuss the subject and ask questions. A seminar is an advanced or postgraduate class in which students do independent research and then compare their results informally with the professor and other students.

Exercises

80.1 Read these sentences spoken by college students. What subject is each person studying?

1. "I'm concentrating on the modernist style and the work of Le Corbusier and Frank Lloyd Wright." _architecture_
2. "The way we use fertilizers is much more precise than it was twenty years ago."
3. "Travel and tourism are an important part of this industry."
4. "We're going to concentrate on Freud and Jung this term."
5. "I've been reading some books on time management."
6. "Expressionism was really a reaction to the work of the Impressionists."
7. "We've spent a lot of time on foreign policy and how it is affected by domestic issues."
8. "We're looking at ways that solar energy can be utilized."

Now mark the stress in each of your answers above and practice saying the words. Check the index or a dictionary for help with pronunciation.

80.2 What do you call . . .

1. the money students pay for their courses?   _tuition_
2. the qualification you get at the end of four years at a university?
3. the name we give students during this period at college?
4. teachers at a university/college?
5. an advanced class where students discuss their research with a professor?
6. students studying for a second degree?
7. the study of one subject in great depth and detail, often to get new information?
8. the talks that students go to while they are at university or college?

80.3 Replace the underlined words with different words that have the same meaning in the context.

1. Is he a postgraduate?   _graduate student_
2. Did she receive a college scholarship?
3. He's planning to go to junior college.
4. Where did you go to college?
5. She's studying physics, I think.
6. I think they're doing research into the cause of asthma.

80.4 How similar is higher education in your own country? Answer these questions. If possible, compare your answers with someone else from your own country and/or someone from a different country.

1. Do some students get a scholarship to study at university or college?
2. Is the tuition free in some colleges?
3. At what age do most students go to university or college?
4. How long do most undergraduate courses last?
5. What is your equivalent of the B.A. or B.S.?
6. Do you have similar postgraduate degrees in your country? Explain.

Law and order

A   The police

When someone **commits a crime** [breaks the law and does something **wrong / illegal / against the law**], the police (*note:* plural) **investigate** [try to find out what happened and who is responsible]. If they find a **suspect** [a person who may have committed the crime], they **question** the person [ask questions]. If they are fairly sure the suspect committed the crime, they **arrest** that person [take him/her to the police station] and **charge him/her with** the crime [the police make an official statement that the suspect committed the crime]. The suspect may go to **court** for **trial**.

B   The court

In **court**, the **prosecutor** [the lawyer for the government] must **prove** [provide facts to show something is true] that the person charged with the crime (now called the **defendant**) committed the crime; in other words, prove that the defendant is **guilty** [≠ **innocent**]. The **defense attorney** [the lawyer for the defendant] presents evidence showing that the defendant is not guilty. The **jury** listens to all the **evidence** [information about the crime, for and against the defendant] and then makes a decision.

C   Punishment

If the defendant is **convicted of** the crime [the jury says "guilty"], the judge will give the **sentence** [the punishment]. For example, if a person is convicted of murder, the sentence may be many years in **prison** [a large building where people are locked in]. The defendant then becomes a **prisoner** and lives in a **cell** [a small room in a prison].

For crimes that are not so serious (often called **minor offenses**, e.g., illegal parking), the punishment is usually a **fine** [money you have to pay].

Exercises

81.1 Put this story in the correct order.

Last week $100,000 was stolen from a bank on Main Street.

1. they found both men guilty.
2. and charged them with the robbery.
3. Last week $100,000 was stolen from a bank on Main Street.
4. After the jury listened to all the evidence,
5. They were sent to prison for seven years.
6. The trial took place six months later.
7. They finally arrested two men
8. The police questioned a number of people about the crime.

81.2 Answer the questions.

1. Who investigates crimes?   *the police*
2. Who sentences people?
3. Who lives in prison cells?
4. Who decides if someone is innocent or guilty?
5. Who presents evidence in court?
6. Who commits crimes?

81.3 Fill in the blanks.

1. I have never .....*broken*........... the law and .... a crime.
2. In the U.S., it is .... the law to drive a car without a driver's license.
3. If you park illegally, you will have to pay a ....
4. The police were fairly sure the woman had committed the crime, but they knew it would be difficult to .... it in court.
5. The jury must decide if the defendant is innocent or ....
6. In order to reach their decision, the jury must listen carefully to the
   ....
7. If a defendant is .... of murder, the .... may be life in prison.
8. He has been in trouble with the police once before, but it was only a minor
   ....

81.4 Read this short article. Then write your responses to the questions, based on your knowledge of the law in your own country. If possible, discuss your answers with someone else.

> Two 15-year-old girls broke into a house in the middle of the day when the homeowner was out, and took money and jewelry worth about $900. The homeowner reported the crime to the police when she returned home at 6 p.m.

1. Will the police investigate this crime?
2. How will they investigate? What will they do?
3. If the two girls are caught, what crime will they be charged with?
4. Can the girls be sent to prison? What do you think their sentence would be?

UNIT 82 Crime

 A **Against the law**

If you do something **illegal** [wrong / **against the law**], then you have **committed a crime.** Most people commit a minor crime at some time in their lives, e.g., driving above the speed limit, parking illegally, stealing candy when they were children, etc.

B **Crimes**

Crime	Criminal [person]	Verb
theft [general word for stealing]	thief	steal (also **take**)
robbery [steal from people or places]	robber	rob
burglary [**break into** a store/home and steal things]	burglar	burglarize / burgle / break into
shoplifting [steal from stores while pretending to shop]	shoplifter	shoplift
murder [kill someone by intention]	murderer	murder
manslaughter [kill someone without intention]	–	–

C **Crime prevention**

What can communities do to **fight crime** [take action to stop crime]? These things happen in some places, although some people may think they are not a good idea:

Police **carry** guns. [have]
Police **are allowed to** stop anyone on the street and question them. [are permitted to]
The courts give **tougher punishments** for crimes committed than in the past (e.g., bigger fines or longer prison sentences than in the past].
There is **capital punishment** for some crimes, such as murder. [death, e.g., by electric chair or lethal injection]

What can individuals do to **prevent** a crime **from** happening? [stop a crime from happening] Here are things some people do to **protect themselves** and their **property** [home, land, things they own]:

Don't walk along dark streets **late at night** (e.g., midnight) **by yourself** [alone].
Lock all doors and windows when you leave the house.
Don't wear expensive jewelry when you go out.
Leave lights **on** at home when you go out.
Install [put in] a **burglar alarm** [a machine that makes a loud noise if someone enters your home by force].

Make sure your money is safe, e.g., wear a **money belt** or a **money pouch.**

a money pouch

Put money and **valuables** [valuable possessions] in a **safe.** [a strong metal box, which is very difficult to open or break]

a safe

Exercises

These exercises also review some vocabulary from Unit 81.

82.1 Organize the words in the box into three groups: crimes, people, and places.

Example: Crimes: murder, . . .

murder	thief	prison	attorney	robbery
burglar	cell	criminal	court	police station
manslaughter	judge	prisoner	jury	shoplifting

82.2 Respond to the statements/questions, confirming the crime in each.

1. A: He broke into the house, didn't he?
   B: Yes, he's been charged with .*burglary*.................... .
2. A: He killed his boss?
   B: Yes, he's been charged ....
3. A: She stole jewelry from that department store while she was shopping, didn't she?
   B: Yes, and she's been ....
4. A: The woman on the motorbike didn't mean to kill the bicyclist.
   B: No, she didn't. That's why she's been charged ....
5. A: He took the money from her bag?
   B: Yes, but they caught him, and he's been ....

82.3 How safe and secure are you? Answer these questions *yes* or *no*.

1. Do you often walk in areas that are not very safe?	*yes* = 1	*no* = 0
2. Do you often walk by yourself in these areas late at night?	*yes* = 2	*no* = 0
3. Do you wear a money belt or money pouch when you go out?	*yes* = 0	*no* = 1
4. Do you wear an expensive watch or expensive jewelry?	*yes* = 1	*no* = 0
5. Do you check doors and windows before you go out when your home is empty?	*yes* = 0	*no* = 2
6. Do you have a burglar alarm?	*yes* = 0	*no* = 1
7. Do you leave lights on when you go out?	*yes* = 0	*no* = 1
8. Is there someone who protects the building while you are out?	*yes* = 0	*no* = 2
9. Do you have a safe in your home?	*yes* = 0	*no* = 1

Now add up your score: less than 3 = very, very safe; 3–5 = fairly safe; 6–8 = you should be a lot more careful; more than 8 = you are in danger!

82.4 Fill in the blanks with a logical word.

1. Do you think the police should .... guns?
2. Do you think the police should be .... to stop and question people without a special reason?
3. Do you agree with capital .... for certain crimes, such as murder?
4. Do you think tougher punishments will help .... crime?

What is your opinion on these questions? Discuss them with another person, if possible.

UNIT
83   **Politics**

Types of government

democracy: Leaders are chosen by the people.
monarchy: A country ruled by a king or queen. There are countries that have a
    monarchy, but the monarch is not the ruler, e.g., the United Kingdom.
dictatorship: One person rules the country with total power. This person is called
    a **dictator.**

B   **Political beliefs**

Abstract noun	*Personal noun/adjective*
conservatism	conservative
socialism	socialist
liberalism	liberal
communism	communist

C   **Political positions**

What does it mean to be a **liberal** or a **conservative?** Often it means different
things in different countries, but people in the U.S. sometimes talk about
someone's political position like this:

on the left /	**middle of the road /**	**on the right /**
left of center [liberal]	**in the center** [moderate]	**right of center** [conservative]

D   **Elections**

In a democracy, people **vote for / elect** [choose in a formal way] the person, called
a **candidate,** that they prefer, for president, senator, governor, mayor, etc. Usually
at least two candidates **run for office** [try to be elected]. They do this in an
election. In many countries, national elections **take place / are held** [happen]
every four or five years. Candidates usually belong to a **political party,** e.g.,
Republican, Democrat.

Forty-six percent **voted for** the Democrats in the last Congressional **election.** [The
    Democrats got 46% of the **votes.**]
The President **was elected** two years ago.

E   **Political systems and government**

Political systems are different all over the world. In the U.S., the President is
chosen in national elections every four years. The **Congress** [the legislature /
group of lawmakers] is elected separately, and sometimes (though not usually),
the President and Congress may belong to different political parties. This type of
system is called **presidential government.** In some countries, such as the U.K.,
when a political party wins a **majority** [51% or more] of **seats** [official positions
in Parliament] in a national election, their **leader** [the head of the party] becomes
Prime Minister, and they are **in power.** This system is called **parliamentary
government.**

Exercises

83.1 Complete this word-building table. Use a dictionary to help you, if necessary.

Abstract noun	Person	Adjective
politics	politician	political
dictatorship	....	....
socialism	....	....
conservatism	....	....
liberalism	....	....

83.2 Fill in the blanks to complete this description of the political systems in the U.S. and the U.K. Write one word in each blank.

In the U.S., the President and the (1) ..Congress.......... are elected separately. The political (2) .... with more than 51% of the seats has a (3) .... in Congress; the President may or may not belong to the same party. Presidential (4) .... take place every four years.

In the U.K., elections are (5) .... every five years. (An election could take place sooner, but five years is the maximum.) The political (6) .... in the U.K. is different from that in the U.S.; in the U.K., the political (7) .... that wins a (8) .... of the seats in Parliament will be in power, and their leader becomes (9) .... Minister.

83.3 Answer these questions about your own country. If possible, ask someone else the same questions.

1. Which party is in power at the moment?
2. When was this party elected?
3. Who is the leader of this party?
4. Is this person the President or Prime Minister of your country?
5. How many major (important) political parties are there?
6. Do you think the party that is currently in power will win the next election?
7. Would you describe yourself as left of center, right of center, or moderate?
8. Do you think your political views have changed much during your lifetime? Do you think they might change in the future? (How?)

83.4 How to increase your English vocabulary in politics:

Buy three newspapers (in English if possible, or in your own language), and find the same story about politics in each one. Read the articles and underline any words that appear in all of them, and any other words you think are important.

If you are reading a newspaper in English, try to guess the meaning of these words from the context, and then use a dictionary to check. This exercise is equally useful if you read articles in your own language. Use a bilingual dictionary to find the English translation/explanation for your words. Then look them up in an English-English dictionary too.

UNIT 84 Bureaucracy

A What is it?

Bureaucracy refers to official systems with rules and procedures used by officials [**bureaucrats**] in an organization or a government. For many people it is a negative word, because it often means unnecessary rules, waiting in long lines, and lots of documents and forms.

B Documents

When you need to **obtain** [get] or show documents, it is important that you know the names of them. Here are some important documents:

passport: official identification that allows you to leave your country and enter others
driver's license: the official document that permits you to drive on public roads
visa: gives you permission to enter, pass through, or leave a country
certificates: official pieces of paper stating certain facts, e.g., a **birth certificate** gives
　facts about your birth; a **marriage certificate** states that two people are married

Officials often **check** [look at and examine] your documents, e.g., the police may check your driver's license; customs officials may check your passport. Sometimes you will be asked for **identification/ID** [any document that shows who you are; usually a driver's license or passport is adequate for identification].

Some documents are for a fixed period of time, e.g., a visa may be for six months. At the end of that time, your visa **runs out / expires** [it finishes / comes to an end]. If you want to stay in the country, you must **renew** it [get a new one for a further period of time]. You can renew a visa, a passport, a membership card for a club, etc.

C Forms

Sometimes you need to **fill in / fill out forms** [write in information in the spaces].

landing card: a form you may have to fill out when you enter another country
registration form: a form you often fill in when you take a course or go to school
application form: a form to write details about yourself, often when applying for
　a job, for a credit card, for admission to a school, etc.
income tax forms: forms you must fill out when you pay your income taxes

With almost all forms, you will need to **sign** them [write your signature], e.g.:

signed *Luis Santos*

D Formal language

Forms often ask for the following information:

date of birth (When were you born?)
country of origin (Where do you come from?)
sex (Are you male or female?)
marital status (Are you single or married?)
date of arrival/departure (When did you arrive/leave?)

Exercises

84.1 Write at least two words that can be used before these nouns.

1. *identification* .... card

3. .... license

2. .... certificate

4. .... form

84.2 Complete these sentences.

1. Will you need to *get/obtain* .... a visa if you go to Canada?
2. I was surprised that nobody .... my passport when we arrived in France.
3. Could you .... this form, please?
4. They sent the form back to me because I had forgotten to .... it at the bottom.
5. Unfortunately my visa .... next week, so if I want to stay here I'll have to .... it. But I don't think it'll be a problem.
6. You should get there early because there are always long ...., and you may have to wait a long time.
7. I want to take an English course in California, so I wrote to a few schools and asked them to send me an .... form.

84.3 How many of these documents do you have?

a passport   an insurance card
a driver's license   a marriage certificate
a birth certificate   a hunting or fishing license

84.4 Complete these sentences with a logical paraphrase.

1. What's your date of birth? In other words, when *were you born* ....?
2. What's your country of origin? ....?
3. What's your sex? ....?
4. What's your marital status? ....?
5. What was your date of arrival? ....?
6. When's your date of departure? ....?

84.5 Here are some complaints people often make about bureaucracy. Have you ever had these problems? Which ones? What other problems have you had with bureaucracy?

1. waiting in one line, then discovering you should be in another line
2. not being able to get through on the telephone
3. delays, e.g., getting a new passport
4. being asked to explain the same information over and over again to different officials, especially over the telephone
5. officials losing information you have given them
6. officials who act like police officers

War and peace

A

The outbreak [start] of war

Wars often start because of a **conflict** [strong disagreement] between countries or groups of people, about **territory** [land that belongs to one group or country]. Look at the diagram on the right and read the description on the left.

Country A **invades** country B [A enters B by force and in large numbers], and **captures** (also **takes / takes control of**) the city of X. Soldiers from country B have to **retreat** [go backward; ≠ **advance**] to the city of Y. A's army and air force continue to **attack** the city of Y [take violent action to damage it], but B's soldiers **defend** it [take action to protect it] successfully.

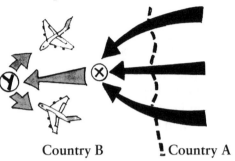

Country B   Country A

B

A war zone

The area around the city of Y is now the main **war zone** [the area where the fighting is happening]. Country B has asked for help from its **allies** [countries that are friends with country B]. The allies send **aid** [help] in the form of extra **troops** [large groups of soldiers] and **supplies** [food and other things that are needed, e.g., blankets and medicine]. There is

shelling [firing of **guns** and **explosives**] of the city every day, and hundreds of soldiers are either killed or **wounded** [injured]. Many **civilians** [ordinary people who are not in the army] are also killed.

C

Peace talks

For the civilians who are still **alive** [≠ dead], the situation gets worse. As winter approaches, food supplies **run out** [they are almost gone/finished]. The soldiers get tired, and both sides begin to see that neither side can win the war; they agree to meet for **peace talks** [*pl.*, talks to try to negotiate a **peace settlement** / an end to the war]. Finally they agree to a **cease-fire** [a period of no fighting].

D

Terrorism

Terrorism is violent action for political reasons. People who do this are **terrorists,** and a common terrorist crime is **hijacking** [taking control of a bus, train, ship, or plane; the people on board then become prisoners]. The main purpose of hijacking is to use the prisoners (called **hostages**) in order to **bargain** for something [to demand something in exchange for the hostages]. The terrorists may agree to **release** the hostages [permit them to go free] if a government agrees to give the terrorists money or release other terrorists.

Exercises

85.1 Match the words on the left with the correct definition on the right.

1. ally	a. land controlled by a country
2. release	b. stop fighting
3. conflict	c. permit to go free
4. troops	d. injure
5. invade	e. large groups of soldiers
6. wound	f. friendly country
7. territory	g. strong disagreement
8. cease-fire	h. enter another country by force, in large numbers

85.2 Use opposites to contradict what the speaker says.

1. A: Is the soldier dead?
   B: No, he's ..*still alive*...

2. A: Will they agree to a cease-fire?
   B: No, they'll ....

3. A: Do you think the army will try to advance when the weather improves?
   B: No, I think ....

4. A: Do the people still have lots of food?
   B: No, they're beginning to ....

5. A: Is the town mostly full of soldiers?
   B: No, they're ....

6. A: Do you think they'll keep the hostages for a long time?
   B: No, I'm sure they'll ....

85.3 When we repeat an idea in a text, we often try to avoid using the same word twice. Read this text and find examples of words being used as synonyms for previous ideas. The first one has been done for you (food and medicine = supplies).

THERE is a desperate need for food and medicine, but with the town surrounded, the trucks are unable to bring in essential supplies. We have seen ordinary people in the street giving some of their meager rations of food to the soldiers who are defending them, but very soon the troops will be just as hungry as the civilians if the situation gets any worse.

Meanwhile, the center of the town is being slowly destroyed. There is almost daily shelling of the buildings that still stand, and this morning we witnessed gunmen firing at almost anyone who dared to go out into the streets. One old woman was hit in the leg, and we saw at least two others who were badly wounded as well.

Aid agencies have appealed to the soldiers to allow them to enter the town, but so far the General in command has refused to let anyone in, including doctors and nurses. Many fear it is now only a matter of days before the town is captured, and if this happens, the army could take control of the whole region within weeks.

85.4 Can you answer these questions with two reasons for each one? If possible, discuss your answers with someone else.

1. Why do terrorists take hostages?
2. Why do some governments always refuse to agree to terrorist demands?

Pollution and the environment

A   Important definitions

Many people are worried about the **environment** [the air, water, and land around us] as a result of the **harmful** [dangerous/**damaging**] effects of human activity. Some of these activities cause **pollution** [dirty air, land, and water], and some are **destroying** the environment [damaging it so badly that soon parts will not exist]. Here are some of the problems:

the ozone layer: a layer of gases that stops the sun's harmful radiation from reaching the earth. Recent research shows that there are now holes in parts of the ozone layer.

the greenhouse effect: when gases (from pollution) trap the sun's heat, in the same way that the glass of a **greenhouse** [a glass building for growing plants in winter] holds in heat. This may lead to **global warming.** (See below.)

global warming: an increase in world temperature caused, in part, by an increase in carbon dioxide and other gases.

acid rain: rain that contains dangerous chemicals; this is caused by smoke from factories.

B   Common causes of damage

smoke from **factories**

car exhaust fumes

dumping [throwing away] industrial **waste** [unwanted material] in seas and rivers

aerosol cans (also called **spray cans**): Some of these contain **CFCs** [a type of chemical], which can damage the ozone layer.

C   Protecting [stopping damage to] the environment

- Don't **throw away** bottles, newspapers, etc. Instead, take them to a **recycling center/bin** so they can be **recycled** [used again].
- Walk, bicycle, or use **public transportation** (buses, subways, etc.), if possible.
- Join a **carpool** [a group of car owners who agree to share their cars; a different car is used for the group each day] if you must drive to work or school.
- Don't **waste** [use badly] **resources** [e.g., water, gas]. Try to **conserve/save** [≠ waste] them.

Note: A **resource** is a valuable possession. There are **natural resources,** e.g., water and gold, and **human resources,** e.g., knowledge and skills. These phrases are often plural.

Exercises

86.1 Fill in the blanks to form a compound noun or phrase from the opposite page.

1. the ..*ozone*.............. layer
2. .... rain
3. aerosol ....
4. .... transportation
5. .... warming
6. .... fumes
7. the greenhouse ....
8. natural or human ....

86.2 Complete these tables. If necessary, use a dictionary to help you.

Noun	Verb
waste	..*waste*.............
....	conserve
....	destroy
pollution	....
damage	....

Noun	Adjective
damage	....
....	environmental
harm	....
danger	....
....	natural

86.3 Complete the definitions.

1. Conservation is the protection of natural things, e.g., *plants* and ....
2. Acid rain is rain that contains dangerous chemicals. It is caused by

   ....
3. The ozone layer is a layer of gases that stops dangerous radiation from the sun
   from reaching ....
4. The greenhouse effect takes place when certain gases in the atmosphere trap

   ....
5. Global warming is an increase in ....
6. CFCs (chlorofluorocarbons) are a type of chemical that ....

   ....

86.4 If we want to protect the environment, there are certain things we should and shouldn't do. Complete these two lists.

We should:
..*recycle*............... paper, bottles, and clothes.
.... public transportation instead of cars, if possible.
.... water and energy.

We shouldn't:
.... paper, bottles, and clothes.
.... the ozone layer.
.... water and energy.

86.5 Test your knowledge of conservation issues. *True* or *false*?

1. CFCs protect the ozone layer.
2. Aluminum cans cannot be recycled.
3. A hole in the ozone layer could increase skin cancer.
4. Cutting down trees increases carbon dioxide in the atmosphere.

Air travel

Departure

At the airport, you first go to the **ticket counter** to **check in** [report that you have arrived]. The **ticket agent** [airline representative] **checks** [examines] your ticket and **identification (ID)** [any document that shows who you are] and gives you a **boarding pass** for the plane with the **gate** number (e.g., gate 14) and your seat number on it. If you have luggage to **check** [the luggage is taken on the plane separately], you are given a **claim ticket** [a piece of paper that shows the luggage is yours]. If you are taking an

international flight, an official checks your passport. International passengers can buy things in the **duty-free shops** without paying sales tax, e.g., perfume, watches, and packaged foods. About half an hour or so before **takeoff**, you **board** [get on] the plane and find your seat. If you have **carry-on luggage,** you can **store** [put] it under the seat in front of you or in the **overhead compartment** above you. The plane then **taxis** [moves slowly] toward the **runway,** and when it has permission to **take off** [leave the ground], it accelerates along the runway and takes off.

Note: The verb **to taxi** is generally used only in this context.

The flight

You may want or need to understand announcements; these come from the **captain** [the pilot] or from the **cabin crew / flight attendants** [people responsible for the safety and comfort of the passengers]:

Please **fasten your seat belts** and put your seat
   in the **upright position.**
We are now **cruising** [flying at a steady speed]
   at an **altitude** [height] of 30,000 feet.
We would like to **remind** you [ask you to
   remember] that this is a nonsmoking flight.
The **flight attendants** are now coming through the aircraft with **landing cards.**
   (These are cards you may have to fill out when you enter certain countries.)
At this time, please **discontinue the use of** [stop using] and **stow** [put away] any
   portable electronic items [electronic articles that you can carry, e.g., a laptop].

Arrival

When the plane **lands** [arrives on the ground], you have to wait for it to stop / to come to a full stop. When the doors are open, you **get off** the plane and walk through the **terminal building** [where passengers arrive and depart] and go to the **baggage claim** area, where you get your luggage. After international flights, you then **pass through customs** [where your bags are checked for illegal goods or large purchases]. If you are lucky, you can then get a bus, taxi, or train to the center of town without waiting too long. You can also **rent** a car at most airports.

Exercises

87.1 Complete the words or phrases below using words in the box.

off	counter	free	pass
in	luggage	claim	compartment

1. ticket ~~counter~~
2. baggage ....
3. carry-on ....
4. boarding ....
5. duty- ....
6. overhead ....
7. take ....
8. check- ....

87.2 What do you call . . .

1. the place where you go when you arrive at the airport with your luggage?
   ticket counter
2. the card they give you with the seat number on it?
3. the bags you carry onto the plane with you?
4. the place above your head where you can store luggage you took on the plane?
5. the part of the airport where the plane accelerates and takes off?
6. the people who take care of your safety and comfort on the plane?
7. the part of the airport you walk through when you arrive or depart?
8. the place where you get your luggage after you land?

87.3 Complete this part of a letter about an unpleasant flight.

> Dear Tom,
>
> I've just arrived in Seoul, but I'm still recovering from a really terrible flight. We (1) *took off / departed* two hours late because of bad weather, and then over the ocean we hit more bad weather. The (2) .... announced that we had to (3) .... our seat belts and remain seated, which got me worried, and for half an hour we (4) .... through a terrible storm. It was still raining and very windy when we (5) .... in Korea, and I was really glad to (6) .... the plane and get into the terminal.
>
> Fortunately things have improved since then, but I really hope the return (7) .... is a lot better.

87.4 Think about the whole experience of flying (from check-in to the time you leave the airport at your destination) and answer these questions. If possible, discuss your answers with someone else.

1. What is the most interesting part, and what is the most boring part of a flight?
2. Where do you often have delays, and why?
3. Is there any part that frightens or worries you?
4. What do you usually do during flights?
5. Do you always eat the food they serve you?
6. Is there one thing that would improve flying and make the experience better?

Hotels

A ### Hotels and other lodgings

a hotel: You pay for your room, but meals are usually extra. Most hotels have a
  restaurant and/or a coffee shop.
a motel: Less expensive than a hotel. Parking is free; often you can park your car
  right outside your room. There's usually no restaurant.
a bed and breakfast (B&B): A room in someone's home or in a small inn.
  Breakfast is included in the price.
a youth hostel: Very inexpensive; you share a room with other people.

B ### Staying at a hotel

We stayed at Harrah's Hotel for three nights in July,
but I **made a reservation / reserved a room** [arranged
for a room to be held] three months **in advance**
[earlier; in other words, in April] because it was the
middle of the tourist **season** [period of time]. When
we arrived, we **checked in at the registration desk / at
the front desk;** then the **bellman** [porter] took our
suitcases up to the room. I gave him a **tip** (n., v.) – $1
for each suitcase. The staff was very friendly – we had
a very nice **maid** [a woman who cleans the room, or
cleaner for a man or woman] – and the room was
very comfortable. The only problem was with the TV, which didn't **work** [function]
very well. (You could also say "There was **something wrong with** the TV.")

C ### Useful words and expressions

a single room: For one person.
a double room: For two people. You can ask for two beds
  or a **king-size** [extra large] bed. **Double occupancy**
  means two **guests** [people] stay in the room. Some hotels
  advertise room rates in this way: "$50 per person,
  double occupancy." [The price is $100.]
a nonsmoking room/floor: Smoking isn't allowed.

A king-size bed.

Could I **make a reservation / reserve a room / book a room** for next Thursday?
Could I have **a wake-up call** at 7 a.m., please? [Could you call to wake me at 7
  a.m.?]
Could you **put it on my bill,** please? [add the cost to the bill, e.g., for a meal you
  order in your room]
I'm **checking out.** [leaving the hotel at the end of your stay] Could I **pay my bill,**
  please? [pay for everything]
Could you **call** [telephone for] a taxi for me to go to the airport?
Are you **full / fully booked** [completely full, no rooms available] all next week?
Is breakfast **included?** [Does the price include breakfast?]
Where's the **elevator?** [the machine that takes you from one floor to another]
Excuse me. **How do I get to** the subway station from here?

Exercises

88.1 Put these sentences in a logical order.

I reserved a single room at the hotel.

1. I watched TV until I fell asleep.
2. I paid my bill and checked out.
3. I checked in at the registration desk.
4. I went up to my room.
5. I had a wake-up call at seven o'clock.
6. I reserved a single room at the hotel.
7. I arrived at the hotel.
8. I got up and took a shower.
9. I had breakfast.
10. I tipped the bellman who took my luggage upstairs.

88.2 What would you say in these situations?

1. You want to stay in a hotel for two nights next week with your husband/wife.
   Neither one of you smokes. You call the hotel. What do you ask or say?
   I'd like to make a reservation for a double room, nonsmoking, with a king-size bed for two nights, next Thursday and Friday. or
   Do you have a nonsmoking double room with two beds available for next Friday and Saturday?

2. You are at the hotel registration desk, and you are planning to leave in about 15 minutes. What could you ask the clerk?
   ....

3. You want to wake up at 7 a.m., but you don't have an alarm clock. You call the front desk. What do you ask?
   ....

4. You have coffee in the hotel lobby. The waiter asks how you want to pay. What's your reply?
   ....

5. When you turn on the shower in your room, the water comes out very, very slowly. What could you say at the front desk or when you call downstairs?
   ....

6. You want to go to the nearest bank but don't know where it is. What do you ask at the front desk?
   ....

88.3 You are staying at a good hotel in your country. Would you expect to have the following? What else would or wouldn't you expect?

1. a room without a private bathroom
2. a hair dryer in the bathroom
3. a color television in the room
4. a fax machine in the room
5. a coffee maker in the room
6. air conditioning in the room

If possible, compare your answers with someone from a different country.

A sightseeing vacation

A   Sightseeing

You may **do a little sightseeing** on vacation, or you may **do a lot of sightseeing.** You might go to a museum or an art gallery, or see/visit some of these things:

statue

famous building

palace

cathedral   temple   market

Many people **go on a sightseeing tour** of a town (usually on a bus); they can also **take a tour of the palace / the cathedral / the art gallery,** etc. When you go sight-seeing, it helps to buy a **guidebook** [a book of information for tourists] and a **map.**

B   Things that tourists often do on vacation

go shopping
take photographs/pictures
spend a lot of / lots of **money**
buy **souvenirs** [typical products from the country]
get lost [lose their way]
go out most evenings [go to different places for
    social reasons, e.g., restaurant or disco]
have a good/great time [enjoy themselves]

C   Describing "places"

The word **place** is very common; it can describe a building, an area, a town, or a country: Quebec City is a lovely **place** [city], and we found a really nice **place** [hotel, etc.] to stay. The city is full of interesting **places** [areas/buildings].

Venice is beautiful, but it's always **packed** [very crowded / full] with tourists in
    summer.
New York is very **cosmopolitan.** [full of people from different countries and cultures]
Puerto Rico has lots of **historical monuments.** [places, e.g., forts, built long ago]
Many beautiful cities have become very **touristy.** [negative: "too much tourism"]
São Paolo is a really **lively** place [full of life and activity], and the **nightlife** is great.

Note: If you want to ask if it is "a good idea" to visit a place, you can use **worth + -ing:**

A: If I go to Mexico, is it **worth** spending a few days in Guadalajara?
B: Yes, definitely. And if you want to travel around, it's **worth** renting a car.

Exercises

89.1 Read this letter that John wrote to his family while he was on vacation. Write a word or a phrase in each space.

July 19th

Hi everyone. I've been in Paris for almost a week now and I'm having a
(1) ..*great time*.......... I spent the first few days (2) .... –
the Eiffel Tower, Notre Dame, and all the usual tourist attractions. Most
places are absolutely (3) .... with tourists (it's the time of the
year, I suppose), so yesterday I decided to go (4) .... and
bought a few (5) ....

Today I've been to a couple of very interesting art (6) I
got (7) .... on my way back to the hotel, but it didn't matter
because I discovered a really fascinating (8) .... with lots of
little stalls selling just about everything from apples to antiques.

I ate in the hotel the first night, but usually I (9) .... and
have dinner in a restaurant – the food is fantastic. I guess I've
(10) .... a lot of money, but it's a great place. I've
(11) .... lots of photos, so you'll be able to see for yourself when
I get back home on the 24th.

See you then,
John

89.2 Which of these places do you like to visit when you're on vacation?

museums	movie theaters	markets
discos	theme parks	restaurants
ancient ruins	tourist shops	churches/cathedrals/temples
art galleries	castles/palaces	the theater / the opera / the ballet / concerts

89.3 Confirm the information in the questions without repeating the same words and phrases. Use words and phrases from the opposite page.

1. A: You have quite a few pictures, don't you?   B: *Yes, we took lots of photos.*
2. A: There's a big mix of people in Toronto, isn't there?   B: Yes, it's very ....
3. A: Was it very crowded?   B: Yes, it was ....
4. A: There's a lot to do in the evenings, isn't there?   B: Yes, the ....
5. A: Did you enjoy yourselves?   B: Yes, we ....

89.4 Without using one place more than twice, can you name a town or city in your country that is . . .

lively?	packed with tourists in summer?	very touristy?
cosmopolitan?	famous for its historical monuments?	not worth visiting?

At the beach and in the country

A

Places to stay

When people **go on vacation,** they stay in **various** places [different places]. Some go to hotels, and others rent a "vacation home" – a house or **cabin** [a small wooden house, often in the woods or mountains]. Some prefer sleeping in a **tent** at a **campsite** [an outdoor area for staying a short time].

a cabin

a tent

B

At the beach

Many people spend their vacation at **beach resorts** [towns by the sea for vacationers, e.g., Acapulco, St. Tropez, Okinawa], where they can spend most of their time on the beach. Some people enjoy swimming, others love **sunbathing** [**lying on the beach** in order to **get a suntan**]. If you like sunbathing, you should use **suntan lotion** or **sunscreen/sunblock** to **protect your skin.** If you don't have any protection, you may get a **sunburn,** which is painful and can be dangerous.

Swimming can also be dangerous if there are **rocks** under the water or if the sea is **rough,** e.g., with big **waves.**

cliff

sea

yacht

waves

beach umbrella

rocks

sand

beach

C

In the country

People who live in cities often like to **get away** [leave the place where they live] on weekends or in the summer and enjoy the **peace and quiet** [calm and tranquillity] of **the country** (also called the **countryside**). Some people just like to **put their feet up** [relax and do nothing] and occasionally go for **a stroll** [a slow casual walk], while others enjoy **hiking** [long walks in the country, often across hills and valleys]. And the countryside is a great place to **have a picnic** [eat a prepared meal of cold food outside].

Note: Learners sometimes say "I love to be in the nature." This is not correct in English. Instead we say: "I love being close to nature."   *or*   "I love being in the country."

Exercises

90.1 Write at least five words beginning with *sun*. Use a dictionary for extra ideas. You can check your answers on the opposite page and in the index.

sun *tan* ....   sun ....   sun ....

sun ....   sun ....

90.2 Match a word from the left with a word from the right to form six words or phrases.

1. sandy   waves
2. suntan   bathe
3. beach   beach
4. steep   lotion
5. sun   umbrella
6. big   cliff

90.3 Now answer these questions.

1. Why do most people go to beach resorts?   *to spend time lying on the beach, sunbathing, and swimming*
2. Why do people sunbathe?
3. Why do they use sunblock or sunscreen?
4. How does it feel if you get a sunburn?
5. What sport requires big waves?

90.4 Write a logical word or phrase in each blank in this paragraph.

I live and work in the city, but I like to (1) ..*get away*.............. on weekends, if possible. My parents have a small house in the (2) ...., about 60 miles to the north, and it's a great place to go if you want some peace and (3) .... In the summer, you can just (4) .... by the pool during the hottest part of the day, then in the evening go for a (5) .... through the town or over the fields. Sometimes we go out for the whole day and have a (6) .... somewhere, by the lake or next to one of the many vineyards.

90.5 Fill in the blanks with a logical word. (One word for each space.)

1. Would you prefer a vacation at a beach ..*resort*............... or in the country?
2. Would you prefer to stay in one place, or would you rather [prefer to] go to .... places?
3. Would you prefer to stay in a hotel or a vacation ....?
4. Would you prefer to eat in a restaurant or have a .... outdoors?
5. Would you prefer somewhere that is lively, or would you rather go to a place where there is .... and quiet?

Look at the questions again. Which would you prefer? If possible, discuss your answers with someone else.

Time

A   Prepositions: *at, on, in*

at a specific time: e.g., at 8 o'clock, at 3:30, at midnight
on a day: e.g., on Monday, on July 14, on the third day, on weekdays/weekends
in a period: e.g., in May, in 2001, in the morning/afternoon/evening [*but:* **at night**]

B   Words that are often confused

I will stay here **until/till** she calls. [I will go after she calls.]
I will be in the office **until/till** 4 o'clock. [I will leave the office at 4:00.]
I will be in the office **by** 4 o'clock. [I will arrive at the office not later than 4:00.]

I've worked in this office **for** six months. (**for** + a period of time)
I've worked in this office **since** May. (**since** + a point in time, i.e., a day, year, etc.)

I worked for a newspaper **during** the war / the summer. (This tells you "when.")
I worked for a newspaper **for** four years / **for** six months. (This tells you "how long.") [*not* I worked for a newspaper during four years.]

Note: **During** a period may mean a part of that period or the whole period, e.g., "during the war" can mean part of the war or the whole war. The context usually makes it clear, but if we want to stress or emphasize that an action occupied the whole period, we often use **throughout**, e.g., It rained throughout the night. [It didn't stop raining.]

I'm going back to Brazil **in** ten days. [ten days from now]
We arranged our next meeting **for** April 7th. [to be on April 7th]

C   Approximate times: past and future

I've known my dentist **for ages** [for a long time], but I haven't had a checkup **recently/lately** [e.g., in the last few months].
I haven't seen Tom **recently/lately**. [e.g., in the last few days or weeks]
I used to go to an Australian dentist, but that was **a long time ago.** [e.g., 5–10 years ago]
My sister went to the dentist **the other day.** [a few days ago]
This temporary tooth will be OK **for the time being.** [for now / until I get a permanent one]

D   Periods of time

There are 60 **seconds** in a minute, 60 minutes in an hour, 24 hours in a day, 7 days in a week, about 4 weeks in a **month,** about 52 weeks in a year, 10 years in a **decade,** 100 years in a **century,** 1,000 years in a **millennium.**

E   Time passing: *take* and *last*

My English course **lasts** ten weeks. [It continues for ten weeks.]
How long does the movie **last?** [How long is it from the beginning to the end?]
It **takes** me [I need] half an hour to get to school.
We can walk, but it'll **take** [we'll need] a long time.

Exercises

91.1 Complete the paragraph with *at, on,* or *in.*

> There's one bus from the city that gets here (1) .at..... 10:00 (2) .... the
> morning, and then another that arrives (3) .... 4:00 (4) .... the afternoon.
> That's (5) .... weekdays, but (6) .... weekends the schedule is a little
> different. (7) .... Saturday there are still two buses, but the second one arrives
> (8) .... 5:30. (9) .... Sunday there is just the one bus (10) .... 2:00. And
> (11) .... the winter, the buses don't run at all (12) .... Sundays.

91.2 Circle the correct answers.

1. The teacher told us to finish our homework by / until Monday.
2. We can't leave by / until the others get back.
3. I've been in the army for / since I was eighteen.
4. They've worked here for / since / during six months.
5. She's going back to Thailand in / until three months.
6. He left the office during / throughout the lunch break.
7. I made a reservation at the restaurant by / for next Saturday. I hope that's OK.
8. It was hot during / throughout August; we didn't have one day under 90 degrees.

91.3 Can you complete these sentences with the correct number?

1. Some athletes can run 100 meters in less than *ten*..................... seconds.
2. The Olympic Games usually last about .... weeks.
3. Picasso was born in the ....th century.
4. President Kennedy died in 1963. That's .... years ago.
5. It takes approximately .... hours to fly from Tokyo to New York.

91.4 Replace the underlined time expressions with "approximate" time expressions.

1. I went to the library three days ago.   *a few days ago*
2. This dictionary isn't great, but it'll be OK until I'm more advanced.
3. I haven't been to the movies for the last three weeks.
4. And I haven't been to a concert for three or four years.
5. I went to Hawaii with my parents, but that was ten years ago.

91.5 Complete these sentences about yourself.

1. On weekdays I usually get up at .... and leave home at
   ....
2. I always brush my teeth in .... and at ....
3. I don't go to school/work on ....
4. I usually take a vacation in ....
5. I have been in my current school/job for ....
6. I have been studying English since ....
7. I haven't spoken English since ....
8. It takes me .... to get to school/work.

Numbers

A Cardinal numbers

379 = three **hundred** (and) seventy nine
5,084 = five **thousand** (and) eighty-four
2,860 = two thousand eight hundred (and) sixty
470,000 = four hundred (and) seventy thousand
2,550,000 = two **million,** five hundred (and) fifty thousand
3,000,000,000 = three **billion**

Note: There is no plural **-s** after *hundred, thousand, million,* and *billion* when these words are part of a number. By themselves, they can be plural, e.g., **thousands** of people; **millions** of insects.

B Ordinal numbers and dates

We write **March 4** (or March 4th), but say **March (the) fourth** or **the fourth of March.**
1905 = **nineteen oh five**
2010 = **two thousand (and) ten** or **twenty ten**

C Fractions and decimals

1¼ = one and **a quarter / a fourth**
1½ = one and **a half**
1¾ = one and **three quarters/fourths**
1⅓ = one and **a third**

1.75 = one **point** seven five
1.25 = one point two five
1.5 = one point five
1.33 = one point three three

D Percentages

26% = twenty-six **percent**
More than 50% is the **majority;** less than 50% is the **minority.**

E Arithmetic

There are four basic processes for doing [calculating] math problems:

+ addition   6 + 4 = 10 (six **plus/and** four **equals/is** ten)
− subtraction   6 − 4 = 2 (six **minus** four equals/is two)
× multiplication   6 × 4 = 24 (six **times / multiplied by** four equals/is twenty-four)
÷ division   4 ÷ 2 = 2 (four **divided by** two equals/is two)

F Saying "0"

telephone numbers: 555-0724 = five five five, **oh** seven two four
mathematics: 0.7 = **zero** point seven / point seven; 6.02 = six point **oh** two
temperature: −10 degrees = ten (degrees) below **zero** / minus ten (degrees)
most sports games: 2–0 = two (to) **nothing** / two **oh** / two (to) **zero**

G Talking numbers

The buildings have **odd** numbers (e.g., 3, 5, 7) on the left side of the street and **even** numbers (e.g., 4, 6, 8) on the right.
I got 16 **out of** 20 on our last test. *16/20*

Exercises

92.1 How do you say these numbers in English? Write your answers after each one.

1. 462 *four hundred (and) sixty-two* ....
2. 2½ ....
3. 2,345 ....
4. 6.75 ....
5. 0.25 ....
6. 3⅓ ....
7. 1,250,000 ....
8. 10.04 ....
9. 47% ....
10. September 10 ....
11. July 4 ....
12. 555-8077 (phone number) ....
13. −5 Fahrenheit ....
14. In 1903 ....
15. In 2036 ....

Now practice saying them. If possible, record yourself saying them and then record someone who speaks English very well. Listen to both. How do you sound?

92.2 Correct the mistakes in these sentences.

                                                        thousand
1. After the game, I heard the crowd was over twenty thousands.
2. We arrived on the ten September.
3. I got twenty-five from forty on my test.
4. My birthday is thirty-one August.
5. The class is two and half hours long.

92.3 Write answers to these math problems.

1. 23 and 36 is *59* .
2. 24 times 8 equals ....
3. 80 minus 20 is ....
4. 65 divided by 13 equals ....
5. Add 10 and 6, multiply by 8, then subtract 40, and divide by 11. What number do you get?
6. Divide 33 by 11, multiply by 7, add 10, and subtract 16. What number is left?

92.4 Answer these questions. Write your answers in words.

1. When were you born?
2. How much do you weigh?
3. What is the number of the apartment or house where you live?
4. Is that an odd or even number?
5. What is the approximate population of your city or town?
6. What is the approximate population of your country?
7. What is the normal temperature of a healthy person?

Distance, size, and dimension

A Distance

How far is it?	**Not very far.**
Is it **a long way**?	No, **just around the corner.** / No, **a short walk.** [very near]
Is it **very far**?	No, **not far.** / No, just **a five- or ten-minute walk.** [fairly near]
Is it a long way?	Yeah, **a fairly long way.** / Yeah, **over a mile.**
Is it very far?	Yes, it's **a long way.** / Yes, **it's miles.** / Yes, it's **too far to walk.**

B Size and dimension

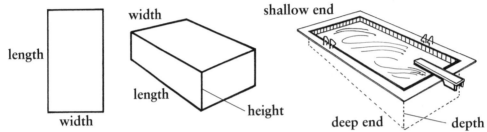

We can describe size using the nouns above or the adjectives formed from them, like this:

What's the **length/width/height/depth/size** of . . .?   *or*
How **long/wide/high/tall/deep/big** is . . .?

Note:
- We generally use **tall** to describe people, trees, and buildings; and **high** to describe mountains. We also say **high-rise buildings.**
- Notice that in the answer to these questions, an adjective follows the measurement:

  The yard is about thirty feet **wide.** [**The width** is about thirty feet.]

C Size in people and things

a **tall** girl [≠ a **short** girl]
a **fat** person [≠ a **thin/slim** person] (See Unit 44 for more details.)
a **long** book [many pages] [≠ a **short** book]
a **deep** lake [many feet deep] [≠ a **shallow** lake]

a **thick** book [≠ a **thin** book]

a **wide** road [≠ a **narrow** road]

Note: We can use **big** or **large** to describe size in English, but not **great.** For English-speaking people, **great** *(informal)* often means "wonderful," e.g., a great movie. But we can use **great** before **big** to say that something is very big, e.g., a **great big** dog. If you want to ask about size in clothes, you can say: **What size are you?** *or* **What size (shoes) do you take/wear?** If you don't know, you need someone to **measure** you.

Exercises

93.1 Think about the room/place you are in now and answer these questions, using some of the expressions from the opposite page.

1. How far is it to the nearest store?
2. How far is it to a bank?
3. Is it very far to the nearest bus stop?
4. Is it very far to a post office?
5. Is it a long way to the nearest swimming pool?
6. Is it a long way to the next big town or city?
7. How far is the nearest train station?
8. Is it far to the downtown area?

If possible, ask someone else the same questions and compare your answers.

93.2 Write down eight different questions you could ask about the distance, size, or dimensions of the person and things in the pictures.

Example: How tall is she?

93.3 Contradict [say the opposite of] the speaker in the sentences below.

1. A: Is it a long movie?
   B: *No, it's pretty short.* ....
2. A: Is he fat?
   B: No, he's ....
3. A: The water's fairly deep, isn't it?
   B: No, ...
4. A: Their office is in a low building, isn't it?
   B: No, ...
5. A: Is the road very wide at that point?
   B: No, ...
6. A: It's a pretty boring book, isn't it?
   B: No, ...
7. A: She's fairly tall, isn't she?
   B: No, ...
8. A: They live in a small place, don't they?
   B: No, it's ....

Shapes, colors, and patterns

A **Shapes**

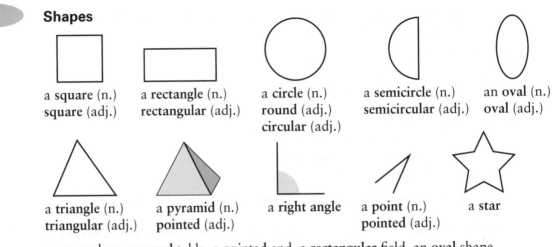

a **square** (n.)
square (adj.)

a **rectangle** (n.)
rectangular (adj.)

a **circle** (n.)
round (adj.)
circular (adj.)

a **semicircle** (n.)
semicircular (adj.)

an **oval** (n.)
oval (adj.)

a **triangle** (n.)
triangular (adj.)

a **pyramid** (n.)
pointed (adj.)

a **right angle**

a **point** (n.)
pointed (adj.)

a **star**

a **square** box, a **round** table, a **pointed** end, a **rectangular** field, an **oval** shape

Note: We can also form adjectives to describe shapes in this way: The ball was
egg shaped; a **heart-shaped** wedding cake; a **diamond-shaped** pin.

B **Colors**

You will already know most of the common colors. Here are some that are less
common:

Mix black and white to form **gray.** Mix red and blue to form **purple.**
Mix green and blue to form **turquoise. Pink** is a color between red and white.
Beige is a very light brown with some yellow in it.

C **Shades of color [degrees and variation of color]**

She bought a **dark** green skirt.
He was wearing **light** blue jeans.
My new shirt is **pale** yellow.

*Shades
of gray*

dark gray   light/pale gray

Note: With some colors, we use **pale** rather than **light,** e.g., pale yellow, pale pink.

D **Patterns (also called "designs")**

striped shirt

plaid skirt

floral tie

checked dress

E **Use of the suffix** *-ish*

When we want to say that a shape is almost round or a color is nearly green, we
can express this idea by adding the suffix -ish: a roundish face; a greenish tie; a
yellowish color.

Exercises

94.1 Describe these pictures using the correct noun and adjective.

Example: 1. a rectangular table

1.

2.

3.

4.

5.

6.

7.

8.

9.

94.2 What object is described in each sentence?

1. It has a point at one end, and that's the end you use to write with.
   a pencil or pen
2. The shape is rectangular and it's usually green. There are lines on it, and people play on it.
3. At certain times of the month it's completely round; at other times, it's closer to a semicircle.
4. It's orange, fairly long, usually pointed at one end, and you eat it.
5. It can look pale blue, more often dark blue, and sometimes almost turquoise. It really depends where it is and whether the sun is shining on it.
6. It's oval-shaped, white or beige or light brown in color, hard on the outside, and you usually eat it when it is cooked.
7. It's usually made of wire or plastic, and the bottom part is triangular. At the top there is another piece in the shape of a semicircle. You put things on the triangular part and hang them up, using the semicircular part.
8. It has four equal sides and four right angles.
9. It has three sides and three angles. No more than one angle can be a right angle.
10. It's grayish on the outside, pink on the inside, it swims, and you eat it.

94.3 What are you wearing? Write a detailed description of what you are wearing, including the exact color of everything. If there is a color or design you cannot describe, try to find it using a bilingual dictionary.

Partitives

Many different words can describe a part or quantity of something [**partitives**], usually followed by *of*.

A

Containers and contents (a *box* of *chocolates*)

a **box** of
chocolates

a **can**
of cola

a **cup** of
coffee

a **tube** of
toothpaste

a **bowl**
of sugar

a **carton** of
orange juice

a **glass**
of water

a **bottle** of
cough syrup

a **jar**
of jam

a **vase** of
flowers

B

With uncountable nouns

When we use uncountable nouns (e.g., **advice**), we sometimes want to talk about *one* of something. We cannot say "an advice" or "one advice," but we can use certain words to make these nouns singular: **a piece of advice, a sheet of paper** [one piece of paper], **a slice of bread** [one piece of bread]. We can use the word **piece** with many nouns:

a **piece**
of cake

a **piece**
of wood

You can use **piece** with some abstract nouns, e.g., **a piece of information.**

A very common partitive is **a little bit** (or sometimes **a bit**), which usually means a small amount but can be fairly general. It can be used with the examples above and more: **a little bit of butter, a little bit of time, a bit of luck,** etc.

C

A pair of . . .

Some nouns have two parts, e.g., pants (two legs) and shoes (left and right). You can use a **pair of**, e.g., **a pair of skis, two pairs of shoes, three pairs of gloves.**

D

Groups of things

a **bunch** of
flowers

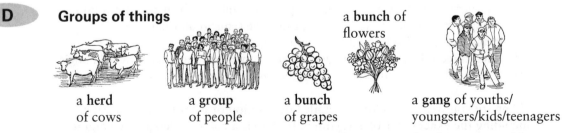

a **herd**
of cows

a **group**
of people

a **bunch**
of grapes

a **gang** of youths/
youngsters/kids/teenagers

Gang has a negative meaning: It suggests a group of young people who cause trouble.

Exercises

95.1 Some of these containers do not look exactly the same as the ones on the opposite page, but the names are the same. Can you decide what the missing words are?

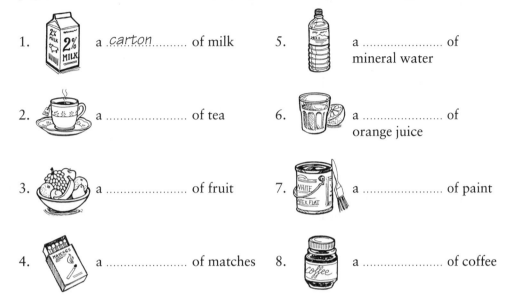

1. a *carton* .... of milk

2. a .... of tea

3. a .... of fruit

4. a .... of matches

5. a .... of mineral water

6. a .... of orange juice

7. a .... of paint

8. a .... of coffee

95.2 Contents come in different containers. Would you be surprised to see any of the following?

a glass of soup	a vase of coffee	a bowl of milk
a tube of milk	a can of tomatoes	a bag of soup
a jar of mustard	a bag of salt	a cup of toothpaste

95.3 Complete these sentences with a logical noun.

1. They gave her a big ...*bunch*.......... of flowers for her birthday.
2. A .... of teenagers may be responsible for the damage.
3. I cut about six .... of bread for the sandwiches.
4. They own a large .... of land in the country.
5. She told us to take out a blank .... of paper, then write our names at the top.
6. A small .... of people gathered outside the embassy.
7. Have you seen that old .... of boots I use for hiking?
8. I have a little .... of time, so I can help you now if you like.

95.4 Circle the correct answer. Sometimes both answers are correct.

1. I ordered a (piece)/ sheet of cake for dessert.
2. I asked her for a bit / piece of advice.
3. My lunch consisted of two slices / pieces of bread and a small bunch / group of grapes.
4. I read a little piece / bit of a novel last night; then I fell asleep.
5. There's a herd / group of people waiting to see you.

Abbreviations and abbreviated words

A Letters or words?

Some abbreviations are spoken as individual letters:

UN	United Nations	PC	personal computer
USA	United States of America	ATM	automated teller machine
EU	European Union	ID	identification

Other abbreviations are read as words:

OPEC /'oʊˌpek/ Organization of Petroleum Exporting Countries
AIDS /eɪdz/ acquired immune deficiency syndrome
PIN /pɪn/ personal identification number

B Written forms only

Some abbreviations are written forms only; they are
still pronounced as full words.

MAIN ST.

Mr. /'mɪs·tər/
Mrs. /'mɪs·əz/ [a married woman]
Ms. /mɪz/ [a woman who may be single or married]

St. Mark (Saint Mark)
Main St. (Main Street)
Dr. (Doctor)

C Abbreviations as part of the language

Some abbreviations (from Latin) are used as part of the language.

Abbreviation	Pronunciation	Meaning*	Latin
etc.	/et'set·ə·rə/ or /et'se·trə/	and so on	et cetera
e.g.	E-G	for example	exempli gratia
i.e.	I-E	that is to say; in other words	id est

*Note: This is also how we say them; we write "e.g." but we say "for example."

D Shortened words

Some English words can be shortened, especially in spoken English. Here are
some common ones:

phone (telephone)	bye (good-bye)	bike (bicycle)
math (mathematics)	exam (examination)	TV (television)
board (blackboard)	plane (airplane)	a paper (newspaper)
photo (photograph)	mom (mother)	vet (veterinarian)
ad (advertisement)	dad (father)	sales rep (sales representative)

the flu (influenza) [an illness like a cold but more serious]
lab (laboratory) [a special room where scientists work]
language lab [a room where students can listen and repeat using recording equipment]

Note: Most of these words are explained in other parts of the book. Use the index
at the back of the book to find them.

Exercises

96.1 What do these letters stand for? Complete each one.

1. EU = European _Union_
2. PC = personal ....
3. USA = United ....
4. ATM = automated ....

5. UN = United ....
6. OPEC = Organization of Petroleum ....
7. PIN = ...

96.2 Rewrite this note, making it more informal by using shortened words and abbreviations where possible.

> Michael,
>
> ~~math~~
> Peter had a ~~mathematics~~ examination this afternoon, and then he had to take his bicycle to the repair shop, so he'll probably get home a little late. You can watch television or read the newspaper while you're waiting for him. If there's a problem (for example, if Doctor Brown calls about the influenza vaccination), my telephone number is next to the photographs in the dining room. I should be home myself by about five o'clock.
>
> Margaret (Peter's mother)

96.3 What abbreviations in written English are often used for these words or phrases?

1. and so on   _etc._
2. for example

3. Street
4. in other words

5. Mister
6. Doctor

96.4 Complete these sentences with abbreviations or shortened words.

1. If you go to any of the Mediterranean islands, _e.g._ ...., Sardinia or Corsica, it's a good idea to rent a car.
2. When you pay by check in a store, they usually ask you for some ....
3. A: Do you always listen to tapes in the classroom?
   B: No, sometimes we listen in the ....
4. I asked the teacher to write the word on the ....
5. If you go there, you can buy books, pens, writing paper, ...
6. She stayed home from school last week because she had the .... I think she's better now, though.
7. When I decided to sell my car, I put an .... in the paper and got three replies the same day.
8. You can't get into the nightclub unless you're of legal age, ..., over 21.

96.5 Here are some more abbreviations. What does each one stand for? Where would you see them?

Example: FYI   _stands for "for your information"_

RSVP   c/o   ASAP   P.S.   p.m.

The senses

A   The five basic senses

The five senses are: **sight, hearing, taste, touch,** and **smell.**

The following verbs are related to the five senses. They are followed by an
adjective or a noun in these constructions. They do not usually take **-ing** forms.

Sight:	It **looks** terrible. (from what I could see)	It **looks like** a wedding cake.
Hearing:	He **sounds** Chinese. (from what I heard)	It **sounds like** a good idea.
Taste:	It **tastes** strange. (from tasting it)	This **tastes like** bread.
Touch:	It **feels** soft. (from touching it)	It **feels like** a blanket.
Smell:	It **smells** wonderful. (from smelling it)	This **smells like** garlic.

We can also use the verbs as nouns. These are very common:

I didn't like **the look of** the fish.   I love **the feel of** silk.
I really like **the sound of** organ music.   I hate **the smell of** gasoline.
I don't like **the taste of** olives.

B   *See, look (at),* and *watch*

See is the ability to use your eyes. (The verb is not usually used with the **-ing**
form.) **Look (at)** often means to look carefully / pay attention to something that is
not moving. **Watch** often means to pay attention to something that is moving.

I can't **see** a thing without my glasses. [I'm not able to see. / I am nearsighted.]
I can't find my keys, and I've **looked** everywhere. [searched / looked carefully]
The police have been **watching** the suspect for weeks. [watching secretly]
I **watched** the game and then went out with friends.
He ran into me because he wasn't **looking.** [paying attention; the speaker seems
    angry]
He ran into me because he didn't **see** me. [wasn't able to see me; the speaker is
    not angry]
I **saw/watched** a great program last night. [on TV; we can use either verb here]
I **saw** a great movie last night. [at a movie theater; we cannot use **watch** here]

C   Hear and listen (to)

Hear means "*able* to hear"; **listen (to)** means to "*pay attention* to things you hear":

I couldn't **hear** what she said. [I was physically unable to hear.]
I don't know what she said because I wasn't **listening.** [I wasn't paying attention.]
I usually **listen to** the evening news on television. [I decide to listen.]
I was **listening to** the radio when I **heard** a loud noise outside.

Sometimes it is possible to use **hear** (but not with the **-ing** form) to mean "listen
to":
I know he's dead – I **heard** it on the radio last night. [I heard it when I was listening.]

D   Touch

Don't **touch** those wires – they're dangerous.
You have to **press** that button to start the machine.
I'm frightened. Could you **hold** my hand?

Exercises

97.1 Complete the sentences using words from the box. Use a dictionary to help you.

water	donkey	photo	silk	fresh
new	laundry detergent	ripe	doorbell	horrible

1. I don't think I'll eat this peach; it doesn't feel *ripe.*
2. Those shoes look .... Did you just get them?
3. This milk smells .... I'll open another carton.
4. This coffee tastes like .... It's very weak.
5. I love the smell of .... bread.
6. That painting is so realistic that it looks like a ....
7. I know it's a horse, but it looks like a ....
8. I'm sure it's expensive perfume, but to me it smells like ....
9. Your telephone sounds just like a ....
10. This blouse was very cheap, but it feels like ....

97.2 Complete the sentences below the pictures using *looks/tastes/feels* + adjective.

1. That man ....   2. This pillow ....   3. This apple ....

97.3 Circle the correct answer. Sometimes both answers are correct.

1. I was listening to / hearing the radio when I listened to / heard a terrible noise outside.
2. The city council is going to introduce new laws about noisy neighbors – I listened to / heard it on the radio this morning.
3. She turned up the volume, but I still couldn't listen to / hear it.
4. They wanted to stay and watch / look at the TV program, but it was getting late.
5. I was very angry with Tom – he just wasn't hearing / listening when I spoke to him.
6. You have to touch / press the eject button if you want to get the video out.
7. Could you touch / hold this vase for a moment while I move the table?
8. If you watch / look carefully, you can look / see how he does the card trick.

97.4 Write a smell, a sound, and a taste that you like and hate. If possible, compare your answers with someone else.

I love the smell of ....   I hate the smell of ....
I love the sound of ....   I hate the sound of ....
I love the taste of ....   I hate the taste of ....

Signs, warnings, and notices

A Informative signs

Some signs give you information:

OUT OF ORDER
for a machine that is not working, usually in a public place, e.g., a pay phone or a public toilet.

NO VACANCY
outside a motel. It means the motel is full – there are no rooms left.

SOLD OUT
outside a theater or concert hall. There are no tickets left – all the tickets are sold.

B Don't do this!

Some notices tell you *not* to do certain things:

NO SMOKING

Thank You For Not Smoking

SMOKING PROHIBITED

PLEASE DO NOT DISTURB

NO PARKING

Keep off the grass

Do not feed the animals.

DO NOT LEAVE LUGGAGE UNATTENDED

C Watch out!

Some signs and notices are warnings – they tell you to be careful because something bad may happen:

FRAGILE HANDLE WITH CARE
[Be careful; this will break easily.]

CAUTION! WET FLOOR
[Be careful not to slip on the floor; it was just washed.]

WATCH YOUR STEP
[Be careful not to fall, e.g., when getting off a bus.]

BEWARE OF PICKPOCKETS
[Be careful; there are people here who will steal things from your bag or pocket without you knowing.]

D Notices and warnings on food and medicine

 Keep this and all other medications out of the reach of children.
[Don't leave this medicine or other medicines in a place where children can get to it.]

Do not exceed recommended dosage.
[Don't use more of this medicine or take it more often than your doctor or the label on the package says.]

 Not to be taken by mouth.
[Do not eat or drink this.]

 Best if used before May 5.
[Don't eat or drink this after the date.]

Exercises

98.1 Complete these signs, warnings, and notices without looking at the opposite page.
(Sometimes there is more than one possibility.)

1. | BEWARE OF *pickpockets* |

2. | WATCH YOUR .... |

3. | DO NOT .... |

4. | NO .... |

5. | THANK YOU FOR .... |

6. | HANDLE WITH .... |

7. | OUT OF .... |

8. | KEEP .... |

98.2 Where would you expect to see these signs, warnings, and notices?

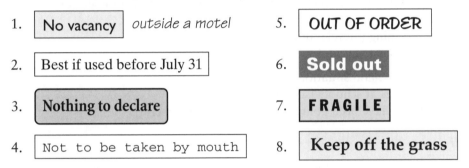

1. | No vacancy | *outside a motel*

2. | Best if used before July 31 |

3. | **Nothing to declare** |

4. | Not to be taken by mouth |

5. | OUT OF ORDER |

6. | **Sold out** |

7. | **F R A G I L E** |

8. | **Keep off the grass** |

98.3 What signs, warnings, or notices are possible in each of these places?

1. a zoo   *Do not feed the animals.*
2. a waiting area in a busy airport
3. the door of a hotel or motel room at 8 o'clock in the morning
4. in front of a driveway
5. inside a theater
6. on a bus

98.4 Now write some different signs of your own. Think of six possible signs,
warnings, and notices you could put in one of these places:

1. a school   3. a language school
2. a hospital   4. a place where people work, e.g., bank, factory, office

Where would you put these signs? If possible, do this activity with another person
or show it to another person.

98.5 Look for other signs, warnings, and notices (in English or your first language).
Can you understand the English signs? Can you translate the ones in your own
language? Try to find six more signs, warnings, and notices in the next week.

(See also Unit 62.)

Vague language

In spoken English, we often use words that are **vague** [not clear/precise/exact].

I have a **vague idea** where it is. [I know the general area, but I don't know exactly where.]
I have a **vague memory** of the game. [I can remember some of it, but not very clearly.]

Thing(s)

- To refer to actions, ideas, and facts:
  The main **thing** [fact] about John is that he likes everything to be well organized.
  Hitting that child was a terrible **thing** [action] to do.

- To refer to *countable* objects (often the speaker and listener know what the object is, or the speaker has forgotten the name of it at the moment of speaking):
  What's that **thing** (bicycle) doing in the house?
  Put those **things** (cups and saucers) in the cupboard.

- To refer to a general situation:
  How are **things** at school? [school in general]
  Lately, **things** have been going really well. [life in general]

Stuff

We sometimes use **stuff** *(informal)* to refer to *uncountable* nouns (or a group of countable nouns) when it is not necessary to be precise and give the exact name. Often the listener knows what the speaker is talking about.

Just leave that **stuff** [different items of clothes]
  on the floor. I'll clear it up.
I never use that chemical **stuff** [laundry
  detergent] in my machine.

Kind of / Sort of . . .

The walls are **kind of** yellow. [not exactly yellow, but similar to yellow]
I'm **kind of** hungry. [a little bit hungry]
He gets . . . uh . . . **sort of** . . . nervous when you mention the word *exams*. [a little bit nervous]
A: Did you like the concert?   B: Yeah, **sort of / kind of.**

Approximately

These words have the same meaning, but **approximately** is more formal than the others:

The train should arrive in **approximately** twenty minutes.
It's **about** three miles to the house.
I'll see you **around** noon.
We are expecting 100 guests, **more or less.**

Exercises

99.1 What could *thing(s)* and *stuff* mean in these sentences?

1. I never wear that stuff; it has such a strong smell. *perfume or after-shave lotion*
2. This thing is stuck in the lock.
3. We don't need these things. We can eat the chicken with our fingers.
4. What's that white stuff called that you mix with water to make bread?
5. Can you turn that thing off? That music is giving me a headache.
6. I couldn't get any more stuff in my suitcase.
7. It's a wonderful thing and keeps my young children occupied for hours.
8. It's good stuff. My hair feels really soft, and it didn't cost a lot.

99.2 Add a few words and phrases from the opposite page to make some of B's answers in this conversation less precise and more natural.

A: How many people were at the conference?
B: Four hundred. *Around/About/Approximately four hundred. or Four hundred, more or less.*
A: Did you enjoy it?
B: Yes.
A: You don't seem very sure.
B: Well, there were some good events, but it was too long.
A: And how did John's talk go?
B: Well, he was nervous at the beginning, but then he got more confident, and I think it went really well.
A: Did he have a big audience?
B: Seventy-five.
A: That's pretty good.
B: I think John was disappointed – he wanted at least a hundred.

99.3 Reply to each of these questions with a "vague" response.

1. A: Was the party fun?
   B: Yeah, *kind of* ....
2. A: Did you get everything you wanted?
   B: Yeah, ...
3. A: Did you say the walls were blue?
   B: Yeah, ...
4. A: Will there be twenty chairs in the room?
   B: Yeah, ...
5. A: Is it a serious movie?
   B: Yeah, ...
6. A: Do you remember your first birthday party?
   B: Yeah, I have ....

99.4 Think about similar words that you use in your own language. How many direct translations can you find for the words and phrases on the opposite page?

Formal and informal English

Most of the English that you learn can be used in many different situations. But you will also hear or see language that is formal or informal, and sometimes very formal or very informal. You need to be careful with this language because it may not be appropriate in certain situations. (It is marked *formal* and *informal* throughout this book.)

A Formal English

Formal English is more common in writing than in speaking. It is found in signs, notices, business letters, and legal English; but you will also hear examples in spoken English.

Cafe notice: Only food **purchased** [bought] here may be eaten on the **premises** [here].
Police statement in court: I **apprehended** [stopped] **the defendant** [the person charged with the crime] outside the supermarket.
Theater announcement: The play will **commence** [start] in two minutes.
Formal business situation: The meeting will **resume** [start again] this afternoon at 2 p.m.
Lawyer: My client had a broken ankle. **Thus** [so] he could not have driven the car.
Formal letter: I **regret to inform you** [I am sorry to say] that we **are unable to** [can't] **grant** [give] you . . .
Announcements: If you **require** [need] **further assistance** [more help], please contact . . .
Outside a restaurant: Parking for **patrons** [customers] only.

B Informal English

In general, informal language is more common in spoken English than in written English. Certain types of language are often informal:

- Most uses of **get** are informal. (See Unit 22 for more details.)
- Many **phrasal verbs** are informal. (See Units 17 and 18 for more details.)
- Many **idioms** are informal. (See Unit 19 for more details.)

Here are some examples using words from above and other common informal words:

Those **kids** [children or young people] like to **hang out** at the park [spend a lot of time at a place].
We always keep a first-aid kit **handy** [nearby, easy to reach].
I offered the **guy** [man] thirty **bucks** [dollars] for the **bike** [bicycle], but he wasn't interested.
I **bet** [think probably] we'll **get** [obtain] the money **pretty** [fairly] soon.
What's up? [What's the matter? / What's new?]
Do you feel like going out? [Do you want to go out? / Would you like to go out?] (Note the **-ing** form after **feel like**.)
Take care. [Good-bye.]

Slang is a form of *very* informal language (e.g., **slammer** = "prison or jail"). Many people think slang words are impolite and unacceptable in most situations. You should probably not use these words.

Exercises

100.1 Put the words on the left into the correct columns in the table.

purchase	handy
kids	resume
thus	guy
five bucks	commence
apprehend	patron

Formal	Informal
purchase	

For each of the words below, find a synonym from the table above.

Example: buy – *purchase*

buy	catch/stop	dollar	man	nearby / easy to reach
start	start again	therefore	customer	children

100.2 Rewrite these sentences in more informal English.

1. Is that your bicycle?   *Is that your bike?*
2. I think the show will commence fairly soon.
3. Would you like to go out for dinner?
4. What's the matter?
5. The man in the market sold me this ring for twenty dollars.
6. Where did you purchase that book?
7. They'll never apprehend him.
8. On our vacation, we're going to spend time at the pool every day.
9. Where did the children obtain that cat?

100.3 Rewrite this letter in more appropriate formal English.

> Dear Ms. Kim:
>   *We regret to inform you*
>   ~~We're really sorry to say~~ that we can't lend you the sum
> of five hundred bucks that you need, but it may be
> possible to give you a loan for some of the money.
>
> If you are still interested, perhaps you will feel like
> contacting our assistant manager. She will be happy to
> talk to you about it.
>
> Take care,

100.4 Dictionaries often tell you if a word is formal or informal. Use your dictionary to find out if the underlined words are formal or informal.

Example: I thought the movie was a drag.   *(informal)* "boring / a bore"

1. I couldn't attend the meeting.
2. Someone lifted my bag.
3. He talks too much; I wish he would shut up.
4. Smoking isn't permitted.

Phonetic symbols

Vowel sounds

Symbol	Examples		Symbol	Examples
/ɑ/	hot, father, sock, star		/ɔ/	saw, thought, ball
/æ/	hat, last, bag		/ɔɪ/	boy, join
/ɑɪ/	bite, ride, sky, height		/oʊ/	go, boat, below
/aʊ/	house, now		/ʊ/	put, good
/e/	let, head, said		/u/	food, blue, shoe, lose
/eɪ/	late, name, say		/ʌ/	*stressed:* sun, love, under
/i/	sleep, me, happy		/ə/	*unstressed:* alone, label, collect, under
/ɪ/	fit, pin, if		/ɜ/	*before* /r/: bird, turn, earn

Consonant sounds

Symbol	Examples		Symbol	Examples
/b/	bid, rob		/r/	read, carry, far, card – *In some parts of North America /r/ is not always pronounced at the ends of words or before consonants.*
/d/	did, under			
/ð/	this, mother, breathe			
/dʒ/	judge, gentle			
/f/	foot, safe, laugh		/s/	see, mouse, recent
/g/	go, rug, bigger		/ʃ/	shoe, cash, nation
/h/	house, behind, whole		/t/	team, meet, matter, sent
/j/	yes, useful, music		/tʃ/	church, rich, catch
/k/	kick, cook, quick		/θ/	think, both
/l/	look, ball, feel, pool		/v/	visit, save
/ᵊl/	settle, middle – *a syllabic consonant*		/w/	watch, away, wear; which, where – *Many North American speakers pronounce /w/ in such words, and many pronounce /hw/.*
/m/	many, some, damp			
/n/	none, sunny, sent			
/ᵊn/	kitten, button, mountain – *a syllabic consonant*		/z/	zoo, has, these
/ŋ/	ring, think, longer		/ʒ/	measure, beige, Asia
/p/	peel, soap, pepper			

Pronunciation problems

when "a" is /eɪ/	when "i" is /ɑɪ/	when "o" or "oo" is /ʌ/	when "u" is /ʌ/
patient	pilot	glove	punctual
Asia	virus	oven	luggage
dangerous	dial	month	hungry
pavement	hepatitis	front	discuss
bacon	minus	color	function
phrase	license	government	publish
engaged	diet	dozen	customs
came	striped	flood	luck
lately	tiny	blood	corrupt

When ow is /oʊ/, e.g., throw, blow, show, know, elbow
When ou or ow is /ɑʊ/, e.g., round, drought, blouse, now, towel, shower
When ou is /u/, e.g., soup, group, through, wound (n.), souvenir, routine
When ou is /ʌ/, e.g., cousin, couple, trouble, tough, rough, enough
When ir, or, or ur is /ɜr/, e.g., bird, shirt, worth, work, purple, burn, burglary, curtain
When er or or is /ər/, e.g., under, cover, mother, advisor, color, doctor
When a, au, or aw is /ɔ/, e.g., tall, fall, cause, audience, exhausted, draw, raw, law
When a or o is /ɑ/, e.g., calm, father, wallet, star, hot, stopped, possible
When a or u is /ɪ/, e.g., busy, business, damage, stomach, orange*, minutes*, lettuce*
When o is /u/, e.g., move, prove, improve, lose, choose, loose
When ea is /e/, e.g., dreadful, jealous, health, dead, bread, instead, pleasant, weather, weapon

*These sounds may be pronounced /ɪ/ or /ə/.

Silent letters (the underlined letters are silent):
island, knee, knife, know, knock, knowledge, wrong, wrist, muscle, castle, whistle, fasten, listen, bomb, lamb, thumb, comb, scissors, science, psychology, honest, hour, cupboard, answer, guess, aisle, half, should, would, Christmas, mortgage

Disappearing syllables (the underlined letters often disappear or are reduced to a /ə/):
fattening, miserable, temperature, vegetable, every, several, comfortable, favorite, laboratory, chocolate, restaurant

Problem pairs:

quite /kwɑɪt/ *and* quiet /ˈkwɑɪ·ət/	desert /ˈdez·ərt/ *and* dessert /də'zɜrt/
soup /sup/ *and* soap /soʊp/	lose /luz/ *and* loose /lus/

Note: The pronunciation of these letters at the end of words is often like this:
-ous /əs/, e.g., famous, dangerous, unconscious, ambitious, cautious, jealous
-age /ɪdʒ/, e.g., luggage, baggage, village, damage, cabbage, bandage, message, manage
-able /ə·bəl/, e.g., comfortable, reliable, suitable, unbreakable, vegetable, fashionable, miserable
-tory, -tary /tə·ri/, e.g., directory, history, documentary
-ture /tʃər/, e.g., picture, signature, departure, capture, temperature, literature, feature
-ate /eɪt/ at the end of verbs, e.g., educate, operate, communicate
-ate /ət/ or /ɪt/ at the end of nouns and adjectives, e.g., graduate, approximate, certificate

Index

*The numbers in the index are **Unit** numbers, not page numbers.*

credit card /ˈkred·ət ˈkard/ 12, 58

crime /kraɪm/ 81, 82

criminal /ˈkrɪm·ən·ᵊl/ 82

critic /ˈkrɪt·ɪk/ 72, 74

crosswalk /ˈkrɔˌswɔk/ 62

crowd /kraʊd/ 71

crowded /ˈkraʊd·əd/ 61

cruise /kruz/ 87

cry /kraɪ/ 43

cucumber /ˈkjuˌkʌm·bər/ 59

cuff /kʌf/ 57

cup /kʌp/ 95

cupboard /ˈkʌb·ərd/ 51

curly /ˈkɜr·li/ 44

currency /ˈkɜr·ən·si/ 54

current /ˈkɜr·ənt/ 75

current affairs/events 75

curtain /ˈkɜrt·ᵊn/ 51, 72

customer /ˈkʌs·tə·mər/ 69

cut (n., v.) /kʌt/ 56, 74, 77

cyclist /ˈsaɪ·kləst/ 63

dad /dæd/ 96

daily /ˈdeɪ·li/ 74

dairy production /ˈder·i prəˈdʌk·ʃən/ 40

damage (n., v.) /ˈdæm·ɪdʒ/ 11, 62

damaging /ˈdæm·ə·dʒɪŋ/ 86

dancer /ˈdæn·sər/ 9

danger /ˈdeɪn·dʒər/ 10

dangerous /ˈdeɪn·dʒə·rəs/ 10, 61, 69

dark /dark/ 9

dark brown/skin/complexion 44, 94

darkness /ˈdark·nəs/ 9

data /ˈdeɪt·ə, ˈdæt·ə/ 77

database /ˈdeɪt·əˌbeɪs, ˈdæt·əˌbeɪs/ 77

date (of arrival/departure) /deɪt/ 84

date of birth 84

day /deɪ/ 91

day shift 64

deal with 64

decade /ˈdekˌeɪd/ 91

decide /dɪˈsaɪd/ 29

decision /dɪˈsɪʒ·ən/ 20

decrease (v.) /dɪˈkris/ 68

deep (end) /dip/ 93

defeat /dɪˈfit/ 71

defend /dɪˈfend/ 85

defendant /dɪˈfen·dənt/ 81, 100

defense (attorney/lawyer) /dɪˈfens/ 81

definite /ˈdef·ə·nət/ 5

definition /ˌdef·əˈnɪʃ·ən/ 3, 4

degree /dɪˈgri/ 80

delayed /dɪˈleɪd/ 24

deliver /dɪˈlɪv·ər/ 67

democracy /dɪˈmak·rə·si/ 83

dentist /ˈden·təst/ 65

deny /dɪˈnaɪ/ 29

department store /dɪˈpart·mənt ˈstoʊr/ 58

depend (on) /dɪˈpend/ 15

depressed /dɪˈprest/ 31

depressing /dɪˈpres·ɪŋ/ 31

depth /depθ/ 93

desert /ˈdez·ərt/ 38

desk /ˈdesk/ 67

despite (the fact that) /dɪˈspaɪt/ 35

dessert /dɪˈzɜrt/ 60

destroy /dɪˈstrɔɪ/ 86

dial /ˈdaɪl/ 76

diamond-shaped /ˈdaɪ·məndˌʃeɪpt/ 94

diarrhea /ˌdaɪ·əˈri·ə/ 55

dictator /ˈdɪkˌteɪt·ər/ 83

dictatorship /dɪkˈteɪt·ərˌʃɪp/ 83

diet (n., v.) /ˈdaɪ·ət/ 11

different (from) /ˈdɪf·rənt/ 15, 36

dime /daɪm/ 54

dining room /ˈdaɪ·nɪŋ ˌrum/ 12, 51

dinner /ˈdɪn·ər/ 49

direct object /dəˌrekt ˈab·dʒɪkt/ 5

director /dəˈrek·tər/ 9, 72

Directory Assistance /dəˈrek·tə·ri əˈsɪs·təns/ 76

dirt /dɜrt/ 10

dirty /ˈdɜrt·i/ 3, 10, 61

disagree /ˌdɪs·əˈgri/ 8

disappear /ˌdɪs·əˈpɪr/ 8

disappointing/disappointed /ˌdɪs·əˈpɔɪn·tɪŋ/ /ˌdɪs·əˈpɔɪn·təd/ 31

disaster /dəˈzæs·tər/ 38

discontinue /ˌdɪs·kənˈtɪn·ju/ 87

discuss /dɪsˈkʌs/ 9, 30

discussion /dɪsˈkʌʃ·ən/ 9, 80

dish /dɪʃ/ 49

dishonest /dɪsˈan·əst/ 45

dishwasher /ˈdɪʃˌwaʃ·ər/ 51

disk /dɪsk/ 77

dislike (v.) /dɪsˈlaɪk/ 8

dismiss /dɪsˈmɪs/ 66

distribution /ˌdɪs·trəˈbju·ʃən/ 69

divide (by) /dəˈvaɪd/ 92

division /dəˈvɪʒ·ən/ 92

divorce /dɪˈvɔrs/ 22, 48

do /du/ 2

do (s.o.) a favor 20

do a lot of / a little (skiing/ sightseeing/etc.) 71, 89

do homework 2, 3, 20

do not feed the animals 98

do not leave luggage unattended 98

do nothing 49

do paperwork 64, 67

do research (into/on) 20, 80

do something/anything/nothing 20

do the housework/shopping/ laundry/etc. 20, 49, 52, 58

Do you feel like (going out)? 100

Do you mind if I . . . ? 25

doctor /ˈdak·tər/ 65

Doctor of Philosophy /fəˈlas·ə·fi/ 80

document /ˈdak·jə·mənt/ 77

documentary /ˌdak·jəˈmen·tə·ri/ 75

dog /dɔg/ 41

dollar /ˈdal·ər/ 54

don't mind 29

don't worry 24

doorbell /ˈdɔrˌbel/ 50

double occupancy /ˈdʌb·əl ˈak·jə·pən·si/ 88

double room 88

down /daʊn/ 32, 68

download /ˈdaʊnˌloʊd/ 78

downtown area 61

Dr. (doctor) /ˈdak·tər/ 96

drag /dræg/ 100

drama /'drɑm·ə/ 75

dramatic drop /drə'mæt·ɪk 'drɑp/ 68

draw /drɔ/ 71

drawer /drɔr/ 67

dreadful /'dred·fəl/ 3

dream (n., v.) /drim/ 11

dresser /'dres·ər/ 52

drink /drɪŋk/ 20

drink up /drɪŋk 'ʌp/ 17

drinkable /'drɪŋ·kə·bəl/ 10

drive (v.) /draɪv/ 63

driver /'draɪ·vər/ 9, 63

driver's license /'draɪ·vərz ˌlaɪ·səns/ 84

driveway /'draɪv·weɪ/ 50

drizzle /'drɪz·əl/ 39

drop (n., v.) /drɑp/ 53, 68

drop out /'drɑp 'aʊt/ 79

drop sharply 68

dropout /'drɑp·aʊt/ 79

drought /draʊt/ 39

drugstore /'drʌg·stɔʊr/ 58

drummer /'drʌm·ər/ 73

drums /drʌmz/ 73

dry (adj., v.) /draɪ/ 11

dub /dʌb/ 72

due to 37, 63

dumb /dʌm/ 45

dump /dʌmp/ 86

during /'dʊr·ɪŋ/ 91

dust /dʌst/ 52

duty-free shop /ˌdut·i'fri 'ʃɑp/ 87

eagle /'i·gəl/ 41

earache /'ɪr,eɪk/ 55

early teens 48

earn /ɜrn/ 64

earring /'ɪr,rɪŋ/ 12, 57

Earth /ɜrθ/ 38

earthquake /'ɜrθ,kweɪk/ 38

easygoing /ˌi·zi'goʊ·ɪŋ/ 13, 45

eat up /it 'ʌp/ 17

economic /ˌek·ə'nɑm·ɪk/ 68

economic stability 68

economical /ˌek·ə'nɑm·ɪ·kəl/ 10

economics /ˌek·ə'nɑm·ɪk s/ 10

economist /ɪ'kɑn·ə·məst/ 9

economy /ɪ'kɑn·ə·mi/ 9, 68

edition /ɪ'dɪʃ·ən/ 74

editor /'ed·ət·ər/ 74

educate /'edʒ·ə,keɪt/ 9

education /ˌedʒ·ə'kɑɪ·ʃən/ 9, 80

effective /ɪ'fek·tɪv/ 1

effectively /ɪ'fek·tɪv·li/ 1

e.g. /'i·dʒi/ 96

eggplant /'eg,plænt/ 59

egg-shaped /'eg,ʃeɪpt/ 94

Egypt /'i·dʒəpt/ 42

Egyptian /ɪ'dʒɪp·ʃən/ 42

El Salvador /ˌel 'sæl·və,dɔr/ 42

elbow /'el,boʊ/ 43

elect /ɪ'lekt/ 9, 83

election /ɪ'lek·ʃən/ 9, 83

elective /ɪ'lek·tɪv/ 79

electrical outlet /ɪˌlek'trɪ·kəl 'aʊt·lət/ 7

electrician /ɪˌlek'trɪʃ·ən/ 65

electronic mail /ɪˌlek,trɑn·ɪk 'meɪl/ 78

elementary school /ˌel·ə'men·tri ˌskul/ 79

elephant /'el·ə·fənt/ 41

elevator /'el·ə,veɪt·ər/ 50, 88

elderly /'el·dər·li/ 48

e-mail /'i,meɪl/ 78

e-mail address 78

embarrassing/embarrassed /ɪm'bær·ə·sɪŋ/ /ɪm'bær·əst/ 31, 46

embarrassment /ɪm'bær·ə·smənt/ 46

emotional /ɪ'moʊ·ʃən·ᵊl/ 45

employee /ɪm,plɔɪ'i/ 66

employer /ɪm'plɔɪ·ər/ 9

engineer /ˌen·dʒə'nɪr/ 63, 65

engineering /ˌen·dʒə'nɪr·ɪŋ/ 80

English /'ɪŋ·glɪʃ/ 42, 79

enjoy /ɪn'dʒɔɪ/ 2, 29

enjoyable /ɪn'dʒɔɪ·ə·bəl/ 10

enormous /ɪ'nɔr·məs/ 31, 50

enough /ɪ'nʌf/ 57

entertainment system 51

environment /ɪn'vaɪ·rən·mənt/ 86

equal /'i·kwəl/ 92

equator /ɪ'kweɪt·ər/ 38

equipment /ɪ'kwɪp·mənt/ 28

erase /ɪ'reɪs/ 1, 7

eraser /ɪ'reɪ·sər/ 7

etc. /et'set·ə·rə, et'se·trə/ 96

EU /'i'ju/ 96

even /'i·vən/ 92

even though 35

eventually /ɪ'ven·tʃə·wə·li/ 34

evidence /'ev·əd·əns/ 81

exam /ɪg'zæm/ 96

examine /ɪg'zæm·ən/ 67

exceed /ɪk'sid/ 98

except (for) /ɪk'sept/ 36

exciting/excited /ɪk'saɪt/ /ɪk'saɪt·əd/ 31, 69

excuse (n.) /ɪk'skjus/ 24

excuse me /ɪk'skjuz ˌmi/ 27

ex-girlfriend /'eks'gɜrl,frend/ 47

exhaust fumes /ɪg'zɔst 'fjumz/ 86

exhausting/exhausted /ɪg'zɔ·stɪŋ/ /ɪg'zɔ·stəd/ 31

exhibit /ɪg'zɪb·ət/ 73

exhibition /ˌeg·zə'bɪʃ·ən/ 73

ex-husband /'eks'hʌz·bənd/ 47

expand /ɪk'spænd/ 68

expect /ɪk'spekt/ 29

expect a baby 48

expenditure /ɪk'spen·də·tʃər/ 68

expensive /ɪk'spen·sɪv/ 54

experience /ɪk'spɪr·i·əns/ 66

expire /ɪk'spaɪr/ 84

explain /ɪk'spleɪn/ 30

explosive /ɪk'sploʊ·sɪv/ 85

expressway /ɪk'spres,weɪ/ 62

extremely /ɪk'strim·li/ 33

eyebrow /'aɪ,braʊ/ 43

fabulous /'fæb·jə·ləs/ 31

factory /'fæk·tə·ri/ 61, 67, 86

fairly /'fer·li/ 33, 54, 93

fairly expensive 54

fairly often 33

fall (n., v.) /fɔl/ 2, 68

fall asleep 49

fall down 17

fall in love 48

fall slowly/sharply 2, 68

falls (n.) /fɔlz/ 38

fame /feɪm/ 10

lung cancer /'lʌŋ 'kæn·sər/ 55
luxury /'lʌk·ʃə·ri/ 69
lying (on the beach) /laɪ·ɪŋ/ 90

M.A. /'em'eɪ/ 80
maid /meɪd/ 88
main course 60
maintain (sth.) /meɪn'teɪn/ 1
major (n., v.) /'meɪ·dʒər/ 80
majority /mə'dʒɔr·ət·i/ 83, 92
make /meɪk/ 2
make a mistake/decision/mess 2, 14, 20
make a profit 68
make a reservation 60, 88
make coffee 51
make dinner/money/friends/ noise/progress 20, 49
make do 19
make it 19
make money 64
make phone calls / a collect call 67, 76
make s.o. do sth. 29
make stops 63
make (sth.) up 18
make up your mind 19
make your own clothes 70
mall /mɔl/ 58, 61
manage /'mæn·ɪdʒ/ 9, 18, 29
management /'mæn·ɪdʒ·mənt/ 9
manager /'mæn·ɪdʒ·ər/ 9, 69, 71
Mandarin Chinese /'mæn·də·rən tʃaɪ'niz/ 42
manslaughter /'mæn,slɔt·ər/ 82
manufacture /,mæn·jə'fæk·tʃər/ 67
map /mæp/ 89
march (n., v.) /martʃ/ 46
marital status /'mær·ət·ºl 'steɪt·əs, 'stæt·əs/ 84
market /'mar·kət/ 69, 89
market leader/research/share 69
marketing department/ manager/mix 69
marriage certificate /'mær·ɪdʒ sər'tɪf·ɪ·kət/ 84
marvelous /'mar·və·ləs/ 31

mass-produced /'mæs·prə'dust/ 69
Master of Arts /'mæs·tər əv 'arts/ 80
Master of Science /'mæs·tər əv 'saɪ·əns/ 80
matchbooks /'mætʃ,bʊks/ 70
math /mæθ/ 79, 96
math teacher 12
meal /mil/ 20
mean (adj., v.) /min/ 29, 45
meaning /'mi·nɪŋ/ 2, 3
measure /'meʒ·ər/ 93
meat /mit/ 59, 60
mechanic /mə'kæn·ɪk/ 65
medium /'mid·i·əm/ 44, 60
medium-rare 60
meet the required standards 67
meet with 64
meeting (n.) /'mit·ɪŋ/ 67
melon /'mel·ən/ 59
menu /'men·ju/ 60
metal /'met·ºl/ 40
Mexican /'mek·sɪ·kən/ 42
Mexico /'mek·sɪ,koʊ/ 42
microwave /'maɪ·krə,weɪv/ 51
middle name 47
middle of the road 83
middle school /'mɪd·ºl ,skul/ 79
middle-aged /,mɪd·ºl'eɪdʒd/ 48
mid-twenties (in your mid-twenties) 48
millennium /mə'len·i·əm/ 91
million /'mɪl·jən/ 92
mine /maɪn/ 40
minimum wage /'mɪn·ə·məm 'weɪdʒ/ 64
mining /'maɪ·nɪŋ/ 40
minor offense /'maɪ·nər ə'fens/ 81
minority /mə'nɔr·ət·i/ 92
minus /'maɪ·nəs/ 92
minute (n.) /'mɪn·ət/ 91
mirror /'mɪr·ər/ 52
miserable /'mɪz·ə·rə·bəl, 'mɪz·rə·bəl/ 45
misread (present tense) /mɪs'rid/; misread (past tense) /mɪs'red/ 8
miss a class 14
miss a person 14

miss the bus 14, 53, 63
misspell /mɪs'spel/ 8
mistake /mə'steɪk/ 20
misunderstand /,mɪs,ʌn·dər'stænd/ 8
modem /'moʊd·əm/ 78
moderately /'mad·ə·rət·li/ 33
mom /mam/ 96
monarchy /'man·ər·ki/ 83
money /'mʌn·i/ 20
money belt /'mʌn·i 'belt/ 82
money pouch /'mʌn·i 'paʊtʃ/ 82
monitor /'man·ət·ər/ 67, 77
monkey /'mʌŋ·ki/ 41
month /mʌnθ/ 91
monument /'man·jə·mənt/ 89
moon /mun/ 38
more or less 99
mortgage /'mɔr·gɪdʒ/ 50
mosquito /mə'skit·oʊ/ 41
motel /moʊ'tel/ 88
mother tongue /'mʌð·ər 'tʌŋ/ 12
mother-in-law /'mʌð·ər·ən,lɔ/ 12, 47
motorist /'moʊt·ə·rəst/ 62
mountain /'maʊnt·ºn/ 38
mountain range /'maʊnt·ºn 'reɪndʒ/ 38
mouse /maʊs/ 77
movie star /'mu·vi 'star/ 12
moving (adj.) /'mu·vɪŋ/ 72
mph 62
Mr. /'mɪs·tər/ 96
Mrs. /'mɪs·əz/ 96
Ms. /mɪz/ 96
M.S. /'em'es/ 80
multiplication /,mʌl·tə·plə'keɪ·ʃən/ 92
multiply (by) /'mʌl·tə,plaɪ/ 92
murder (n., v.) /'mɜrd·ər/ 11, 82
murderer /'mɜrd·ər·ər/ 82
muscle /'mʌs·əl/ 55
muscular /'mʌs·kjə·lər/ 44
museum /mju'zi·əm/ 73
mushroom /'mʌʃ,rʊm/ 59
music /'mju·zɪk/ 10, 73
musical (adj., n.) /'mju·zɪ·kəl/ 10, 72

twist your ankle *56*
two-hour (delay) *13*

ugly /ˈʌg·li/ *2, 44*
umpire /ˈʌm·paɪr/ *71*
UN /juˈen/ *96*
unable (to) /ʌnˈeɪ·bəl/ *8, 100*
unambitious /ˌʌn·æmˈbɪʃ·əs/ *45*
unattended /ˌʌn·əˈten·dəd/ *98*
unbreakable /ʌnˈbreɪ·kə·bəl/ *10*
uncle /ˈʌŋ·kəl/ *47*
uncomfortable /ʌnˈkʌm·fərt·ə·bəl, ʌnˈkʌmf·tə·bəl/ *10*
unconscious /ʌnˈkɑn·tʃəs/ *56*
uncountable /ʌnˈkɑʊn·tə·bəl/ *5*
uncountable noun *5*
under /ˈʌn·dər/ *32*
under s.o. *66*
undergraduate /ˌʌn·dərˈgræʤ·ə·wət/ *80*
undrinkable /ʌnˈdrɪŋ·kə·bəl/ *10*
unemployed /ˌʌn·ɪmˈplɔɪd/ *8, 66*
unfriendly /ʌnˈfren·dli/ *8, 45*
unhappy /ʌnˈhæp·i/ *3, 8*
United States /juˌnaɪt·əd ˈsteɪts/ *42*
unkind /ʌnˈkaɪnd/ *45*
unknown /ʌnˈnoʊn/ *8*
unless /ənˈles/ *36*
unlike /ʌnˈlaɪk/ *36*
unlock /ʌnˈlɑk/ *8*
unpack /ʌnˈpæk/ *8*
unpleasant /ʌnˈplez·ənt/ *45*
unreasonable /ʌnˈri·zə·nə·bəl/ *8*
unreliable /ˌʌn·rɪˈlaɪ·ə·bəl/ *10, 45*
until /ənˈtɪl/ *91*
up /ʌp/ *32, 68*
upmarket /ˈʌpˈmɑr·kət/ *69*
upright position /ˈʌpˌraɪt pəˈzɪʃ·ən/ *87*
upscale /ˈʌpˈskeɪl/ *69*
upset /ʌpˈset/ *46*
URL /ˌjuˌɑrˈel/ *78*
USA /ˌjuˌesˈeɪ/ *96*

use (up) *(v.)* /juz/ *17, 98*
use of /ˈjus əv/ *87*
useful /ˈjus·fəl/ *10*
useless /ˈjus·ləs/ *10*
user friendly /ˈju·zər ˈfrend·li/ *77*
usually /ˈju·ʒə·wə·li/ *33*

vacancy /ˈveɪ·kən·si/ *98*
vacation /veɪˈkeɪ·ʃən/ *64*
vacation pay *64*
vacuum /ˈvæk·jum/ *52*
vacuuming /ˈvæk·jum·ɪŋ/ *49, 52*
vague (idea/memory/etc.) /veɪg/ *99*
valley /ˈvæl·i/ *61*
valuables /ˈvæl·jə·bəlz/ *82*
value /ˈvæl·ju/ *54*
variety (of stores) /vəˈraɪ·ət·i/ *61*
vase /veɪs, veɪz, vɑz/ *51, 95*
VCR /ˌviˌsiˈɑr/ *51*
veal /vil/ *59*
vegetable /ˈveʤ·tə·bəl, ˈveʤ·ə·tə·bəl/ *40*
vehicle /ˈvi·ɪk·əl, ˈviˌhɪk·əl/ *63*
Venezuela /ˌven·əzˈweɪ·lə/ *42*
Venezuelan /ˌven·əzˈweɪ·lən/ *42*
verb /vɜrb/ *5*
very /ˈver·i/ *31, 33, 54*
vet /vet/ *65, 96*
veterinarian /ˌvet·ə·rəˈner·i·ən/ *65*
video /ˈvɪd·iˌoʊ/ *7, 49, 58*
video (rental) store *58*
videocassette /ˌvɪd·iˌoʊ·kəˈset/ *7*
videotape /ˈvɪd·iˌoʊˌteɪp/ *7*
Vietnam /viˌetˈnɑm/ *42*
Vietnamese /viˌet·nəˈmiz/ *42*
view /vju/ *50*
vinegar /ˈvɪn·ə·gər/ *59*
violent /ˈvaɪ·ə·lənt/ *72*
violin /ˌvaɪ·əˈlɪn/ *73*
violinist /ˌvaɪ·əˈlɪn·əst/ *73*
virus /ˈvaɪ·rəs/ *55, 77*
visa /ˈvi·zə/ *84*
visit /ˈvɪz·ət/ *64*
V-neck /ˈviˌnek/ *57*

vocational high school /voʊˈkeɪ·ʃən·ᵊl ˈhaɪ ˌskul/ *79*
volcanic eruption /vɑlˈkæn·ɪk ɪˈrʌp·ʃən/ *38*
volcano /vɑlˈkeɪ·noʊ/ *38*
volleyball /ˈvɑl·iˌbɔl/ *71*
vomit /ˈvɑm·ət/ *55*
vote (for) *(n., v.)* /voʊt/ *83*

waist /weɪst/ *43*
wait (for) *(n., v.)* /weɪt/ *15*
waiting room /ˈweɪt·ɪŋ ˌrum/ *12*
wake up /ˈweɪk ˈʌp/ *17, 18, 49*
wake-up call /ˈweɪˌkʌp ˈkɔl/ *88*
walk *(n.)* /wɔk/ *93*
want /wɔnt/ *29, 30*
war /wɔr/ *85*
war movie *72*
war zone /ˈwɔr ˈzoʊn/ *85*
warehouse /ˈwerˌhaʊs/ *67*
warm /wɔrm/ *39, 45*
warn /wɔrn/ *30*
wash (my hair/face) /wɑʃ/ *49, 52*
wash the dishes *52*
washable /ˈwɑʃ·ə·bəl/ *10*
washing machine /ˈwɑʃ·ɪŋ məˈʃin/ *12*
waste *(n., v.)* /weɪst/ *54, 86*
wastebasket /ˈweɪstˌbæs·kət/ *67*
watch /wɑtʃ/ *97*
watch out *27*
watch videos *49*
water *(v.)* /ˈwɔt·ər/ *40*
wave *(n., v.)* /weɪv/ *46, 90*
wavy /ˈweɪ·vi/ *44*
we could . . . *25*
We were wondering if you'd like to . . . *25*
weak /wik/ *9, 45*
weakness /ˈwik·nəs/ *9*
weapon /ˈwep·ən/ *56*
weather /ˈweð·ər/ *2, 28*
weather forecast /ˈweð·ər ˈfourˌkæst/ *74*
Web /web/ *78*
Web pages/sites *78*
week /wik/ *91*
weekly /ˈwi·kli/ *74*

Answer Key

Unit 1

1.3
1. true
2. true
3. false: A **routine** means doing certain things in the *same* way each time.
4. true
5. false: If something is **effective**, it *works* very well.
6. false: **At least** fifty people means a *minimum* of fifty people.
7. true
8. true
9. false: **Reviewing** means studying something for the *second* or *third* time (or more!).
10. true

Unit 2

2.1 *Suggested answers:*

Clothes/Accessories	Transportation/Travel	Adjectives with **-ful** or **-less** suffix
tie	ticket	painful
jeans	fare	helpful
scarf	platform	homeless
dress	trip	useless
blouse	station	careful
put on	train	thoughtless
jacket	get on	useful

2.2   1. c   2. b   3. c   4. b   5. c   6. a   7. a and c   8. b

2.3   The answers will depend on your first language. A translation may or may not be appropriate for all of the words. Example sentences are a good idea for most words, and often something else is useful to know. Here are some suggestions:

dream: noun and verb (regular). As a noun it is used with the verb *have;* also useful to learn *nightmare* [bad dream].

empty: ≠ full. It's also useful to learn *half-empty* [a more negative way of saying *half-full*].

concentrate: The main stress is on the first syllable. It is sometimes followed by the preposition *on,* e.g., you concentrate on your exams. The noun is *concentration.*

forget: irregular verb (forget/forgot/forgotten); ≠ remember.

beard: a picture is the best way to show meaning; it is pronounced /bɪrd/; also useful to know is *mustache.*

rescue: synonym = *save;* noun and verb (regular).

nearly: synonym = *almost;* usually goes before the main verb except the verb *to be,* e.g., We nearly lost the game. It is nearly 4 o'clock.

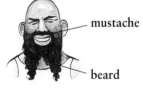

knife: a picture is the best way to show meaning; the letter **k** is silent; also important to know are *fork* and *spoon.*

2.4 *Possible answers:*

take: a picture/photo, time, a bath, a taxi, an exam
do: your homework, research, someone a favor, one's best, the shopping, the laundry
make: a mistake, a decision, a mess, noise, friends, money, coffee
have: breakfast/lunch/dinner, a drink, a party, a good time, fun, a baby

Unit 3

3.1 *Suggested answers:*

2. the same as *choose*; o = /u/
3. a verb
4. an adjective
5. uncountable
6. complete/total/utter
7. two
8. *ch* = /k/, as in *character*
9. between/from
10. You have to choose between A and B. *or*
    You can choose from ten different colors.

3.2

2. advise
3. piece
4. chaotic
5. clean
6. **Homework** is schoolwork that you do at home; **housework** is work that is necessary in a home (e.g., washing, ironing, cleaning).
7. win a game
8. **gain / put on** weight
9. order
10. Take a seat. / Have a seat.

3.3 cas<u>t</u>le; bom<u>b</u>; dou<u>b</u>t; <u>p</u>sychology; <u>w</u>rist; recei<u>p</u>t; <u>k</u>nife

3.4 *bye-bye:* informal/spoken   *put someone down:* informal
    incision: technical   *childish:* disapproving
    thereby: formal

Unit 4

4.1

2. children/animals/crops – to take care of children until they are fully grown
3. increase
4. children/animals/crops – to take care of crops until they are fully grown
5. improve
6. increase – speak loudly and angrily; **raise your voice** is a highlighted phrase.
7. raise a question/objection, etc. – to begin to talk or write about something that you want someone to consider
8. move; **raise your hand** is a highlighted phrase.

4.3 The answers will vary, depending on the dictionary used.

4.4 *Suggested answers:*

2. cold   3. sad   4. worried, impatient, nervous   5. two

Unit 5

5.1

2. **in** Seville (preposition)
3. **I** spent (pronoun)
4. **a** beautiful city (indefinite article)
5. **expensive** hotel (adjective)
6. **of** money (preposition)
7. wonderful **hotel/place** (noun)
8. **to** Spain (preposition)
9. **never** stays (adverb)

5.2 *uncountable noun:* time; traffic
    plural noun: clothes; shorts; jeans
    phrasal verb: put on
    idiom: get a move on

5.3 2. intransitive   3. intransitive   4. transitive   5. transitive   6. intransitive

5.4 *Syllables and main stress (underlined)*
one syllable: noun
two syllables: <u>Eng</u>lish; be<u>fore</u>; de<u>cide</u>
three syllables: under<u>stand</u>; <u>adj</u>ective; <u>opp</u>osite; in<u>form</u>al; <u>comf</u>ortable (Four syllables are
    possible here, but the **or** is silent for most English speakers most of the time:
    /ˈkʌmf·tə·bəl/)
four syllables: prepo<u>si</u>tion; edu<u>ca</u>tion
five syllables: pronunci<u>a</u>tion

5.5
1. adjective
2. happily; correctly; luckily; surely; possibly
3. happy = content; correct = right; lucky = fortunate; sure = certain; no clear synonym
    for *possible,* although *maybe* and *perhaps* (both adverbs) are similar.
4. unhappy; incorrect; unlucky; unsure; impossible
5. cor<u>rect</u>

Unit 6

6.1 The vowel sounds are underlined:

1. row /roʊ/; cow /kaʊ/
2. back /bæk/; bacon /ˈbeɪ·kən/
3. soup /sup/; soap /soʊp/
4. pot /pɑt/; pole /poʊl/

6.2
1. **dream** is pronounced /drim/
2. **flood** is pronounced /flʌd/
3. **fast** is pronounced /fæst/
4. **wound** is pronounced /wund/ as a noun
5. **since** is pronounced /sɪns/
6. **symptom** is pronounced /ˈsɪm·təm/

6.3 Schwa /ə/ appears in all of the words.

First syllable	*Second syllable*	*Third syllable*
opposite /ˈɑp·ə·zət/	cathedral /kəˈθi·drəl/	understand /ˌʌn·dərˈstænd/
policy /ˈpɑl·ə·si/	police /pəˈlis/	competition /ˌkɑm·pəˈtɪʃ·ən/
palace /ˈpæl·əs/	attractive /əˈtræk·tɪv/	education /ˌedʒ·əˈkeɪ·ʃən/
desert (n.) /ˈdez·ərt/	assistance /əˈsɪs·təns/	
organize /ˈɔr·gəˌnɑɪz/		

Note that in some cases, the reduced sound /ə/ may be pronounced as /ɪ/, which is often a
reduced sound too. For example, **policy** can be /ˈpɑl·ə·si/ or /ˈpɑl·ɪ·si/, and **palace** can be
/ˈpæl·əs/ or /ˈpæl·ɪs/.

6.4

Same	*Different*
know/knife	listen/western (**t** in **listen** is silent)
muscle/scissors	island/Islam (**s** in **island** is silent)
climb/bomb	answer/swear (**w** in **answer** is silent)
wrong/wrist	honest/hope (**h** in **honest** is silent)
	cold/could (**l** in **could** is silent)

Unit 7

7.1
1. plug
2. (electrical) outlet
3. notebook
4. briefcase
5. file
6. tape recorder / cassette player

7.2
2. a cassette (tape)
3. to photocopy / make copies of things
4. notes/papers
5. notes/books/files (Some people carry all sorts of things in a briefcase, e.g., their lunch.)
6. a plug

7. usually to look up the meaning of a word; also to look up the pronunciation, to find synonyms, etc.
8. to erase writing

7.3
2. turn up the tape recorder
3. borrow a dictionary
4. share with a classmate
5. videotape a program
6. do an exercise
7. make mistakes
8. plug in the OHP

7.5
A: What does *borrow* mean?
A: How do you pronounce it?
A: How do you spell it?
A: What's the difference between *borrow* and *lend*?

Unit 8

8.1

unhappy	impatient	impolite	illegal
incorrect	irregular	invisible	impossible
illegible	unfriendly	unemployed	dishonest
unpack	unlock	disagree	disappear

8.2
1. it's illegal
2. overcharged
3. invisible
4. it's illegible
5. she's very impatient
6. impolite

8.3
2. unpacked
3. disappeared
4. disagree
5. redo
6. overslept
7. unlock
8. disliked
9. retake
10. unwrap
11. undressed
12. misspell

Unit 9

9.1

Noun	*Noun*
improvement	stupidity
discussion	darkness
government	weakness
spelling	similarity
hesitation	punctuality
arrangement	happiness
	popularity

9.2
1. television
2. election
3. education
4. administration
5. weakness
6. stupidity
7. management
8. improvement

9.3
2. employer
3. actor
4. singer
5. driver
6. psychologist
7. economist
8. translator
9. manager

9.4 *Suggested answers:*
1. dances in ballets
2. writes reports/articles for newspapers, magazines, or TV news
3. directs movies
4. manages a bank
5. employs/hires people (employees)
6. sings pop songs / makes recordings / gives concerts
7. translates books, articles, and speech from one language to another
8. takes pictures (photographs)

Unit 10

10.1

industrial	dirty	painful, painless	(un)comfortable
attractive	careful, careless	knowledgeable	famous
creative	dangerous	(in)comprehensible	(un)reliable
foggy	political	sunny	washable
homeless	enjoyable	musical	(un)breakable

10.2

1. careful
2. famous
3. knowledgeable *or* helpful
4. dangerous
5. painful
6. reliable
7. industrial
8. undrinkable
9. inflexible
10. homeless

10.3   painless; tactless;* useless; hopeless; thoughtless

*If someone is *tactful* they are diplomatic, i.e., they always say the right thing. If you are *tactless,* you always say the wrong thing and might offend someone.

Opposites for the other words:
beautiful (≠ ugly); wonderful (≠ terrible, awful); awful (≠ wonderful, fantastic)

10.4   *Possible answers:*

2. dangerous, careless, thoughtless, awful
3. musical, creative, famous
4. industrial, famous, beautiful, dirty, attractive
5. famous, creative, knowledgeable
6. reliable, comfortable, economical
7. political, enjoyable, thoughtful, incomprehensible, hopeful
8. ?

Unit 11

11.1

1. We waited a long time.
2. Can you answer my question?
3. This orange tastes strange.
4. The vacation cost about $800.
5. I replied to his letter yesterday.
6. When the door gets stuck, you have to push it.

11.2

1. If I put on weight, I go on a diet, but then I always gain it back again.
2. It was very hot, so we took/had a rest after lunch.
3. I hit the brakes, but I still couldn't stop in time.
4. I had a dream about you last night.

11.3

1. same meaning
2. similar (but not exactly the same because *to water* means "to pour water over something that is growing")
3. completely different (the verb *to book* means "to reserve," e.g., a flight, a hotel room)
4. completely different (*a break* is "a rest"; *to break a leg* means "to fracture a bone in the leg")
5. similar (but not exactly the same because a *run* here is not just the action of running; it is a recreational activity)

Unit 12

12.1   *Possible answers:*

Money: credit card, parking meter, income tax, checkbook, box office, ticket office, personal computer
Roads: traffic light, parking meter, stop sign, traffic jam, traffic cop

People: math teacher, movie star, brother-in-law (also sister/father/mother-in-law), baby-sitter, pop star, rock star, traffic cop

Things we wear: earring, T-shirt, running shoes, raincoat, sunglasses

Note: Other words may fit into these categories, depending on your point of view.

12.2 *Suggested answers:*

1. traffic jam	3. alarm clock	5. baby-sitter	7. income tax
2. movie star	4. waiting room	6. sunglasses	8. parking meter

12.3 *Possible answers:*

3. pop star; rock star
4. birthday card; postcard
5. toothbrush [what you brush your teeth with]
6. living room; waiting room
7. traffic jam; traffic cop
8. suntan [when your skin gets darker from the sun]; sunburn [when your skin gets red and inflamed from too much sun]
9. postcard; postmark [official mark on mail showing the date and place it was sent from]
10. hairdresser/hairstylist [person who cuts/styles your hair]; hairdo [way the hair is cut and arranged]

12.4 *Possible answers:*

notebook [a book of plain paper to write notes]
textbook [a book used for study, especially in schools]
cookbook [a book that explains how to prepare and cook food]
telephone book / phone book [a book with names and telephone numbers; also called a telephone directory]

bookcase [a piece of furniture with shelves for books]
bookstore

greeting card, e.g., birthday card, Christmas card
phone card [to use with telephones]
business card
postcard
identification/ID card
playing cards [used in card games]

Unit 13

13.1

good-looking	well-known
easygoing	northeast
ten-dollar	short-sleeved
brand-new	badly written
part-time	left-handed
firsthand	second-class

13.2 *Possible answers:*

well-made; well-dressed
part-time; full-time
badly written; badly paid
northeast; southeast
right-handed; left-handed
first-class; second-class

13.3
1. five-star
2. left-handed
3. brand-new
4. southeast/southwest
5. badly behaved
6. part-time
7. badly written
8. well off
9. twenty-minute
10. good-looking
11. hundred-dollar
12. easygoing

Unit 14

14.1 *Possible answers:*

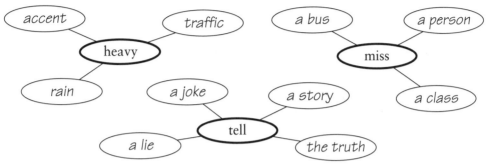

14.2 *Suggested answers:*
2. weak coffee
3. a loud voice
4. get off the bus
5. tell a lie
6. miss the bus

14.3 *Suggested answers:*
1. terribly/awfully; missed
2. told
3. start
4. runs
5. start
6. made
7. commits
8. heavy; highly
9. humanly
10. missed

14.4
1. large size
2. wide range
   (broad range *is also possible*)
3. broad shoulders
   (wide shoulders *is also possible*)
4. vast majority

Unit 15

15.1 *Possible answers:*
1. for; Her brother, I think.
2. for; Assistant manager.
3. to; I think it's a documentary.
4. about; She said the room was too cold.
5. for; For being late twice last week.
6. to; No, I think it belongs to her friend.
7. at; One of the other students.
8. in; Yes, she likes jazz and classical music.
9. on; How much it costs, I suppose. (*Note:* **depend upon** is also possible.)
10. of; Climbing ladders. She's afraid of heights.

15.2
2. (j) She wasn't aware of her mistakes.
3. (f) I was very surprised at his choice.
4. (i) He complained about the bad service.
5. (h) That suit is similar to the one she's wearing.
6. (c) She applied for a job in Puerto Rico.
7. (a) He threw a book at me, but it missed.

8. (d) He said it depends on me.
9. (g) The suitcase was full of clothes.
10. (e) She apologized for the mistake.

15.3 *Possible answers:*

2. at English/math/etc.
3. for a job at a travel agency / for a job with an airline
4. to my brother/sister
5. from hay fever / from the heat
6. in astrology/languages/etc.
7. of flying / of death / of going to the dentist / etc.
8. from people in the U.S. / Canada / the U.K. / etc.

15.4 *Suggested answers:*

fond **of**, e.g., He's very fond of animals.
concentrate **on**, e.g., If you want to improve your English, you'll need to concentrate on your listening skills.
responsible **for**, e.g., That gang is responsible for the robbery.
rely **on**, e.g., I rely on you for good advice.

Note: Some other prepositions are possible with these words, but the ones listed above are the most common.

Unit 16

16.1

1. on	5. by	9. on	13. in	17. at
2. by	6. by	10. by	14. by	18. at
3. on	7. for	11. in	15. on	19. by
4. on	8. in	12. on	16. in	20. at

16.2

1. in time (for the movie / to see the movie)
2. on the phone
3. on TV
4. by mistake
5. in the end
6. at the end
7. at the moment
8. by chance

16.3 *Suggested answers:*

1. No, she hit him by accident.
2. No, they went on foot (*or* by bus, by taxi, by train).
3. No, they're here on business.
4. No, I saw it on TV (*or* I heard about it on the radio).
5. No, he went by himself.
6. No, I'm in a hurry.

Unit 17

17.1

2. found	4. getting	6. look	8. runs
3. get	5. went	7. go	

17.2 *Possible answers:*

2. bread/coffee/sugar/etc.
3. in a dictionary
4. my boss / my parents / the neighbors / my teacher / etc.
5. his coat / his jacket / his gloves / etc.
6. the fire
7. on time / early / late / etc.
8. by fifty dollars / next week / etc.

17.3   2. definition 3   3. definition 7   4. definition 5   5. definition 1

17.4   *See section C in Unit 17 (page 36) for examples.*

Unit 18

18.1   *Possible answers:*
2. late last night / all night
3. the TV / the radio / the light
4. my apartment / our house / the bank
5. the last sentence / the final part
6. just outside the city / on a deserted road
7. on your salary / on so little money / on $1,000 a month
8. in a small town / in poverty / in a large family

18.2
1. yes (**put** the fire **out**)
2. yes (**turn** the radio **on**)
3. no
4. yes (**made** that story **up**)
5. no
6. no
7. yes (**turned** the light **off**)
8. yes (**leave** this question **out**)
9. no
10. yes (**Pick** your toys **up**)

18.3
1. going up; get by
2. come in; take off; put out
3. make up; leave out
4. brought up; going up

18.4   *Possible answers:*
Unit 22: get along (with someone); get to know; get up
Unit 48: grow up; go out (with); split up; break up
Unit 49: wake up; get up; go out; come over
Unit 57: put (something) on; take (sth.) off; hang (sth.) up; try (sth.) on
Unit 63: get on; get off; get in; get out
Unit 75: plug (something) in; turn (sth.) on/off; turn (sth.) up/down; switch (sth.) on/off

Unit 19

19.1
1. **feel like** = want/desire
2. **for good** = forever
3. **change my mind** = change my decision/plan
4. **tied up** = busy
5. **make do** = manage / get by

19.2
2. make it   4. get a move on   6. keep an eye on
3. What's up?   5. make up your mind

19.3
1. starters; matters   3. offhand   5. do; run
2. turns   4. small

19.4   *Suggested answers:*
have something/nothing/little in common = to have or not to have similar interests (If you have nothing/little in common, it means you don't have similar interests.)
crazy about something = to like something very much
get on someone's **nerves** = to make someone angry or irritable by your behavior

Unit 20

20.1 *Correct answers:*

1. do	3. make	5. take	7. made	9. make
2. have	4. do	6. take	8. take	10. doing

20.2 *Suggested answers:*

1. took	5. I'm thirsty.	9. had a good time
2. make	6. do my shopping	10. making progress
3. do the housework	7. make a lot of money	
4. had	8. make a decision	

20.3 *Suggested answers:*

2. Maria does/did her homework after dinner.
3. Bill takes a nap after lunch most afternoons.
4. The Lees took a lot of photos/pictures on their vacation.
5. Nancy is having a baby / going to have a baby next month.

20.4 Check page 42 for expressions with these verbs.

Unit 21

21.1
break a record / the law / a promise
catch the ball / a bus / a cold
keep a record / a promise / in touch
give me a hand / my regards to . . .

21.2 *Suggested answers:*

1. see	5. See / I'll see	9. see	13. give
2. keep	6. keep	10. give	14. broke
3. give	7. caught	11. give	
4. see	8. break	12. keep	

21.3 1. catch the (*or* a) bus   2. break a record   3. break the ice

Unit 22

22.1

1. buy/obtain*	5. find/obtain*	9. receive
2. bring	6. receive	10. arrive
3. arrive	7. becoming	
4. became	8. buy / pick up	

***Obtain** is used more frequently in written English than in spoken English.

22.2

2. I'm getting hungry.   5. It's getting dark.
3. I'm getting hot.   6. It's getting crowded.
4. It's getting late.

22.3

1. getting ready to go out   4. get along (very) well with my boss
2. get dressed very quickly   5. get rid of most of these chairs
3. get to know people in this country   6. get it, do you

Unit 23

23.1 2. coming
3. go

4. bring (**Bring** is most likely because Jim would be speaking from his own home; but **take** is also possible if the speaker is thinking of Jim's home as another place.)
5. bring
6. go
7. come

23.2   1. How are you?   3. takes me/you
             2. lead   4. How are you getting along?

23.3   2. for breakfast   4. sightseeing; for a drive
             3. swimming (*or* for a swim)   5. riding

23.4   1. deaf   2. bankrupt   3. gray   4. bald   5. crazy/nuts

Unit 24

24.1   2. I'm / to be; held; problem   5. apologize; matter
             3. keep; mind   6. long; Never
             4. kind   7. beg; worry

24.2   *Possible answers:*

2. I'm sorry I'm late, but I missed the bus.
3. Oh, thank you. That's very kind of you.
4. Don't worry. It doesn't matter.
5. Thank you for inviting me. / Thank you for a lovely dinner/evening.
6. Please accept our apologies for the delay in sending the information we promised you. Unfortunately we have experienced a much higher volume of business this month than usual, and this has resulted in . . .

24.3   *Possible answers:*

1. I'm terribly sorry. / I beg your pardon. I'll get you a cloth / some paper towels.
2. I'm sorry about the mess. I'll clean it up.

Unit 25

25.1   B: I wish I could, but I don't have any money.
             A: That's OK, I'll pay. How about going to a movie?
             B: Yeah, great.
             A: Why don't we go see that new romantic comedy playing downtown?
             B: I don't know. Sounds kind of boring. (Omit *like* after *sounds*.) I think I'd rather see an action movie. (Omit *to* after *rather*.)
             A: Well, what about the latest disaster movie?
             B: Great! I'd love to.

25.2   *Suggested answers:*

1. Could; sure / of course
2. wondering; love to
3. should; don't; good/great idea
4. should; How/What about; could; rather; like
5. would; about; Sounds

25.3   *Possible answers:*

2. No problem.   *or*   I'm sorry, but I'm in a terrible hurry.
3. I'm sorry, but I don't have one to spare.   *or*   Yes, sure.
4. Yes, I'd love to.   *or*   I wish I could, but I have other plans.

5. I'd love to, but I have to work late.   *or*   Yeah, great.
6. Sounds good.   *or*   I'm sorry, I can't.
7. I think I'd rather work in the language lab.   *or*   Yes, that's a good idea.
8. Yes, if you like.   *or*   I don't know. I'd prefer to practice one-on-one.

Unit 26

26.1   *Any combination of these question beginnings:*

What do you think of . . .
How do you feel about . . .
What are your feelings about . . .
What's your (honest) opinion of . . .

26.2   1. of; personally (*actually* would also be correct here)
2. opinion
3. extent
4. concerned
5. totally (*completely* would also be correct here)
6. mean

26.3   *Suggested answers:*

2. In my opinion, the club needs to buy a new computer.
3. Yes, I agree with you.
4. How do you feel about our new workplace?
5. I agree with her to a certain extent. / I agree with her somewhat.

26.4   *Possible answers:*

2. Yes, I think you're right.   *or*   Yes, I agree to some extent, but how do you decide if someone doesn't want to work?
3. Yes, it makes them lazy.   *or*   Yes, maybe, but there are lots of educational shows too.
4. I agree. We can't allow animals to suffer.   *or*   Yes, I agree somewhat, but don't forget that it leads to cures for many human diseases.
5. Yes, education should be a priority.   *or*   I see what you mean, but I don't know if we can really afford it in the long run.

Unit 27

27.1   *Suggested answers:*

1. Happy birthday! / Congratulations! [because your friend has achieved a milestone: 21 years]
2. Happy New Year.
3. Congratulations.
4. Good luck!
5. See you later/soon.

27.2   *Possible answers:*

1. Nice to meet you. / Nice to meet you too.
2. Have a nice weekend.
3. Bless you.
4. Cheers. / To your health. [*or possibly:* To us.]

27.3   *Suggested answers:*

1. "Excuse me (please)" is enough here, but you could add a little more, e.g., "Excuse me for a moment" or "Excuse me. This won't take long."
2. Excuse me? / I beg your pardon? / Pardon me? (with rising intonation)

3. Excuse me. / I beg your pardon. / Pardon me.
4. Good night. (See you tomorrow / in the morning.)
5. Congratulations.
6. Good luck.
7. Good-bye. Nice to meet you. / Nice meeting you.
8. Hi. How're things? / Nice to see you. / Good to see you.

27.4
1. We ask people to "say cheese" to get them to smile when we are about to take a photograph of them.
2. We say "Watch out" as a warning, e.g., to warn someone crossing the street that a car is turning the corner and could hit them if they aren't careful.
3. We say "I have no idea" to show that we definitely do not know the answer to a question. Sometimes we say it to show annoyance at being asked the question.
4. We say "Good for you" if we are pleased with someone's actions, e.g., "I was offered a job and I've decided to take it." "Good for you!"

Unit 28

28.1
2. We had great weather.
3. I'm looking for a new pair of jeans.   *or*   I'm looking for some new jeans.
4. Your hair is getting very long.
5. I can't find my sunglasses.
6. We had a lot of homework yesterday.
7. Do you think she's making (any) progress with her English?
8. These pajamas are too big for me.

28.2
countable: cup; grape; people

uncountable: butter; spaghetti; paperwork; insurance; money; vocabulary

countable and uncountable:
coffee	U:	I love coffee.
	C:	I sat down and ordered a coffee. [i.e., a cup of coffee]
work	U:	Most people enjoy their work.
	C:	The *Mona Lisa* is a famous work of art.
television	U:	Television has too much violence.
	C:	We bought a new television yesterday.

28.3
1. a pair of scissors / some scissors
2. a pair of sunglasses / some sunglasses
3. some advice
4. some furniture
5. some headphones / a pair of headphones
6. homework/work

28.4
uncountable nouns: traffic; construction; news (*News* looks like a plural noun because it ends in **-s**, but it's an uncountable noun, e.g., "The news is good.")
plural nouns: outskirts; authorities (*Authorities* has a singular form – *authority* – but it has a different meaning. *The authorities* are the people with official responsibilities in an area. *Authority* is the right to exercise power, e.g., "I don't have the authority to let you in.")

Unit 29

29.1
2. to help	5. to drive / driving	8. going
3. going	6. eating	9. to finish
4. to make	7. to work / working	10. smoking

29.2 *Possible answers:*

1. to be happy; to have a successful career; to have children
2. doing housework; waiting at bus stops; going to the dentist
3. getting up late; walking in the country; going shopping
4. to live a long life; to have some disappointments; to meet someone they will love
5. making their bed; cooking meals; cleaning the house
6. come home at a certain time; clean their own room; get up at a certain time
7. get up when they like; do what they like; have parties at their home

29.3 *Suggested answers:*

1. He let her go on vacation with her friends.
2. He offered to lend her the money for a hotel.
3. He refused to pay for the flight and her entertainment.
4. She promised to bring him back a present and repay the loan in six months.
5. They decided to go to the Caribbean for two weeks.

Unit 30

30.1 2. He told me (that) it was not possible.
3. Can you explain what to do?
4. He suggested (that) we go to an Italian restaurant. / He suggested going to an Italian restaurant.
5. I want him to leave.
6. I need to confirm the flight.
7. I apologized for my mistake.
8. She advised me to buy a dictionary.

30.2 *Suggested answers:*

2. complain	4. warn	6. insisted	8. blamed
3. apologize	5. persuaded/convinced	7. confirm	

30.3 *Possible answers:*

1. that we go out to eat. / going out to eat.
2. them to be quiet.
3. (that) it was great.
4. it in class.
5. on going with her. / that we go together.
6. them to go.
7. him to go home.
8. the manager for the loss.
9. them not to drink it.
10. how it works.

30.4 *order*
1. + object: We ordered two coffees.
2. + object + infinitive: He ordered us to leave.

recommend
1. + object: She recommended the school highly.
2. + *(that)* clause: He recommended that we stay in a hotel.
3. + preposition: What would you recommend for young children?
4. + **-ing:** I recommend reading the book before you see the movie.

prevent
1. + object: I couldn't prevent the accident.
2. + object + preposition: They prevented us from leaving.

Unit 31

31.1 2. exhausted   3. terrifying   4. astonished   5. freezing

31.2   2. disappointed   3. embarrassed   4. confused   5. astonished/excited

31.3   2. cold/freezing   5. bad/terrible *or* awful *or* horrible
            3. surprised/astonished   6. frightened/terrified
            4. hot/boiling

31.4   *Suggested answers:*

> Dear Sandy,
>   Arrived Sunday evening. We were <u>starving</u> and had dinner
> right away. The hotel is fabulous - we have an <u>enormous</u> room
> and the food is <u>terrific</u>. It's been <u>boiling</u> every day so far, so we've
> spent most of the time on the beach. But the water is actually
> <u>freezing</u> - that's because it's the Pacific coast, I suppose.
>   Tomorrow we're going to walk to a small town about
> three miles from here – I'm sure I'll be <u>exhausted</u> by the time
> we get back, but it sounds like a <u>fascinating</u> place and I'm
> looking forward to it. It's so small that I was <u>astonished</u> to
> find it on a map!
>   I'll write again in a couple of days and tell you about it.
>   Best regards,
>   Benita

Unit 32

32.1   2. at   3. at   4. in   5. on   6. at   7. on   8. in

32.2   2. No, down the hill.   5. No, above the clouds.
            3. No, under the fence.   6. No, the apartment below me.
            4. No, out of the car.

32.3   2. in   4. across/over   6. across   8. at/in
            3. past   5. into/to   7. along (*or* down) 9. across

Unit 33

33.1   2. She hardly ever calls me.
            3. I hardly saw him during his visit.
            4. I occasionally get up early. (*Occasionally* could also begin or end the sentence.)
            5. I have never smoked.

33.2   2. hardly   3. nearly   4. fairly / somewhat / rather   5. terribly/incredibly

33.3   *Possible answers:*
            2. They said it was a bit / a little bit / slightly boring.
            3. The clothes were fairly / somewhat / rather expensive.
            4. I thought they were extremely / terribly / incredibly good.
            5. He's been getting very good marks on his exams.

33.4   *Possible answers (they depend on you):*
            2. I polish my shoes occasionally.
            3. I hardly ever remember my dreams.
            4. I often give money to people on the street if they ask me.
            5. I rarely speak to strangers on buses and trains.
            6. Sometimes I'm rude to people who are rude to me.

Possible answers (they depend on you):

2. I usually have coffee in the morning.
3. I sometimes listen to music in the evening.
4. I would never comb my hair in public.
5. I would like to go dancing more often, but I hardly ever have a chance to.

Unit 34

34.1 2. while   3. leaving   4. eventually/finally   5. After that,

34.2 *Possible answers:*

2. I'm finished here.
3. you leave.
4. I was getting out of the car.
5. John looked up the other half.

6. the bus arrived.
7. you don't have a driver's license.
8. I was coming around the corner.

34.3 *Suggested answers:*

1. And for another, I've got lots of work to do.
2. Finally, we stopped in Kyoto for a couple of days.
3. besides/anyway, we can't really afford it.

34.4 *Possible answer:*

```
Ms. M. Watson
Manager, Park Royal Hotel

Dear Ms. Watson:

I have just returned from a weekend at the Park Royal Hotel, and
I am writing to express my dissatisfaction with the food and
service in your restaurant.

To begin with, there was very little variety in the food and
sometimes no choice at all. Secondly, the service was very slow
most of the time, and we had to wait half an hour between
courses. And finally, when we complained to the waiter, he was
very rude and the service did not improve.

I hope that something will be done about this situation.

Sincerely,
(Your name)
```

Unit 35

35.1 1. Although   4. even though   7. However,
2. in spite of   5. whereas   8. too / as well
3. in spite of / despite   6. In addition,

35.2 He went to school today even though he didn't feel very well.
He always did his best at school, whereas most of his classmates were very lazy.
He has the right qualifications. What's more, he's the most experienced.

He didn't pass the exam in spite of the help I gave him.
He decided to take the job. However, the pay isn't very good.

35.3
2. whereas
3. Furthermore / In addition / What's more
4. although / even though / though / despite the fact that
5. however / on the other hand
6. as well / too

35.4 *Possible answers:*

2. the others couldn't.   5. I think I passed.
3. the bad weather.   6. I wasn't bored at all.
4. it's much cheaper.

Unit 36

36.1 *Suggested answers:*

2. unlike / different from
3. a lot in common
4. in common
5. live at home / have jobs / like sports / want to become managers
6. goes to college

36.2
1. Hong is very different from her sister.
2. The apartments are a very good value compared with/to the houses.
3. Everyone in the class passed the exam except (for) Carla.   *or*   Everyone except (for) Carla passed the exam.
4. The two boys have nothing in common.

36.3   2. in case   3. unless   4. as long as   5. otherwise

36.4 *Possible answers:*

2. have to do it over the weekend   4. my cousin comes to stay for a few days
3. pay me back by next week   5. I have to

Unit 37

37.1 *Suggested answers:*

2. I turned up the radio in the living room so (that) I could hear it in the kitchen.   *or*   I turned up the radio in the living room in order to hear it in the kitchen
3. The restaurant was full, so we went to the coffee shop next door.   *or*   We went to the coffee shop next door because/since/as the restaurant was full.
4. The company's poor management has caused / is responsible for / has led to / has resulted in a drop in profits.
5. It is a very large city, so you have to use public transportation a lot.   *or*   You have to use public transportation a lot because/since/as it is a very large city.
6. I learned to drive so (that) my mother wouldn't have to take me to school every day. *(purpose)*   I learned to drive, so my mother didn't have to take me to school every day. *(result)*

37.2
2. She got the job because of her excellent qualifications.
3. We couldn't eat outside because of the awful weather.
4. She had to stay home because of a broken ankle.
5. The flowers died because of the dry weather / the dryness.

6. I was half an hour late because of the heavy traffic.
7. The referee had to stop the game because of the rain.

Note: It is also possible to use **due to** in all the above sentences.

37.3   2. cause / lead to / result in   4. cause / lead to / result in
3. so that   5. Therefore/Consequently

37.4   *Possible answers:*

2. I bought myself a personal stereo so that I can/could listen to English cassettes on the bus.
3. I study English on weekends since I am very busy during the week.
4. I always write words down in my notebook in order to help me remember them.
5. I don't get many opportunities to practice my English. Consequently, I find it difficult to remember everything I study.
6. My brother has a lot of American and Canadian friends. As a result, he gets a lot of opportunities to practice his English.

Unit 38

38.1   2. moon   4. stars   6. North Pole   8. Earth
3. sun   5. equator   7. South Pole

38.2   1. an ocean   6. a sea
2. a mountain range   7. a group of islands
3. a country   8. a continent
4. a desert   9. a continent / an island / a country
5. a jungle / a rain forest (*also:* a river)   10. mountain

38.3   3. Ø   5. Ø   7. Ø   9. Ø
4. the   6. Ø   8. the   10. the

38.4   1. hurricane   2. flood   3. earthquake   4. volcano / volcanic eruption

38.5   *Possible answers:*

Other natural disasters include **famine** [many people starving]; **drought** [extreme dryness because of lack of rain]; **epidemic** [widespread disease]; **tornado** [violent storms with wind that spins in the shape of a funnel]; **typhoon** [violent storms in tropical areas with severe winds moving in circles]; **tidal wave** [an extremely large wave caused by the movement of the earth under the sea when there is an earthquake or a volcanic eruption].

Unit 39

39.1   1. cloudy   2. windy   3. raining/rainy/pouring   4. sunny

39.2   2. true
3. true
4. true
5. false: A shower is a short period of rain.
6. true
7. false: When it is humid, the air is very wet/moist/damp.
8. true
9. false: Drought is a long period without rain.
10. false: When it's foggy, you don't need sunglasses.   *or*   When it's sunny, you need sunglasses.

39.3 breeze; gale
boiling; freezing

39.4 2. hot 3. winds 4. snows 5. spell 6. heavy 7. humid

Unit 40

40.1 *Suggested answers:*

1. plant crops/trees/wheat
2. water crops/trees/wheat
3. pick apples/crops
4. extract coal
5. grow wheat/apples/crops/trees
6. raise animals (We also say *raise crops*.)

40.2 2. false: Animals are slaughtered for food. *or* Plants are harvested for food.
3. true
4. false: The harvest is the period when we collect and bring in crops.
5. true
6. false: Iron is used to make steel.

40.3 2. a silver spoon
3. a knife with a steel blade
4. a frying pan with a copper bottom
5. a gold ring
6. strong iron bars

40.4 2. vegetable 3. metal 4. dairy 5. Grains 6. crop(s)

Unit 41

41.1 1. same /aɪ/
2. different /e/, /i/
3. same /oʊ/
4. different /g/, /dʒ/
5. same /aɪ/
6. same /ʌ/
7. different /æ/, /eɪ/
8. different /ər/, /ɑr/

41.2 *Suggested answers:*

Farm animals: horse, goat, sheep, cow, pig, chicken
Wild animals: monkey, tiger, lion, gorilla, elephant, leopard, bear
Insects: butterfly, bee, fly, ant, mosquito

41.3 *Possible answers:*

2. Whales *or* sharks
3. Monkeys *or* dogs
4. Leopards, lions, tigers (and other big cats); giraffes; horses; dogs
5. Camels
6. Whales
7. Monkeys *or* giraffes
8. snakes
9. elephants
10. sheep

Note: Other creatures, not listed in this unit, could also complete these sentences.

41.4 *Possible answers:*

2. pigs/horses/chickens/goats
3. leopards (*Panthers* and *cheetahs* would also be possible.)
4. ants/flies/bees (Spiders are not technically insects, although many people call them insects. *Cockroaches* and *beetles* would also be possible.)
5. camels

41.5 golden eagle = 168 mph when they dive [fly in a downward direction]
lion = 50 mph
shark = 40 mph
rabbit = 35 mph
elephant = 25 mph
pig = 6.5 mph
spider = 1.17 mph
snail = 0.03 mph

Unit 42

42.1 *Suggested answers:*

1. Australia, Canada, Great Britain, New Zealand, the Philippines, the United States
2. Portuguese
3. Salvadoran(s)/Salvadorian(s)
4. Arabic
5. Thai
6. Spanish
7. Korean(s)
8. China and Taiwan
9. Argentina, Chile, El Salvador, Mexico, Panama, Spain (There are many others.)
10. Philippine/Filipino(s)

42.2

Ja<u>pan</u>	Japa<u>nese</u>	Bra<u>zil</u>ian	E<u>gyp</u>tian	<u>Ar</u>abic
Chi<u>nese</u>	Aus<u>tra</u>lia	Indo<u>ne</u>sia	Indo<u>ne</u>sian	Vietna<u>mese</u>

Words ending -ian: The main stress is on the second syllable from the end because in these words, **-ian** is pronounced as one syllable. However, some words pronounce **-ian** as two syllables (e.g., Canadian, Hungarian, Salvadorian). In those cases, the main stress is usually on the third syllable from the end.
Words ending -ese: The main stress is usually on the final syllable, i.e., on the **-ese**.

42.3 *Suggested answers:*

3. Canadians   5. (the) Mexicans   7. the British
4. The French   6. The Japanese   8. Brazilians

42.4

2. Argentina   5. the Philippines   8. Russia
3. Turkey   6. Taiwan   9. Spain
4. South Korea   7. Greece   10. Japan

Unit 43

43.1

2. cheek   8. knee   14. waist
3. chin   9. foot   15. buttocks
4. arm   10. toes   16. wrist
5. chest   11. neck   17. hand
6. hip   12. shoulder   18. finger
7. thigh   13. elbow   19. heel

43.2

2. nod your head   4. fold your arms   6. shake hands
3. comb your hair   5. bend your knees   7. bite your nails

43.3 *Possible answers:*

2. running or exercising
3. someone says something funny
4. they're nervous
5. they have a cold or after a sneeze
6. they want to say "no"
7. they mean "yes"
8. they're tired or bored

43.4

Words across: elbow, neck, ankle, chest, cheek
Words down: chin, toe, lip, back, knee, eye, nail, arm, heel

Unit 44

44.1
2. skin	5. shoulders	8. arms/legs
3. hair	6. chests	9. looking
4. height/build	7. beard/mustache	10. hair/skin/complexions/eyes

44.2
1. beautiful/pretty	3. overweight	5. good-looking/handsome
2. plain/homely	4. thin	

44.3
1. What does he/she look like?
2. How tall is he/she?
3. How much does he/she weigh? *or* What is his/her weight?

Unit 45

45.1
Positive	*Negative*
cheerful	miserable
nice	unpleasant
generous	stingy
relaxed	tense
hard working	lazy

45.2
unreliable; unfriendly; unambitious; unpleasant
inflexible; insensitive
dishonest

45.3
2. unreliable	6. shy
3. doesn't take initiative	7. flexible
4. punctual	8. sensitive
5. lazy	

45.4
punctuality	optimism/optimist (person)	reliability	laziness
confidence	generosity	ambition	stupidity
sensitivity	strength	flexibility	shyness

Unit 46

46.1 sadness; happiness; pride; jealousy; embarrassment

46.2 2. f   3. e   4. a   5. b   6. d

46.3 *Possible answers:*
1. I would feel embarrassed and upset.
2. I was once a passenger in a speeding car; I was/felt frightened.

3. Sometimes I feel upset or angry when other people want me to do things I don't want to do.
4. I might be embarrassed or I might not worry about it.
5. I'm proud of paying my own way through college / getting good grades in all my classes / being admitted to a good university / etc.
6. I sometimes feel embarrassed when people compliment me too much / when the teacher asks me questions in class and I don't know the answers / when I'm a dinner guest and someone offers me food I don't like.

46.4
1. people strolling
2. people pushing a car
3. someone pressing a button
4. someone whispering
5. people waving

46.5   2. whispered   3. strolled   4. marched   5. stared

Unit 47

47.1
2. Michael is Jill's **nephew.**
3. Rita and Ana are Michael's **cousins.**
4. Rita is Vicki's **niece.**
5. Don Graham is Tom's **grandfather.**
6. Barry is Rita's **uncle.**
7. Susan is Michael's **aunt.**
8. Paul died in 1997, making Jill a **widow.**
9. Tom is Karen's **grandson.**
10. John and Vicki are related **by marriage.**

Unit 48

48.1
2. retired
3. mid-twenties
4. in her late forties / middle-aged
5. their early thirties
6. senior citizen / senior
7. baby
8. teenager
9. adult
10. adolescence

48.2
2. true
3. true
4. false: They split up because they had lots of fights.
5. true
6. false: Marie got pregnant a year after they got married.
7. false: Marie is now expecting her second child.
8. false: Sam left Marie.

48.3   *Suggested answers:*
1. e   2. c   3. a   4. f   5. d   6. g   7. h   8. b

Unit 49

49.1   *Possible answers:*

have breakfast/lunch/dinner; a snack; friends over
take a nap/shower/bath; take a lunch break / coffee break; take out the garbage/trash
do nothing; the shopping; the laundry; the ironing; the dishes; the vacuuming

49.2
1. brush my teeth
2. do the shopping
3. stay home
4. fall asleep
5. get up early
6. feed the dog

49.5   1. The man / He is getting up.
2. The girl / She is brushing her teeth.
3. The woman / She is leaving for work / leaving home / leaving the house.
4. The two people / They are taking a (coffee) break.
5. The two people / They are taking out the garbage/trash.

Unit 50

50.1   1. yes   3. yes   5. yes   7. no, on the ground floor / first floor
2. no   4. shut   6. no   8. no, a view of a park

50.2   1. front door; doorbell   3. view   5. belongs; condition
2. climb; elevator   4. rent   6. mortgage

50.3   *Possible answers:*

Positive   *Negative*
a good view   no view
quiet   noisy
large/huge rooms   small/tiny rooms
big/enormous closets   small/tiny closets
in good condition   in bad condition
a balcony/porch   no balcony/porch

Unit 51

51.1   *Possible answers:*

1. bath; shower
2. sleep
3. cooking/dishes
4. sit; relax (and watch TV, listen to CDs/music, read)
5. eat/have meals
6. guests sleep / you keep things you don't use all the time
7. work/study
8. under/below the house

51.2   *Suggested answers:*

2. in the oven/microwave/broiler; in a frying pan on the stove
3. in the freezer
4. in the dishwasher / in the sink
5. in the cupboard
6. in the cupboard
7. on the counter (*Note:* You might use a cutting board.)
8. in a blender

51.3   2. out; back   3. on; in   4. at/through; on   5. in   6. out; on

51.5   *Possible answers:*

1. radio, CD player, stereo, dishwasher, oven, microwave, blender, broiler
2. plates, cups, saucers, saucepans, frying pans, glasses, knives, forks
3. chair, armchair, sofa
4. teakettle, saucepan

Unit 52

52.1
1. I brushed my teeth.
2. I went to sleep.
3. I set the alarm clock.
4. I turned out the light.
5. I took a bath.
6. I put on my pajamas.
7. I got into bed.

Possible order: 5, 1 (*or* 1, 5), 6, 3, (*or* 3, 6), 7, 4, (*or* 4, 7), 2. There are, of course, other variations.

52.2 *Suggested answers:*

2. He vacuumed the carpets. / He did the vacuuming.
3. He did the ironing. / He ironed a shirt. / He ironed his clothes.
4. He did the laundry/wash/washing.
5. He washed the dishes. / He did the dishes.
6. He made the bed.

Unit 53

53.1

Infinitive	Past tense	Past participle
to break	broke	broken
to forget	forgot	forgotten
to run	ran	run
to lose	lost	lost
to leave	left	left

53.2   1. d   2. f   3. e   4. a   5. b   6. c

53.3
1. Paul broke his glasses.
2. He had/got a stain on his pants.   *or*   He spilled something (on his pants).
3. He burned something he was cooking.

53.4 *Possible answers:*

2. There's something wrong with it. / It isn't working.
3. I lost it.
4. I left it home.
5. It's not (*or* It isn't) working. / It's out of order.

Unit 54

54.1
1. sold; bought
2. lost; cost; found
3. paid
4. gave; spent
5. won
6. wasted

54.2
1. How much is your CD player worth?
2. I'm sorry, but I can't afford it.   *or*   I'm sorry, but I can't afford to go.
3. Could you lend me $5?
4. How much did your dictionary cost?

54.3   1. no   2. no   3. yes   4. no   5. yes   6. no   7. no   8. no

Unit 55

55.1 *Suggested answers:*

2. sneezing, a sore throat, a cough, a runny nose, aching muscles, a temperature/fever
3. sneezing, a runny nose, itchy eyes

4. a stomachache, keep going to the bathroom
5. difficulty breathing / breathing problems

55.2
1. different /ɪ/, /aɪ/
2. same /k/
3. same /ɜr/
4. different /aɪ/, /ɪ/
5. same /f/
6. different /ɔ/, /ʌ/

55.3 *Possible answer:*

I had a terrible toothache, which was very painful, so I went to the dentist. She looked at (*or* examined) the tooth and said it needed a filling. I had an injection (*or* The dentist gave me an injection), so the drilling was painless. Afterward, my tooth felt much better.

55.4
2. attack
3. stomachache
4. pain
5. lung
6. prescription
7. asthma
8. myself (*or* my leg, my arm, etc.)

Unit 56

56.1

Noun	Verb
cut	cut
bandage	bandage
blood	bleed
bruise	bruise

Noun	Verb
injury	injure
shot	shoot
treatment	treat
wound	wound

56.2 2. e   3. d   4. b   5. a

56.3 *Suggested answer:*

Paul somehow fell out of the tree where he was picking apples and knocked himself unconscious. His wife immediately called 911 for an ambulance. It arrived quickly and rushed him to the hospital. He was suffering from a concussion and had to have some stitches for a large cut on the side of his head. Fortunately he's going to be fine.

Unit 57

57.1 *Possible answers:*

boots, socks, jeans, pants, shorts, gloves, pantyhose/stockings, earrings

57.2 *Suggested answer:*

4, 7, 1, 3, 5, 9, 2, 8, 6

57.3 a belt, a pocket, a necklace, (a pair of) gloves

57.4 *Suggested answers:*

1. skirt; blouse *or* top (*top* is a general word)
2. suit; pants
3. tie; shirt
4. enough; size
5. too; enough

57.5 *Possible answers:*

1. *worn by women:* dress, blouse, skirt, pantyhose/stockings, necklace
   worn by both men and women: hat, gloves, jeans, pants, jacket, scarf, coat, overcoat
   (Earrings are worn by both men and women in some places.)

Unit 58

58.1
2. clothes/clothing
3. furniture
4. electrical appliances
5. household goods
6. toys
7. stationery / office supplies

58.2 *Possible answers:*

butcher shop: a chicken
department store: gloves, an armchair, and possibly some of the food items
grocery store: aspirin, grapes, bananas, a loaf of bread, carrots
pharmacy: aspirin, toothbrush
office supply store: envelopes, a notebook

Some other things you could buy in each store:
butcher shop: steak, ground beef, lamb
department store: clothes, washing machines, saucepans, makeup, perfume, TV sets, stereos
grocery store: onions, oranges, lettuce, lemons
pharmacy: soap, shampoo, toothpaste, suntan lotion, cough syrup, medicine
office supply store: pens, pencils, writing paper, paper clips, files, tape

58.3
2. video (rental) store
3. fitting room
4. cashier / checkout counter
5. (shopping) mall
6. window shopping
7. pharmacy/drugstore

58.4
1. looking for   2. size   3. take   4. pay by   5. looking

Unit 59

59.1 *Possible answers:*

	Vegetable	*Fruit*
1.	potato/peas/pepper	peach/pear/pineapple
2.	beans	banana
3.	mushroom	melon
4.	carrot/cauliflower/cabbage/cucumber	cherry
5.	lettuce	lemon

59.2
banana/melon /ə/   onion/mushroom /ʌ/
peach/zucchini /i/   salmon/lamb /æ/
pepper/lemon /e/   oysters/oil /ɔɪ/

59.3
2. Salmon is the only fish; the others are types of shellfish.
3. Eggplant; the others are found (raw) in salad, but eggplant isn't.
4. Peach is the only fruit; the others are vegetables.
5. Oysters are shellfish; the others are types of meat.

59.4 *Possible answers:*

Always	*Sometimes*	*Never*
cherries	apples	pineapples
grapes	pears	bananas
strawberries	oranges	melons
	lemons	mangoes
	peaches	

Unit 60

60.2
2. buttered <u>noodles</u> with zucchini and bacon
3. grilled <u>steak</u> in a pepper sauce
4. baked <u>salmon</u>
5. <u>grilled</u> steak in a <u>pepper</u> sauce
6. baked <u>salmon</u> with spinach and breast of <u>chicken</u> in a white sauce with mushrooms
7. grilled <u>steak</u> in a pepper sauce
8. chocolate <u>mousse</u> and ice cream
9. <u>fruit</u> salad
10. <u>probably</u> the broccoli soup, salmon, and fruit salad

60.3 *Possible answers:*

chicken – bland *or* tender   ice cream – sweet *or* fattening
honey – sweet   steak – tender *or* fatty *or* lean
bacon – salty *or* fatty *or* tasty   chili peppers – hot and spicy
    avocado – bland

Unit 61

61.1 *Suggested answers:*

Big towns and cities	*The country*
dirty, with polluted air	clean, with fresh air
exciting	boring
crowded	lots of open space
lots of nightlife	nothing to do in the evening
dangerous	safe

61.2 *Possible answers:*

Town	*Country*	*Town and country*
traffic	fields	libraries
pollution	tractors	fences
factories	valleys	parking lots
town hall	farmhouses	rivers
suburbs	woods	
shopping malls	hills	
nightlife	paths	

61.3 *Suggested answers:*

2. tractor	4. field	6. woods
3. path	5. valley	7. town

Unit 62

62.1 Go <u>straight</u> and turn <u>left</u> at the intersection. Then you keep <u>going</u> and <u>turn</u> right when you <u>get</u> to the <u>school</u>. Then <u>turn</u> <u>right</u> again at <u>Green</u> Street, and the bank is <u>on your</u> / on the <u>left</u>, just after the <u>movie</u> <u>theater</u>.

62.2 *Suggested answers:*

2. injured; damaged	5. crosswalk	8. passed; lane
3. rush hour	6. broke down	
4. braked; crashed	7. traffic jam	

62.3 2. speed limit   3. slippery   4. airport   5. signal/light   6. construction

Unit 63

63.1   2. get in   3. run   4. fly   5. take   6. missed

63.2   *Suggested answers:*

1. miss the bus; miss the train; miss the plane
2. taxi driver; bus driver; truck driver
3. bus station; train station; gas station
4. get on the bus; get on the train; get on the plane; get on the bicycle; get on the motorcycle
5. get in the car; get in the taxi; get in the minivan
6. bus fare; train fare; airfare; taxi fare

63.3   1. truck   2. minivan   3. bus   4. bicycle/bike   5. motorcycle

63.4   2. track   4. arrival; to   6. line   8. to; stops
            3. full   5. punctual   7. by; took

Unit 64

64.1   2. work overtime   4. attend meetings   6. run a store
            3. pay income tax   5. see clients

64.2   2. What's your job?
3. My salary/income is $35,000.
4. My (total) income is $50,000.
5. I work for an engineering company/firm.
6. I'm in charge of one of the smaller departments.

64.3   *Suggested answers:*

A: Do you ever work/do overtime? / Are you paid extra for working overtime?

A: How much vacation do you get? / How many weeks' vacation do you get?

A: Do teachers earn much? / Do teachers get a good salary? / Teachers don't earn very much, do they?

Unit 65

65.1   *Possible answers:*

1. a doctor, an architect, a lawyer, an engineer, a professor
2. a surgeon, a dentist, a soldier, a sailor, a pilot, a police officer, a firefighter
3. a sailor
4. a mechanic
5. a doctor, a soldier, a sailor, a pilot, a police officer, a firefighter
6. a vet
7. a pilot, a firefighter
8. an accountant
9. a doctor, a nurse, a surgeon, a vet
10. a soldier, a sailor, someone in the air force

65.2   *Possible answers:*

2. teaches in a university
3. keeps and examines financial records of people and companies
4. treats animals
5. advises people on legal problems
6. plans the construction of roads, bridges, machines, etc.

7. builds walls with bricks
8. buys and sells stocks
9. repairs cars
10. operates on people in a hospital

65.3   2. Really? When did she join the army?
3. Really? When did he join the navy?
4. Really? When did he join the air force?
5. Really? When did she join the fire department?

65.4   *Possible answers:*

an architect to design your house
a lawyer to give you legal advice
a carpenter to make cupboards
a plumber to install pipes in the kitchen and bathroom
an electrician to do all the electrical work
an accountant to calculate how much everything will cost

Unit 66

66.1   2. intern   5. promoted   8. employees
3. unemployed   6. prospects   9. raise
4. resigned/quit 7. retired   10. abroad

66.2   1. b   2. e   3. d   4. a   5. c

66.3   *Suggested answers:*

2. training/experience   3. challenge   4. her   5. over

66.4

Verb	General noun	Person noun(s)
promote	promotion	–
employ	employment	employer (boss); employee (worker)
resign	resignation	–
train	training	trainer (gives the training); trainee (receives it)

Unit 67

67.1   *Possible answers:*

1. *write:* a letter, a report, a memo, a check
2. *send:* a letter, a report, a fax, an invoice
3. *make:* phone calls, products, coffee, mistakes
4. *answer:* phone calls, questions, the door, a letter

67.2   2. assembly line   3. filing cabinet; briefcase   4. paperwork   5. wastebasket

67.3   2. automation   4. calendar   6. invoice
3. goods   5. appointment book 7. retailer

67.4   2. put together   4. stored
3. examines/checks   5. deliver (**Send** is also possible.)

Unit 68

68.1   2. interest   4. aims/objectives/goals   6. (in) recession
3. inflation   5. it breaks even

68.2 *Suggested answers:*

2. sharp   4. expanding   6. gone up / increased
3. thriving/prospering   5. aims/goals

68.3 *Suggested answers:*

2. fell slightly / went down / decreased slightly
3. sharp *or* dramatic fall/drop/decrease
4. steady increase / steady rise
5. increased sharply / rose sharply / rose dramatically / increased dramatically
6. increased/rose

68.4 *Possible answers:*

2. political/economic stability   5. raw material(s)
3. make a profit   6. profit and loss
4. interest rate / inflation rate (**Rate of inflation** is also commonly used.)

Unit 69

69.1 product, price, promotion, place

69.2 *Suggested answers:*

sales manager, sales figures, sales department, sales forecast
market leader, market research, market share
marketing manager, marketing department

69.3 2. manager; department   4. leader; share
3. figures   5. force

69.4 2. products   4. competitors   6. customers/clients
3. products   5. consumers

69.5

Noun	Adjective	Noun	Adjective
competition	competitive	glamour	glamorous
danger	dangerous	luxury	luxurious
excitement	exciting	mass production	mass-produced
fashion	fashionable	reliability	reliable

Unit 70

70.1 *Possible answers:*

1. cards, board games, chess, musical instruments
2. stamps, coins, antiques, matchbooks
3. hiking, camping, rock climbing, jogging

70.2 *Suggested answers:*

2. collecting antiques *or* shopping   4. jogging   6. chess
3. playing a musical instrument   5. making clothes   7. carpentry

70.3 2. took up; gave it up   4. collects   6. play   8. do
3. made   5. go   7. joined

Unit 71

71.1 throw it; head it; pass it; hit it; catch it; kick it

71.2 *Suggested answers:*

1. baseball, tennis, table tennis, golf
2. football, soccer, basketball
3. football, baseball, basketball
4. football, soccer
5. soccer

71.3
2. true
3. true
4. false: It has a referee.
5. false: The red team is leading.
6. false: It is played on a court.
7. true
8. true

71.4 *Suggested answers:*

2. lost / been defeated / been beaten
3. winners
4. leading
5. tied
6. score

Unit 72

72.1 1. orchestra   2. C   3. yes   4. yes

72.2
2. the cast
3. the audience
4. clap/applaud
5. director
6. critics/reviewers
7. reviews
8. subtitles
9. to reserve
10. stars

Unit 73

73.1 saxophonist; guitarist; drummer; violinist; cellist

73.2 1. a landscape   2. a portrait   3. an abstract painting

73.3
2. classical; composer
3. playwright; play
4. exhibit/exhibition; gallery/museum
5. write/compose; performs/plays/sings
6. opera
7. novels/books/works
8. artists/painters

Unit 74

74.2
2. The legislature has reduced/lowered taxes.
3. There is a new attempt/try to reduce teenage smoking.
4. The U.S. supports a European plan.
5. A study has made a connection between stress and heart disease.
6. The police have discovered a very important witness.

Unit 75

75.1 *Suggested answers:*

2. Could you turn it up, please?
3. Could you switch/change channels?
4. Could you turn it down?
5. Could you turn/switch it off?

75.2 Drama series: *The X-Files, Law & Order*
Newsmagazine: *60 Minutes*
Game show: *Jeopardy!*
Sports program: *NASCAR Racing*
Talk show: *The Tonight Show*

Cartoon show: *The Simpsons*
Current affairs: *Washington Week in Review, 60 Minutes*
Soap opera: *The Light of Our Lives*
Comedy series: *Seinfeld, The Simpsons*

Unit 76

76.1   *Possible answers:*

telephone number; phone card; pay phone; telephone book; cell phone; on the phone; phone bill

76.2   *Suggested answers:*

A 2. message   3. out / not here / away from his desk
   4. call you back   5. number
B 6. this is   7. be back   8. leave; message   9. call me / call me back
C 10. Is this / Can I speak to   11. This is   12. tried/called/dialed
   13. get through   14. busy   15. on

Unit 77

77.1   *Suggested answers:*

2. software   6. keyboard   9. laser printer
3. floppy disk(s)   7. a computer program/ 10. laptop
4. user-friendly   programmer/game   11. spreadsheet
5. computer-literate   8. CD-ROM   12. back-up copy

77.2

1. paste   2. print   3. cut   4. copy   5. save

77.3   2. printed   5. back-up   8. graphics
        3. crashed   6. graphics   9. save
        4. save   7. cut (*or* deleted)   10. back-up

Unit 78

78.1   *Suggested answers:*

2. the Internet   3. browser   4. e-mail   5. the World Wide Web or WWW

78.2   2. f   3. e   4. g   5. d   6. a   7. h   8. c

78.3   *Suggested answers:*

2. e-mail   6. download
3. modem   7. page/site
4. Net/Internet/Web 8. World Wide Web / Web / WWW
5. e-mail

Unit 79

79.1   1. math   2. history   3. science   4. English   5. art   6. music

79.2   2. 3 or 4   6. English, reading, writing, math, science, social studies
        3. 5 or 6   7. public
        4. kindergarten   8. middle school or junior high school
        5. vocational; specialized

1. to school
2. graduated; to college
3. dropped out
4. compulsory/required

Unit 80

80.1
2. agriculture
3. hotel administration
4. psychology
5. business
6. history of art / art history
7. political science
8. engineering

80.2
2. a degree *or* a B.A./B.S.
3. undergraduates
4. professors, instructors
5. seminar
6. postgraduates / graduate students
7. research
8. lectures

80.3
2. get
3. community college
4. school/university
5. taking
6. conducting

Unit 81

81.1 3, 8, 7, 2, 6, 4, 1, 5

81.2
2. the judge
3. prisoners
4. the jury
5. the prosecutor and defense attorney/lawyer
6. criminals

81.3
1. broken; committed
2. against
3. fine
4. prove
5. guilty
6. evidence
7. convicted; sentence
8. offense

81.4 *Possible answers:*
1. Yes.
2. Visit the person whose home was broken into and take fingerprints if possible; question neighbors.
3. Burglary.
4. No, not at 15. They'd probably receive a **suspended sentence** [the girls won't have to spend any time in prison] or **probation.** [They must see a probation officer regularly, and if they commit another crime in the next year or two, they will receive a much tougher punishment.] They may also have to do **community service** [unpaid work to help others in the same city, neighborhood, etc.] as a punishment. If the girls already have a criminal record, they could be sent to a detention center for young offenders.

Unit 82

82.1

Crimes	People	Places
murder	burglar	cell
manslaughter	thief	prison
robbery	judge	court
shoplifting	criminal	police station
	prisoner	
	attorney	
	jury	

82.2
2. with murder
3. charged with shoplifting
4. with manslaughter
5. charged with theft

82.4
1. carry
2. allowed/able
3. punishment
4. prevent/fight/stop/reduce/cut

Unit 83

83.1

Abstract noun	Person	Adjective
dictatorship	dictator	dictatorial
socialism	socialist	socialist
conservatism	conservative	conservative
liberalism	liberal	liberal

83.2
2. party   5. held   8. majority
3. majority   6. system   9. Prime
4. elections   7. party

Unit 84

84.1 *Possible answers:*

1. identification / landing card
2. birth / marriage certificate
3. driver's / marriage / fishing license
4. application / registration / income tax form

84.2 *Suggested answers:*

2. checked
3. fill in / fill out / sign
4. sign
5. runs out / expires; renew
6. lines
7. application

84.4
2. Where do you come from?
3. Are you male or female?
4. Are you single or married?
5. When did you arrive?
6. When will you leave?

Unit 85

85.1 2. c   3. g   4. e   5. h   6. d   7. a   8. b

85.2 *Suggested answers:*

2. keep fighting / continue to fight
3. they will retreat
4. run out of food
5. mostly civilians
6. release them

85.3

First mention	repeated as . . .
ordinary people	civilians
soldiers	troops
shelling	firing
hit	wounded
soldiers	army
allow them to enter	let anyone in
captured	take control of

85.4 *Possible answers:*

1. Terrorists use hostages for bargaining, e.g., they release hostages if governments give them money or release political prisoners. Hostages also give the terrorists protection.
2. Some governments refuse on moral grounds, i.e., they believe it is wrong to bargain with the lives of hostages. Some governments believe that if you agree to terrorists' demands on one occasion, terrorists will attack again.

Unit 86

86.1
2. acid rain
3. aerosol can(s)
4. public transportation
5. global warming
6. exhaust fumes
7. the greenhouse effect
8. natural or human resources

86.2

Noun	Verb
waste	waste
conservation	conserve
destruction	destroy
pollution	pollute
damage	damage

Noun	Adjective
damage	damaging
environment	environmental
harm	harmful [≠ harmless]
danger	dangerous
nature	natural

86.3
1. plants; animals
2. smoke from factories
3. the earth
4. the sun's heat
5. world temperature
6. damages the ozone layer

86.4
We should:
recycle paper, etc.
use/take public transportation instead of cars.
save/conserve water and energy.

We shouldn't:
throw away paper, etc.
destroy the ozone layer.
waste water and energy.

86.5
1. false   2. false   3. true   4. true

Unit 87

87.1
2. baggage claim
3. carry-on luggage
4. boarding pass
5. duty-free
6. overhead compartment
7. take off
8. check-in

87.2
2. boarding pass
3. carry-on luggage
4. overhead compartment
5. runway
6. flight attendants (*or* cabin crew)
7. terminal building
8. baggage claim

87.3
Suggested answers:
2. captain/pilot
3. fasten
4. flew
5. landed/arrived
6. get off
7. flight

Unit 88

88.1
Suggested answers:
6, 7, 3, 4, 10, 1, 5, 8, 9, 2

88.2
Possible answers:
2. I'm checking out. Could I have my bill, please?   *or*
   Could you order a taxi for me, please?
3. Could I have a wake-up call tomorrow at 7 a.m., please?
4. Could you put it on my bill, please?

5. There's something wrong with the shower in my room.   *or*
   The shower in my room isn't working very well.
6. How do I get to the nearest bank from here?   *or*
   Where's the nearest bank?

Unit 89

89.1
2. sightseeing
3. packed
4. shopping
5. souvenirs
6. galleries/museums
7. lost
8. market
9. go out
10. spent
11. taken

89.3 *Suggested answers:*
2. Yes, it's very cosmopolitan.
3. Yes, it was (absolutely) packed.
4. Yes, the nightlife is fantastic/great.
5. Yes, we had a great time.

Unit 90

90.1 *Possible answers:*

suntan; sunshine; suntan lotion; sun cream; sunburn; sunglasses; sunbathe; sunlight; sunblock; sunscreen; sunset; sunrise; sunshade; sunstroke

90.2
2. suntan lotion
3. beach umbrella
4. steep cliff
5. sunbathe
6. big waves

90.3 *Suggested answers:*
2. because they want a suntan
3. to protect themselves from the sun
4. very painful
5. surfing

90.4
2. country/countryside
3. quiet
4. lie/sit/sunbathe
5. walk/stroll
6. picnic

90.5 *Suggested answers:*
2. different/various   3. home   4. picnic   5. peace

Unit 91

91.1
2. in
3. at
4. in
5. on
6. on
7. On
8. at
9. On
10. at
11. in
12. on

91.2
2. until
3. since
4. for
5. in
6. during
7. for
8. throughout (*During* is possible, but *throughout* is more precise here because it emphasizes that it was hot for the entire month – every day.)

91.3
2. two
3. 19th
4. The answer depends on what year it is, e.g., 40 years in 2003.
5. 12½ hours

91.4 *Suggested answers:*
2. for the time being
3. recently/lately
4. for ages (You could also say "in ages.")
5. a long time ago

Unit 92

92.1
2. two and a half
3. two thousand three hundred (and) forty-five
4. six point seven five
5. zero point two five *or* point two five
6. three and a third *or* three and one third
7. one million two hundred (and) fifty thousand
8. ten point oh four
9. forty-seven percent
10. September (the) tenth *or* the tenth of September
11. July (the) fourth *or* the fourth of July
12. five five five, eight oh seven seven *or* five five five, eight oh double seven
13. five (degrees) below zero *or* minus five (degrees) Fahrenheit
14. nineteen oh three
15. twenty thirty-six *or* two-thousand thirty-six

92.2
2. on the tenth of September / on September (the) tenth
3. twenty-five out of forty
4. the thirty-first of August / August (the) thirty-first
5. two and a half hours long

92.3
2. 192   3. 60   4. 5   5. 8   6. 15

Unit 93

93.2 *Possible questions:*

What size shoes/dress does she take/wear?
How high is the mountain? / What's the height of the mountain?
How far is it from one side of the lake to the other?
How big is the lake? / What's the size of the lake?
How deep is it? / What's the depth of the lake?
How long is the swimming pool? / What's the length of the swimming pool?
How wide is the pool? / What's the width of the pool?
How deep is the pool at the deep end / at the shallow end?   *or*   What's the depth of the pool at the deep end / at the shallow end?

93.3 *Suggested answers:*
2. No, he's fairly thin/slim.
3. No, it's very shallow.
4. No, it's in a tall building.   *or*
   No, it's in a high-rise building.
5. No, it's very narrow.
6. No, it's a great book.
7. No, she's pretty short.
8. No, it's a (great) big place.

Unit 94

94.1
2. a star-shaped ring
3. a round window
4. a checked shirt
5. a plaid tie
6. an oval-shaped mirror
7. diamond-shaped earrings
8. a striped sofa
9. a pointed hat

94.2
2. a football/athletic field (*or possibly* a tennis court)
3. the moon
4. a carrot
5. the sea (*or* a lake / other body of water)
6. an egg
7. a coat hanger
8. a square
9. a triangle
10. salmon

Unit 95

95.1   2. cup   4. box   6. glass   8. jar
3. bowl   5. bottle   7. can

95.2   *Suggested answers:*
The most surprising and unlikely are: a glass of soup, a tube of milk; a vase of coffee; a bag of soup (unless it's dry soup mix in a sealed plastic bag); a cup of toothpaste.

95.3   2. gang   6. group
3. slices (*also* pieces)   7. pair
4. piece (*also* plot)   8. bit
5. sheet (*also* piece)

95.4   *Correct answers:*
2. bit/piece   3. slices/pieces; bunch   4. bit   5. group

Unit 96

96.1   2. personal computer   5. United Nations
3. United States of America   6. Organization of Petroleum Exporting Countries
4. automated teller machine   7. personal identification number

96.2

> Michael,
>
> Peter had a <u>math</u> <u>exam</u> this afternoon, and then he had to take his <u>bike</u> to the repair shop, so he'll probably get home a little late. You can watch <u>TV</u> or read the <u>paper</u> while you're waiting for him. If there's a problem (<u>e.g.</u>, if <u>Dr.</u> Brown calls about the <u>flu vaccination</u>), my <u>phone number</u> is next to the <u>photos</u> in the dining room. I should be home myself by about five o'clock.
>
> Margaret (Peter's <u>mom</u>)

96.3   2. e.g.   3. St.   4. i.e.   5. Mr.   6. Dr.

96.4   2. ID   4. board   6. flu   8. i.e.
3. language lab   5. etc.   7. ad

96.5   **RSVP** means "please reply" (from the French *répondez, s'il vous plaît*) and is found at the bottom of formal invitations, e.g., to a reception or wedding. The French do not use this expression or abbreviation, however.
c/o stands for "care of." You put this on an envelope when you are writing to someone who does not live at the address on the letter but can be reached there.
ASAP stands for "as soon as possible"; it is used when something is urgent. The letters are read individually: A-S-A-P.
P.S. is the abbreviation for "postscript." We use it to add a note to the end of a letter, usually after the closing/signature.
p.m. is the abbreviation for *post meridiem*. It is used after numbers to show times between noon and midnight, e.g., 4 p.m.

Unit 97

97.1
2. new
3. horrible
4. water
5. fresh
6. photo
7. donkey
8. laundry detergent
9. doorbell
10. silk

97.2 *Possible answers:*

1. looks sad/unhappy
2. looks/feels soft
3. tastes horrible/awful

97.3 *Correct answers:*

1. listening to; heard
2. heard
3. hear
4. watch
5. listening
6. press
7. hold
8. watch/look; see

Unit 98

98.1 *Possible answers:*

2. Watch your step
3. Do not disturb; Do not feed the animals; Do not leave luggage unattended
4. No parking; No vacancy; No smoking
5. Thank you for not smoking
6. Handle with care
7. Out of order
8. Keep off the grass

98.2 *Possible answers:*

2. on a container of food, milk, medicine, etc.
3. customs at an airport or port
4. on a package/bottle/tube of medicine
5. public telephone, bathroom, photocopier
6. theater, concert hall, or movie theater
7. on the outside of a parcel/package
8. in a park

98.3 *Suggested answers:*

2. Do not leave luggage unattended; Do not leave children unattended
3. Please do not disturb; Please make up this room early (Sometimes this notice is on the other side of a "Do not disturb" sign.)
4. No parking
5. Thank you for not smoking / No smoking
6. No smoking; Watch your step

Unit 99

99.1 *Possible answers:*

2. a key
3. knife and fork
4. flour
5. stereo/radio
6. clothes *or* belongings
7. a toy *or* game
8. shampoo *or* conditioner

99.2 *Possible additions:*

A: How many people were at the conference?
B: Around/About/Approximately four hundred.   *or*   Four hundred, more or less.
A: Did you enjoy it?
B: Yes, sort of / kind of.

A: You don't seem very sure.
B: Well, there were some good <u>things</u>, but it was <u>kind of</u> long.
A: And how did John's talk go?
B: Well, he was <u>kind of / sort of</u> nervous at the beginning, but then he got more confident, and I think it went <u>really well</u>.
A: Did he have a big audience?
B: <u>About / Around</u> seventy-five.
A: That's pretty good.
B: I think John was <u>kind of</u> disappointed – he wanted at least a hundred.

99.3 *Possible answers:*

2. more or less
3. sort of / kind of
4. more or less / approximately
5. kind of / sort of
6. a vague memory (of it)

Unit 100

100.1

Formal	Informal
thus	kids
apprehend	five bucks
resume	handy
commence	guy
patron	

start – commence; catch/stop – apprehend; start again – resume; dollar – buck; therefore – thus; man – guy; customer – patron; nearby / easy to reach – handy; children – kids

100.2
2. I bet the show will start pretty soon.
3. Do you feel like going out for dinner?
4. What's up?
5. The guy in the market sold me this ring for twenty bucks.
6. Where did you buy/get that book?
7. They'll never catch him.
8. On our vacation, we're going to hang out at the pool every day.
9. Where did the kids get that cat?

100.3 *Possible answer:*

Dear Ms. Kim:

We regret to inform you that we are unable to lend you the sum of five hundred dollars that you require, but it may be possible to grant you a loan for part of the sum.

If you are still interested, perhaps you would like to contact our assistant manager. She will be happy to discuss the matter further.

Sincerely,

100.4
1. attend *(formal)* "go to"
2. lifted *(informal)* "stole"
4. shut up *(informal)* "be quiet"
5. permitted *(formal)* "allowed"